JACQUES COUSTEAU'S AMAZON JOURNEY

JACQUES COUSTEAU'S
BY JACQUES-YVES COUSTEAU AND MOSE RICHARDS

WITH PHOTOGRAPHS BY SCOTT FRIER

AYRTON CAMARGO | ANNE-MARIE COUSTEAU

RICHARD C. MURPHY | JEAN-MICHEL COUSTEAU

AND OTHER COUSTEAU TEAM MEMBERS

AMAZON JOURNEY
HARRY N. ABRAMS, INC. PUBLISHERS NEW YORK

ACKNOWLEDGMENTS

We were helped in the making of this book by several members of the expedition who faithfully recorded their experiences in journals and on tape cassettes. We would also like to thank the following for their generous contributions and comments: Jean-Michel Cousteau, Neal Shapiro, Dr. Richard C. Murphy, Paula DiPerna, Jacques Constans, Silvio Barros, Anne-Marie Cousteau, Laurie Treuhaft, Judith Anderson, Martine Viveros, and Barbara Stover.

CONTENTS

JOURNEY OF A THOUSAND RIVERS

Calypso crosses the junction of the Amazon and the Rio Negro, a tributary nearly four times as large as the Mississippi. Rio Negro water on the left is stained a cola color by decaying foliage; the Amazon is muddied by nearly a billion tons of Andean sediment carried annually to the sea.

Overleaf:
Map of the Amazon basin.

"CALYPSO" | NORTH COAST OF BRAZIL | WESTERN ATLANTIC

Shortly after dawn on May 29, 1982, as he does each morning, steward Maurice Hervé sets up a continental breakfast on the dining table in *Calypso's* mess room, the *carré*—dry toast in baskets, jars of orange marmalade, strawberry jam, peanut butter. There is hot coffee in a large urn on a Formica counter.

The crew members drift in, help themselves to the food, then wander off to begin their day's tasks. The youngest are twenty-one-year-old French diver Xavier Desmier and deck chief Bruno Vidal, from St. Pierre and Miquelon Islands, who is twenty-two and looks younger. Albert ("Bebert") Falco and Raymond Coll are the "elders," and when they enter the *carré* the others defer to them, ask them about the work of the day ahead. The two men joined *Calypso* in Marseilles thirty years ago to help Jacques Cousteau excavate a sunken ship of the third century B.C., the first major undersea archaeological expedition. They were among the first people to make their living as Aqualung divers.

There is a palpable anticipation aboard ship this morning. Ahead, in a few hours, the vessel will cross a liquid barrier, and the adventure called Cousteau's most complicated and ambitious ever will commence. But talk in the *carré* is limited by *Calypso's* engulfing noises as she cuts the heavy seas. Beams creak with each forward lurch, each warp sideward. The thrumming of the diesel engines resonates through the vessel's wooden torso. Outside, a ragged percussion of breaking water coughs past the portholes.

Cousteau enters the *carré*, dressed in a blue cotton workshirt, four pens in a pocket on the arm, a rolled map tucked under his elbow. There is no mystery about his breakfast: orange marmalade and toast, always. He unfurls the map across the table with sacerdotal slowness, studies it while sipping coffee, then, in his meticulous hand, draws for the two men looking over his shoulder the route of the ship during the next few weeks as it sails up the world's mightiest river and into the planet's greatest and least-known jungle.

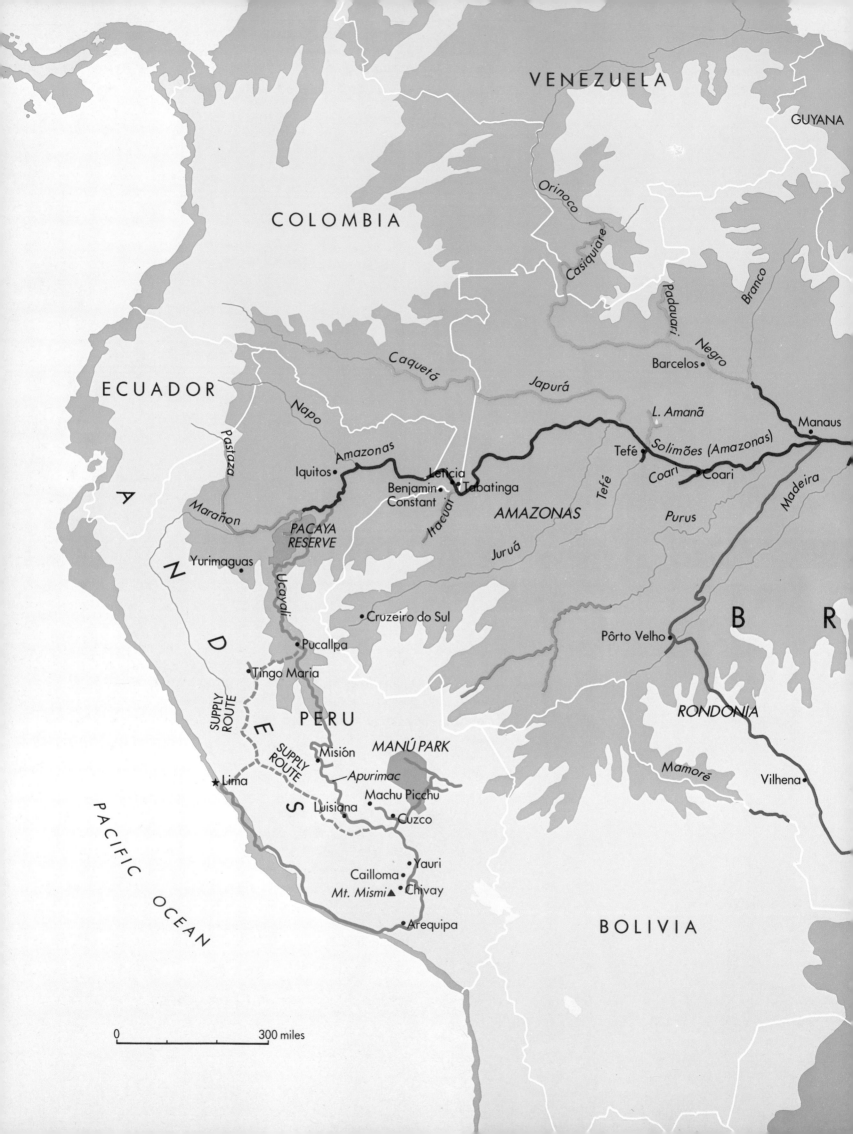

VENEZUELA

GUYANA

COLOMBIA

Orinoco

Casiquiare

ECUADOR

Caquetá

Napo

Japurá

Padauari

Branco

Negro

Barcelos •

L. Amaná

Pastaza

Amazonas

Iquitos •

Leticia

Benjamin
Constant

Tabatinga

Tefé •

Solimões (Amazonas)

Coari

Coari •

Manaus
•

A

Marañon

PACAYA
RESERVE

Itacuai

AMAZONAS

Tefé

Purus

Madeira

Yurimaguas •

N

Juruá

Ucayali

• Cruzeiro do Sul

D

• Pucallpa

Pôrto Velho •

B

R

• Tingo Maria

E

SUPPLY
ROUTE

PERU

MANÚ PARK

RONDONIA

S

SUPPLY
ROUTE

• Misión

Apurimac

★ Lima

Machu Picchu

• Luisiana

•

Cuzco
•

Mamoré

Vilhena
•

• Yauri

Cailloma •

Mt. Mismi ▲

Chivay

PACIFIC

• Arequipa

BOLIVIA

OCEAN

0 |——————————| 300 miles

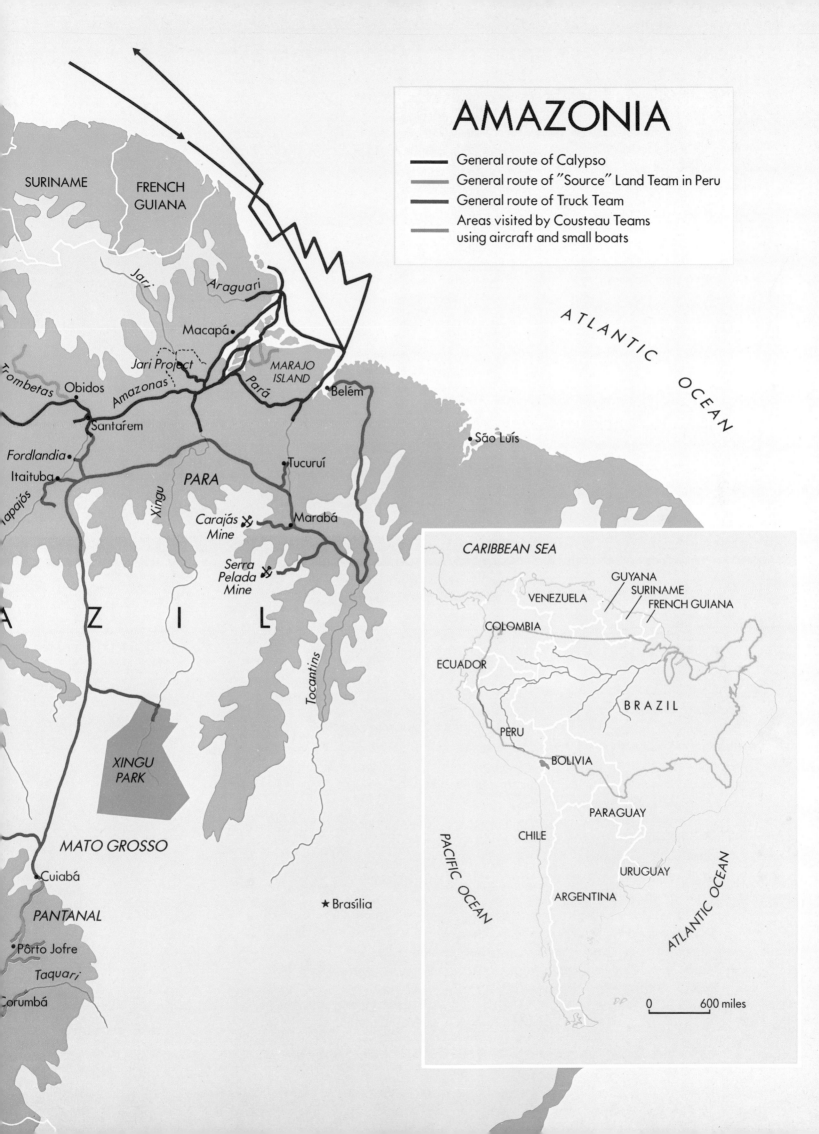

AMAZONIA

- General route of Calypso
- General route of "Source" Land Team in Peru
- General route of Truck Team
- Areas visited by Cousteau Teams using aircraft and small boats

SURINAME

FRENCH GUIANA

ATLANTIC OCEAN

Jari

Araguari

Macapá •

Jari Project

Amazonas

MARAJO ISLAND

Pará

• Belém

Trombetas

Obidos •

Santarém •

• São Luís

Fordlandia •

• Tucuruí

Itaituba •

Tapajós

Xingu

PARA

Carajás Mine ⚓

Marabá •

Serra Pelada Mine ⚓

Tocantins

B R A Z I L

XINGU PARK

MATO GROSSO

• Cuiabá

★ Brasília

PANTANAL

• Pôrto Jofre

Taquari

Corumbá

CARIBBEAN SEA

VENEZUELA

GUYANA
SURINAME
FRENCH GUIANA

COLOMBIA

ECUADOR

PERU

BOLIVIA

B R A Z I L

PARAGUAY

CHILE

PACIFIC OCEAN

URUGUAY

ARGENTINA

ATLANTIC OCEAN

0   600 miles

He marks an X in southern Peru. At this moment on the other side of the continent, his son Jean-Michel and an eight-man Land Team are setting out to follow the great river downward from the trickling waters of its source in the high Andean Cordillera. Today it begins, an expedition for which he and Jean-Michel have over several years sought funding, researched, planned, secured official authorizations, and now organized.

The Amazon.

It is not merely the largest river on earth; it is a moving freshwater sea that dwarfs in size any other river. Nearly one fifth of all the river water in the world is flowing in the Amazon. The immensity of this 4,000-mile-long rolling flood is comprehensible only through a string of staggering comparisons. The volume of water discharged into the sea by the Amazon, 7 million cubic feet per second, could fill Lake Ontario in about three hours. The outflow is nearly twelve times larger than that of the Mississippi, sixteen times greater than the Nile's. There are ten Amazon tributaries larger than the Mississippi. Altogether there are more than a thousand tributaries, seventeen of them more than a thousand miles long.

The Amazon is also the widest of the world's rivers. Even a thousand miles inland the river is often seven miles wide, and that can swell to thirty-five miles during the wet season. At its mouth it is two hundred miles wide. Over a good part of its course, the main river averages one hundred feet deep, enabling oceangoing vessels to navigate 2,300 miles upstream, and nearly across the continent, to the port of Iquitos, Peru, at the eastern edge of the Andes.

The colossal network of Amazon creeks, streams, rivers, swamps, flooded forests, lakes, and lagoons drains a basin twice as large as that of any other river in the world, a continent-size expanse of dense jungle that would barely fit within the contiguous United States. A single island at the river's mouth, Marajó, is as large as Switzerland. Though most of the Amazon system sweeps through Brazil, its drainage area, called Amazonia, includes parts of nine nations.

And the superlatives extend to the jungle itself, the largest forest in the world, accounting for about one third of all the planet's forest. Some botanists consider it the oldest vegetation formation on earth, essentially unchanged from Tertiary times.

The result of a hundred million years of diversification is a bewildering assemblage of plant life—countless species of trees mixed together so densely as to create darkness along the forest floor, liana vines trailing from branches, flowers that survive in the treetops and never touch soil, strangling plants that wrap themselves around huge trees and kill them.

And among the tangled vegetation of the forest exists the most exotic terrestrial animal life on the planet—spiders so large they catch birds, more species of butterflies than anywhere else, nearly half of the world's total bird species. The largest parrots, the largest rodents, the largest ants, the longest snakes, more species of bats, more species of monkeys.

The preeminence of forest life is matched by river life. There are more species of fish in the Amazon than in the Atlantic Ocean. There are five hundred species of catfish alone. There are also electric eels, sharks, dolphins, stingrays, sawfishes, manatees, caimans, anacondas, turtles. The world's largest otter and one of the world's largest freshwater fish. There is a species of catfish so large that river people claim it has swallowed children. And there is the most celebrated Amazon river inhabitant of all: the piranha.

But perhaps the most extraordinary aspect of this prodigious and prolific tract of the earth's surface is its obscurity. Too dense and vast to be easily penetrated by human enterprise, rife with disease-carrying insects and fraught with legends of vicious and venomous creatures, bathed in steamy heat, the Amazon remains one of the last and least-known earthly secrets. Seemingly endless blocks of forest remain unexplored and unmapped. When the Brazilian government initiated a program in 1971 to map Amazonia by means of high-altitude aerial photography and radar imaging, scientists studying the cloud-penetrating images discovered a major 400-mile-long Amazon tributary flowing beneath the forest canopy—a river whose existence had never been suspected. Deep within the interior regions of the rain forest, and beneath the opaque surface of the thousand rivers, dwell an incalculable number of plant and animal species still undiscovered. Scientists estimate that the percentage of unidentified species in Amazonia may represent 30 to 50 percent of the number of species present.

It is a world of enigmatic human life, as well. Amazonia is one of the last tracts of land on earth where tribes of humans persist in lifestyles largely unchanged by the modern world—hunting peccaries, tapir, birds, and monkeys; catching fish by bow and arrow; planting manioc. Their ways of life are gradually disappearing as the world encroaches on the Amazon, but some remote tribes are rarely visited, and it is widely assumed that undiscovered tribes survive in deep reaches of the jungle.

For many, this approaching world that Cousteau studies on his map is the last great terrestrial reservoir of primordial wildness.

Amazon. The word itself evokes a sense of foreboding mixed with seductive possibilities.

J.-Y. C.—*We encounter it at 11:30 A.M., a turbid brown "sea" that extends to the horizon, bordered by a belt of milky green water: the mingling by gradations of blue ocean and silt-laden river. As* Calypso's *stem slices from the Atlantic into the cloudy olive edge of the Amazon's discharge, I note our location. We are at least a six-hour sail from the nearest point of land, Cabo Norte, a lip of Brazilian coastline that juts out at the north edge of the Amazon's mouth. So immense is the outpouring of this great river that it penetrates sixty miles into the ocean and its effects can be detected two hundred miles from the coast. Bebert and I, rushing up to the foredeck for a closer look, amuse ourselves with the realization that we will be sailing in a freshwater river during the balance of the day—while on the high sea! The vast bone-brown flood before us displaces seawater above an area of the continental shelf larger than some European countries.*

I send our cinematographer, Colin Mounier, up in our helicopter, Felix, piloted by Bob Braunbeck. For about twenty minutes they circle above, filming this dramatic juncture of the Atlantic and its largest freshwater root system. As I watch the little aircraft dart about in the heavy equatorial air—seeming as always to dance acrobatically under Bob's control—

Opposite, above:
Monkeys, like this Squirrel Monkey *(Saimiri sciureus),* are a principal food of Amazon Indians and settlers. In contrast with other parts of the world, a large percentage of Amazonia's mammals are tree-dwellers. Some thirty monkey species are unique to the Amazon.

Opposite, below:
Jean-Michel Cousteau steers a Zodiac, followed by a team aboard the expedition's river raft *Pirarucu.*

while Colin leans fearlessly out the open helicopter doorway aiming his camera at us, there is a welling up of anxiety in my mind over the safety of our teams during the coming months. Most of our people are specialists in the ways of the sea. They know its moods and rhythms. They can gauge the danger of a circling shark and the wind-force that is prelude to an ominous storm. But today we embark on a mission into an alien world of jungle and freshwater creatures, of meandering tributaries that can deceive even forest-wise boatmen, of sudden tropical thunderstorms and invisible river hazards such as submerged hardwood tree trunks and shifting sandbars, demons camouflaged by muddy waters. Our two aircraft will roam far from the relative safety of the main river, crossing disorienting expanses of jungle canopy.

The same possibilities that inspire a wisp of dread also exhilarate us. Amazonia harbors certain dangers because it is so remote—and therefore so enticing to our team.

The voyage strikes us as a natural extension of our undersea explorations. In the past thirty-two years we have made fifty-two oceanographic expeditions. It soon became clear to us that the most productive provinces of the sea, the coastal waters, are directly affected by running water of telluric origin. We found that the freshwater arteries of the land were playing a crucial role in the health of the sea, washing human and industrial pollutants into the ocean, the ultimate sewage receptacle. Rivers that used to fertilize the sea with salts and nutrients, like the breasts of Mother Earth, were turned into kidneys soiling the sea with toxic matter.

Therefore, while Calypso's oceanographic studies continue, we have begun to launch parallel surveys of the most important freshwater lakes and rivers. In the past few years we have explored the Nile from Rwanda to the Mediterranean and the St. Lawrence between Lake Superior and Newfoundland. Soon we will study the Mississippi. It seems of paramount importance, now, to investigate the most critical of all earth's rivers and watersheds, and with a certain haste. Here in Amazonia we can evaluate a freshwater-dominated environment where human encroachment is only beginning to change, and slightly so far, the web of natural systems established over millions of years by evolutionary processes.

When Felix returns to the yellow metal grid above the aft deck that serves as her pad, Colin reports a measure of success. He and Bob have succeeded in capturing the first shots of the great river and the olive-green hemline at her edge, but growing cloud cover has partially obscured the dramatic collision of colors at this significant meeting of waters. Storm clouds will be a familiar ceiling above us during the coming months. The hot equatorial sun is vaporizing Atlantic seawater even as we film today, sending the moisture up into prevailing trade winds that carry the steamy air westward, blanketing the Amazon's endless foliage in humidity that usually exceeds 80 percent. Frequently the billowing clouds of Amazonia seem to explode with cascading water, drenching the jungle in thunderstorms forty times more powerful than the rains of Europe or the United States. The average rainfall across Amazonia exceeds 80 inches per year, but in some places the total occasionally surpasses 390 inches—more than 32 feet of rainfall annually!

Opposite, above:
Amazon river snakes inhabit the bankside shallows, feeding on fish, invertebrates, small mammals, and rodents.

Opposite, below:
The largest snake in the world, the anaconda (*Eunectes murinus*) can grow to nearly forty feet. The venomless constrictor kills by enwrapping and strangling its prey. Underwater the anaconda flicks its tongue constantly, tasting for chemical information about its environment.

The crew has prepared for the conditions ahead. Braunbeck has canvas covers for the helicopter blades. Mounier is equipped with specially tailored canvas "jackets" that cloak his 16 mm camera and film magazine. Our still photographer, Scott Frier, has likewise outfitted himself with a roomful of waterproof bags and trunks to protect his Nikons. There is a new canvas roof for the chaland, *our ship's launch. And there are more rain slickers aboard than ever before, more even than during our missions in the stormy North Atlantic.*

Soon the clouds thicken and grow dark, turning the river water below us a dull sepia. Watching Braunbeck fasten the rain covers onto Felix, *and our new diver, Bertrand Sion, remove freshly washed T-shirts from a makeshift clothesline across the foredeck, and my wife, Simone, gather up our little "waterdog," Youki, to keep him in our quarters during the approaching storm, I realize that we are now entering* two *rivers—the Amazon, upon which* Calypso *will sail, and the vertical river of Amazonia's engulfing rains.*

"CALYPSO" | BELÉM | BRAZIL

On May 30, *Calypso* arrives at the port of Belém, Brazil—the first encounter—for three days of protocol, planning, and provisioning. Passports are checked; customs, immigration, and agriculture agents conduct mandatory inspections of the vessel. The ship's stores are replenished, a creative experience for chef Jean-Pierre Hervé, who does a quick study in Amazon meats and produce. Jean-Marie France, the ship's stolid chief engineer for sixteen years, who speaks rarely but breaks into operatic arias while working in the engine room, supervises the refilling of the bunkers of light marine diesel for the main engines, as well as the tanks and drums storing aviation fuel, gasoline for the outboards, lubrication oils, and fresh water. Vidal, Sion, and diver Arturo Calvo hose down salt from the ship to preserve its wood. Maurice Hervé sends the dirty laundry out.

Although it is up an Amazon tributary called the Pará, eighty miles from open sea, Belém is the Amazon's only port of entry. "Gateway to the exotic Amazon," says the brochure from the government office of tourism. The full name is Nossa Senhora de Belém (Our Lady of Bethlehem), and the city has attended to the explorers and exploiters of the Amazon since the year 1616, when it was founded by Portuguese soldiers, who made it their home port for the conquest of Amazonia. Twenty-one years later a Portuguese military expedition led by sixty-two-year-old Pedro Teixeira sailed upstream from Belém, all the way to Quito, claiming for Portugal not only the Amazon river but about half of present-day Brazil. This irritated the Spanish, who had declared rights to the territory. But the Spanish were already occupied with the harvesting of other treasures in a vast colonial empire, so a serious conflict over Amazonia never arose. From Belém's Presépio Fort, Portuguese soldiers made sorties upriver to prevent permanent settlements by the English, French, Irish, and Dutch—hence the enduring influence of tiny Portugal over language and culture throughout the Amazon.

To attract seed-dispersing monkeys and birds, countless Amazon tree species produce colorful fruits, such as these palm fruits seen in a Belém market. Some Amazon Indian tribes harvest as many as sixty varieties of wild fruits.

14

Today Belém has a million inhabitants and is the capital of Pará, a single Brazilian state larger than Portugal, France, England, Italy, Belgium, and Holland combined. The city is a mélange of ancient customs from the jungle and hardware from the invading industrial future. Highrises loom up among the city's mango-lined boulevards. Small fishing boats with multicolored sails, on their way to the docks at Ver o Peso Market, bob past huge container ships five times the length of *Calypso*.

The crew wanders through waterfront shops and stalls, along streets permeated by tropical aromas, past electronic products from Tokyo, contraband whiskey from the British Isles, perfume from Paris, T-shirts emblazoned with the words "New York Mets." And alongside this glittery array, youngsters hawking strange root and herb concoctions from the jungle, mounds of cotton hammocks, necklaces made from the vertebrae of young boa constrictors. The juices and ice creams sold in the marketplace are nearly all derived from Amazon fruits. And perched like ominous pigeons above the crowds, descending to pick at the debris, countless *urubús*, black vultures with gray heads. Not far away, a Hilton is under construction.

Writer Paula DiPerna was the first member of the Cousteau Society team to arrive in Belém. The previous December, DiPerna had moved from New York to Brazil as the expedition's chief researcher and advance person. The scope of the Cousteau project made necessary a blizzard of official paperwork and permissions from government ministries in both Brazil and Peru, the initial theaters of operation. Working with Celso Luiz de Oliveira—a Brazilian friend of Captain Cousteau's whose interest in Amazonia resulted from years spent as a secretary of agriculture in the southern state of Parana and as director of Brazilian farm cooperatives, and whose official contacts made him instrumental in procuring government permissions for the expedition—DiPerna first set up personal audiences in January for Captain Cousteau and Jean-Michel with Brazilian President João Baptista Figueiredo and Peruvian President Fernando Belaúnde Terry. Both chief executives were enthusiastic and streamlined the process of authorization. There were visits as well to ministers of navies and air forces, interior departments, and to the directors of leading scientific institutions in both countries. There were official receptions, press conferences, dinners, cocktail parties. The process was exciting socially but professionally exasperating. DiPerna discovered what was to be a two-year frustration: the Amazon telephone system. As she characterizes it, the network is sometimes astonishingly efficient, permitting collect calls even from the jungle to the U.S. and Europe, and at other times is both casual and fragile. Rain frequently downs wires. Directory numbers are wrong. Voices at each end fade away. Lightning reduces conversations to static. Operators forget you are holding. Sometimes there is a busy signal before the number is dialed. In many jungle towns there may be no phone at all or a Catch-22 aspect to the telephones available. In tiny Barcelos, on the Rio Negro, DiPerna asked the operator in town, who sat before the village's only telephone set, if she could place a call to the United States. Yes, but the connection would take five hours. Okay, she would wait. But it is useless, the operator explained. The telephone office was open for only four hours at a time.

DiPerna's assignment was a formidable one: to feed to Cousteau's sailors, film crews, and office staff everything they would need to know in the ensuing

months—facts about navigation, docking facilities, availability of fuels, customs problems, weather, radio frequencies, local contacts, clear-water rivers for diving, important locations for filming, road conditions, medical precautions, barges, ferries, airlifts, helicopters and jeeps for rent, development projects, Indian tribes and Andean guerrilla groups, and, of course, Amazonian flora and fauna.

In January, DiPerna established a Cousteau office in Manaus, the unofficial capital of the Amazon. The "office" was, in fact, a fourth-floor room at the Hotel Monaco. Bed and dresser were replaced by desks, file cabinets, and telephones. She met and hired an assistant in Manaus, Silvio Barros, a young Brazilian ecologist. The two spent the winter and spring preparing for the expedition, and when *Calypso* eased up against her Belém berth at the end of May, DiPerna and Barros were waiting on the dock.

The overall plan of the expedition is simple. During the first phase, *Calypso* will sail upriver as far as the river's depth permits, at least to Iquitos, perhaps beyond. Meanwhile the Land Team, led by Jean-Michel Cousteau, will trace the headwaters down from the Amazon's source in the Peruvian Andes, using kayaks, rafts, and a support truck, until the Land Team and *Calypso* rendezvous. Then a second phase will begin. *Calypso* will leave Iquitos and head back down the main river at a slow pace, entering the larger tributaries wherever possible and anchoring frequently to conduct scientific studies and to film. Flying and Land Teams, using *Calypso* as a base, will then be dispersed to remote regions beyond the reach of the ship.

The idea is simple but the logistics are not. Travel and communications pose the largest problems. To extend the range of the crew aboard *Calypso*, two new vessels have been acquired. Cousteau has shipped from France a 20-foot-long hovercraft that can carry nine passengers and a 1,500-pound payload at 35 knots over river, swamp, or open ground, gliding on a cushion of air. Jean-Michel has found in Manaus a traditional Amazon riverboat named the *Anaconda*—a two-deck, 50-foot-long "birdcage," as such a boat is called along the river. With bunks to sleep a dozen and a draft of only two feet, *Anaconda* can accompany *Calypso* as a floating dormitory or can sail far up tributaries carrying scientists or a film crew.

There is a need, as well, for another aircraft. *Felix*, a two-passenger helicopter with a maximum range of 350 miles, will be useful for short trips from *Calypso*, but it cannot serve as a workhorse plane to transport people and equipment across wide stretches of jungle. The problem is solved when Atlanta businessman George Montgomey offers support to The Cousteau Society in the form of a new amphibious bush plane (which is dubbed *Papagallo*, Spanish for "parrot"). After an extensive search for a qualified pilot, Jean-Michel meets and hires Guy Gervais in Lima. The strapping six-foot-three French Canadian is one of the world's most experienced bush pilots, with more than 15,000 hours logged over the jungles of Central and South America and New Guinea, as well as the forests of Canada. Once a missionary priest with the Montford Fathers in New Guinea, Peru, Surinam, and Guatemala, Gervais is now married, living in Lima, and flying "mercy missions" for the international humanitarian organization Wings of Hope.

The expedition's communications system is perhaps the most complex part of the project. There will be a routine need for communication between

Calypso and the satellite teams, sometimes across more than two thousand miles of wilderness. DiPerna and Barros, stationed in Manaus but frequently traveling throughout Amazonia, need almost daily contact with the ship, with teams in the field, and with the New York office of The Cousteau Society, where staff members Karen Brazeau and Susan Spencer-Richards handle airline reservations, procure and freight equipment and film, hire ship's agents, and pass messages on to other Cousteau offices in Norfolk, Los Angeles, Paris, and Monaco.

At the center of this global web is a COMSAT terminal in *Calypso*'s radio room, through which radio officer Michel Treboz can send typed telex messages or make phone calls. The communications are relayed anywhere in the world through a Marisat (Maritime Satellite) in geosynchronous orbit above the Atlantic. The system also permits a Cousteau staff member in New York or Paris, for example, to direct-dial *Calypso* in the heart of Amazonia. The telephone calls cost about $10 per minute, however, so expedition messages are routed by telex except in emergencies. Treboz also manages several kinds of radios—VHF, HF, Ultra Sideband, and Single Sideband—through which he can contact a ship's pilot in the next port or the Peruvian Land Team. Expedition trucks, aircraft, and rafts are also equipped with radios.

The Peruvian Land Team will also carry a small plastic domed device about the size of a salad bowl. A transmitter in the white dome beams a pulse to a satellite, which relays data to the National Environmental Satellite Service in Suitland, Maryland, where the information is sorted out and retransmitted to the Argos center of the French Space Agency (CNES) in Toulouse, France, where the coordinates of the Land Team are in turn sent to Cousteau offices in Paris or Monaco and then relayed via satellite to *Calypso*. Although there is no verbal communication involved, Captain Cousteau aboard *Calypso* can determine the precise location of his Land Team at any time by interrogating this system.

While travel and communications involve the most elaborate planning for the Amazon, there are other special preparations. In California, Jean-Michel has supervised the design of new lightweight diving suits for the expedition, constructed of a thin neoprene that will offer protection from river hazards without intensifying the tropical heat. New double air tanks have been built in Italy. Expedition scientific coordinators Jacques Constans and Dr. Richard C. Murphy have ordered new scientific instruments and supplies. There is an electric bug killer in the *carré*. There are mosquito nets and cases of insect repellent aboard. Air conditioning has been installed in the crew's quarters (but not elsewhere on the ship).

To while away the hours on long passages in the remote regions, the crew members have carted aboard a variety of personal items. Cassette players abound. The shelves of the small *carré* library are crowded with new paperback novels, some in French, some in English. There are half a dozen copies of the French comic books *Astérix* and *Tintin*. There are a few 8 mm movie cameras aboard to document the Amazon for families at home. There are chess sets and Rubik's cubes. A new supply of video cassettes fills a shelf below the *carré* television set.

More important, the ship is stocked with tropical medical supplies, administered by the ship's doctor, Jean-Jacques Darnault, who has taken leave

Opposite, above:
This clear-winged butterfly (*Ithomidae*) extracts alkaloid chemicals from plants and converts them internally into a powerful perfume to attract mates.

Opposite, below:
Amazonia's profusion of insects, like this exotic butterfly, results in part from the spectacular diversity of plant species, with which insects have co-evolved.

from his Martinique practice to accompany Cousteau on the Amazon adventure. If there is a major anxiety among the men, it is the peril of insect-borne Amazon diseases. Many of the team have read naturalist Alex Shoumatoff's 1978 book *The Rivers Amazon*, which graphically describes the swarming microbial life of Amazonia and its serious effects: malaria, tuberculosis, hepatitis, Hansen's disease (leprosy), leishmaniasis (which produces subcutaneous ulcers that can ultimately cause disintegration of the nose and palate), yellow fever, schistosomiasis (a liver disease transmitted by river snails), onchocerciasis (a black-fly-carried disease that causes blindness), Chagas's disease (which is initiated by a beetle bite and can result, twenty years later, in cardiac and digestive dysfunction). There are other diseases thriving in Amazonia, too, most of them poorly understood. There are also bothersome ticks, chiggers, stinging ants, bees and wasps, sandflies, and a botfly whose mosquito-carried larvae climb into human hosts after hatching and mature into inch-long maggots.

There are venomous spiders and snakes, though current literature indicates that their abundance in the jungle is widely exaggerated. Anacondas and boas are constrictors that carry no venom but kill their prey by encircling and crushing with formidable muscles. The snake most responsible for human deaths in Amazonia is the *jararaca*, called fer-de-lance elsewhere, which injects a yellow venom that is frequently fatal. There are also bushmasters, rattlers, corals. Silvio Barros has purchased a serum in São Paulo at the Butantan Institute, allegedly the strongest snakebite remedy in South America, and a supply is boarded in Belém. The serum must be stored at cool temperatures, so the transport to *Calypso*, and later to the Peruvian Land Team, demands packing in dry ice. There is initially some confusion over where dry ice might be located in the steamy Amazon. DiPerna finds it at a brewery.

J.-Y.C.—*On June 1, while* Calypso *is still in Belém, we have our first opportunity to enter jungle. The Federal University of Pará has requested our assistance in the evaluation of an area about twenty-five miles southwest of Belém. There are proposals to "sacrifice" the region's rain-forest cover for the construction of a huge metallurgical complex producing aluminum oxides and aluminum. The University has decided to conduct a hydrological survey and to create an adjacent reserve into which flora and fauna of the area to be developed can be transferred. Constans and Coll have been asked to lead a* Calypso *team on a small survey of the area.*

Bebert and Braunbeck make an early-morning helicopter flight over the area, filming and mapping out a route for the team. The crew departs in two Zodiac inflatable boats and an aluminum launch from the University—Coll, Mounier, second cameraman Raymond Amaddio, our sound recording engineer, Yves Zlotnicka, diver Arturo Calvo, Frier, Desmier, Constans, and three University scientists including Paulo Sucasas, who has spent months researching the site.

When the men return at 5:30 P.M., just in time for our first dinner sitting, I eagerly join them to hear their accounts and to solicit their first impressions of the jungle waters. Constans, in his precise manner, reports the route, from one small tributary to another. Coll describes how the team made a sweep of all the sites of interest to the University, diving in the area where the nature reserve is planned. They were underwater a half-hour, at a depth of twenty-five feet initially, where the visibility was only six feet. At forty feet they had the impression that the water was much clearer, but there was almost no light penetration. "It will be difficult for us to film underwater if these are common conditions," remarks Coll.

"And what of insects?"

Constans, who has a keen interest in insects and an extensive collection of coleoptera, is overjoyed by the butterflies he has seen. "Immense neon-blue morphos," he says. "The top of the wings is an iridescent metallic blue and the underside a flat chestnut punctuated with false eyes. In fact their blue coloration is a visual trick, since the effect is created not by pigments but by tiny transparent scales that reflect light."

To his chagrin, Constans had forgotten his butterfly net. When he tried in vain to capture a morpho with his hat, cameraman Mounier recorded a scene rich in comedy.

The men speak excitedly, enumerating other sightings: a pink toad, red dragonflies, tiny crabs. While Coll's team was underwater, the men waiting in the boats were visited by large red bees, swollen with pollen, that stopped to drink water from the wet nylon anchor rope.

Everyone is fascinated by the plant life. Constans describes the profusion of palm leaves, some with the appearance of fireworks rockets bursting. He suggests that Mounier film the abundance of roots and their massive, sumptuous twists and turns.

On the return trip, however, they have had an experience that is more prosaic than these glimpses of exotic life. They are caught unawares by the titanic rise and fall of Amazon waters in the tidal estuary, and they confront for the first time Amazonia's ubiquitous world of mud.

Retracing their morning route, they discover that, in some places where earlier the water was several feet deep, now they are up to their bellies in mud as they pull and carry the boats forward. Frequently they are forced to stop and wait for the returning tide to raise the river water a few inches. Mounier and Zlotnicka, deeply amused by their plight, step onto the riverbank to record on film the slow progress of a laughing team. At one point, plopping through soft mud up to his knees, Coll announces that they have discovered a new mudbath spa. While they are chuckling on the bank, Mounier asks Zlotnicka for a smoke.

"When I turned around to get the cigarette," Colin says, "he was gone. He had stepped sideways into mud and descended about three feet. Each time he tried to move he sank deeper. Our laughter grew hysterical."

The following day, June 2, we depart Belém on a week-long voyage to Manaus. Although our plan is to hurry upriver, making a preliminary reconnaissance, and to investigate it more thoroughly on a leisurely sail back downriver, I cannot resist the temptation to see for myself the realities of the rain forest that looms up solidly along the banks on either side.

Braunbeck and I make daily helicopter flights above the forest canopy. Early in the morning we glide over cottony wisps of fog that seem to cling to the treetops, separate little cloudballs the size of a house which fill in every dimplelike depression in the green carpet of jungle that stretches as

Above, top:
The seeds of this flowering fruit tree (*Pachira aquatica*) are a kind of chestnut known in Amazonia as *Mungubarana*.

Above:
A white substance within the flowers of this mimosoid legume (*Pithecellobium*) attracts animals, which consume and disperse the seeds.

Opposite:
Like water hyacinth, the *Eichornia crassipes* is adapted to a floating life, equipped with bladders. Both plants have been accidentally introduced into Florida, where they multiply rapidly and clog waterways.

far as we can see in every direction. Often we surprise a pair of scarlet macaws, or a small flock of green parrots. They streak off above the trees shrieking raucously, Braunbeck and I in close pursuit. Looking down upon them as the kaleidoscopic plumage of their beating wings flickers above the mottled greens of the canopy, I am awed by the luxuriousness of the beauty we are witnessing.

I am reminded of a vision I have seen thousands of times, of vividly hued fish gliding above reef heads, darting in and out of crevices in the way these parrots plunge among the treetops. The larger flocks, like fish schools, bank and turn so symmetrically and magically that they could be a single organism.

The helicopter flights make a compelling prelude to the adventure of penetrating the jungle for closer examination, and during the week we stop occasionally to gather impressions and to film, making short trips by Zodiac up tributaries.

Always we are engulfed in haunting sounds. A bizarre squeal arises somewhere beyond the wall of trees lining the water, a whine as strident as the electronic wail of microphone and speaker interference. Moments later, the wild braying of a donkey erupts from the dark recesses of the forest. The group of us drifting along the glassy tributary glance at one another, mesmerized, knowing that there can be no donkeys here in this stretch of virgin rain forest.

Coll stills the outboard motor and Mounier pans his camera across the face of the surrounding jungle. But the tangled vegetation is too dense for his lens to penetrate, a thick barrier of foliage and shadows. It is a frustration that will continue to plague us during the months ahead. We are within the most extravagant biological treasury on earth, and yet the infinity of creatures here remains largely hidden from our cameras behind the shroud of fronds, lianas, trunks, and pockets of darkness. The occasional sightings are so brief that Colin has no time to aim and focus. Capybaras, the world's largest rodents, bolt out of the shallows ahead and disappear into a crowd of aquatic plants. A caiman slides into the water from a sandbank and quickly vanishes downriver, its crocodilian eyes flashing what can only be disdain over this interruption of a sunbath. But the actions are sudden and unannounced, and Mounier can capture only a few frames of the capybaras' haunches and of rippling water behind the caiman's powerful tail. (This difficulty amuses our film editor in Paris, Hedwige Bienvenu, who telexes later to ask why we are sending her so much film of ronds dans l'eau, circles in the water.)

We have no problem hearing and taping the voices of this unseen multitude, however. I watch with delight the face of our soundman, Yves, who holds an omnidirectional microphone before him in the wet-hot air. Through earphones he listens to the forest music his tape recorder is capturing. He smiles in awe. It strikes me that this is a rare joy for him, a man whose life is largely spent in an acoustic world, who is as sensitive to sounds as a painter is to colors. We are all enchanted by the sounds enveloping us, but Yves is transported. He passes his earphones to me. Intensified and purified by the recording system, the jungle murmur becomes a symphony of distant hisses, crackles, peals, whistles, wheezes—of un-

Opposite, above:
Wading into a shallow Amazon tributary, Dominique Sumian finds relief from the oppressive heat.

Opposite, below:
Scientists aboard *Calypso* regularly captured samples of Amazon fish for identification. No freshwater environment on earth sustains such a diverse fish population as the Amazon, home to more species than the Atlantic Ocean—perhaps half of them still to be identified and named.

Overleaf:
Diver Arturo Calvo crosses a typical bridge along a trail through dense jungle. Tim Trabon is at left.

known birds, insects, monkeys, and countless other living instruments. The rain forest itself offers an occasional flourish, as limbs crack or a faraway trunk crashes dully through surrounding vegetation. The branches rustle slightly when a rare wisp of breeze sighs through them, Keats's "little noiseless noise among the leaves." Some sounds enthrall. Bebert and Constans have heard the thunderous moans produced by distant troops of howler monkeys. Both men describe the noise as chilling.

We register, these first days of the expedition, our first observations of Amazonian life—the extraordinary sounds, the debilitating humidity that traps us all in endlessly sweat-soaked clothing, and the profusion of insects. When Bebert tries to tether our little Zodiac to a large fig tree, a swarm of bees descends on him. He leaps back into the boat and speeds away with only a few stings. Walking down a jungle slope, I reach out to a tree trunk for support and discover a squadron of furious wasp-size ants streaming up my arm.

We soon realize that Amazonia is a kingdom of small beings—insects, birds, spiders, rodents, butterflies, frogs, lizards, bats. Though she remains away from shore on the main river, Calypso *is quickly covered in spider webs, sheer nets speckled with shiny beads of moisture. Our new friend Silvio Barros tells us a story from his childhood, how he and his boyhood friends would finish each walk through the jungle by lying completely still in a shallow stream while fish cleaned the profusion of ticks from their bodies.*

We sense also that life here is usually a solitary business for the larger animals. Except for monkey troops, peccary herds, and capybara families, most creatures appear to be single hunters, rarely seen in their travels and commonly nocturnal. We are fascinated by the phenomenon and eager to solve the mystery in our minds: why is such a vast, verdant environment principally an empire for the small?

The question suggests an even greater puzzle. For at least a hundred years, visitors to the Amazon Valley have predicted that its fertile ground would feed the world, its native products flood international markets, its hidden mineral wealth enrich the continent. Yet the golden future has not yet materialized, despite the schemes of entrepreneurs and entire governments. Why?

The answers lie somewhere among the patches of green shade, the splinters of light, the barrel-like trunks that surround us. I am most impressed by the mood *of the forest. It is the presence of biological antiquity, powered by the solar engine of the tropics, quickened by the serum of life—water—which pervades, dripping from the canopy above, coursing through bloodstreams and leafstalks, clouding the air, flushing ground nutrients toward taproots below and ocean-bound rivers beyond. I feel here a caress of the life force, of somber energies and a deep jungle intelligence in fundamental matters of life, death, blood, breath.*

Among those who have preceded us, some portray the Amazon as a Green Hell, and others as a Garden of Eden. We wonder which it will be for us.

Opposite, above:
A flock of scarlet ibis (*Eudocimus ruber*) passes below *Calypso's* helicopter.

Opposite, below:
The scarlet macaw (*Ara macao*) is the largest of Amazonia's parrot species. The creature's powerful hooked beak is specially adapted for cracking the tough shells of nuts.

THE COLD BIRTH

LAND TEAM | AREQUIPA DEPARTMENT | SOUTHERN PERU

The yellow truck heading southward out of Lima, following the Pan American Highway along a stark and arid coastline, attracts the attention of nearly everyone it passes. Unlike Peruvian flatbed trucks with their lacquered stakes in flamboyant patterns, the lumbering Italian vehicle bears an odd resemblance to two huge footlockers bolted atop six wheels. The forward box, covered with a canvas roof, carries eight parka-clad men bound for the roof of the Andean Cordillera, the world's second-highest mountain range and the source of the Amazon. Over the haunches is an aluminum container as large as those carried by oceangoing freighters. Within are packed nearly five tons of support equipment.

While Captain Cousteau and *Calypso* sail westward into the river's mouth, this team, led by Jean-Michel and expedition leader Dominique Sumian, will explore the farthest, highest origin of the flood among peaks higher than those of the Alps or the Rockies. To reach the Continental Divide of the Andes, the team has set out in this six-wheel-drive truck dubbed with an appropriate nickname: *Amarillo*, Spanish for "yellow."

The truck's passengers spend their time in the jiggling cabin preparing for the work ahead. Soundman Guy Jouas cleans the heads on his tape recorders, cinematographer Louis Prezelin loads his film magazines, Sumian studies maps and reads research reports supplied by Paula DiPerna. Dick Murphy, a marine biologist who doubles as a still photographer, begins to fill the first of several notebooks with observations that will provide a continuing chronicle of the team's adventure.

After two days of travel, the truck turns eastward into the mountains and halts some sixty miles from the Pacific at Arequipa, Peru's second-largest city and a staging area for adventurers entering the southern ranges of the Andes. Sometimes called the White City, Arequipa is built almost entirely of white volcanic rock.

Two weeks earlier photographer Anne-Marie Cousteau, Jean-Michel's wife, and cinematographer Jean-Paul Cornu spent several days exploring

Amarillo climbs toward Arequipa. The world's second highest mountain range, the Andes form an immense continental barricade, trapping moist Atlantic air currents over the jungle to the east and leaving Peru's western regions among the driest on earth.

31

the region around Arequipa to determine possible film stories and the best routes to the Amazon's source. Just prior to the arrival of the Truck Team, the two return to Arequipa in *Papagallo*, accompanied by pilot Gervais and Jacques Ertaud, a French film director who is also an experienced mountain climber. The assembled team spends three days gathering supplies in Arequipa—candles, plastic containers for salt and sugar, fresh fruits and vegetables.

Their introduction to the world of the Andean visitor takes two forms in Arequipa: cases of dysentery appear, a debilitating problem that will linger for weeks among team members; and the curious realm of the Quechua Indians, direct descendants of the Incas, envelopes the crew. In the Arequipa marketplace, the team marvels at richly hued woven fabrics and wanders among cubicles where produce and eggs and meat and coca leaves are sold by Indian women dressed much alike, all positioned behind their wares with elbows on counters in a uniform position. The exotic sights and smells of the market are entrancing, the cold air and the robust fragrance of the surrounding mountains invigorating. When they look above the low roofs of Arequipa, the team sees bank upon bank of craggy, snow-covered volcanic cones and shafts. Somewhere to the north is their first destination: one of these vertebral peaks of splintered porphyry and granite is shedding precipitation that will journey four thousand miles in a continuous stream that takes nearly a dozen names, sometimes two at a time, the last of them "Amazonas," finally mingling with the salty waters of the Atlantic Ocean.

The actual spot where drops of water form the farthest source of the Amazon has seemed to leap from one peak to another in the past as explorers sought to be the first to pin down the location. The source river was once thought to be the Marañon in northern Peru, which joins with the Ucayali above Iquitos to form the main artery of the Amazon. But further study showed that the Ucayali system was longer than the Marañon (though not as voluminous) and that the Ucayali's longest tributary was the Apurímac. (Technically, the source of a river is generally recognized to be its farthest point of origin, not the largest of its headwater tributaries.)

As if tracing a lineage back to the founding ancestors, explorers were able to determine by 1970 that the farthest source of the Apurímac is a stream known as the Hornillos, which is born on the slopes of a mountain in the Chila Range, some sixty miles north of Arequipa. It was originally assigned to a mountain known as Minaspata but later determined to descend from Mt. Mismi, a snowy, crescent-shaped ridge that rises to 18,363 feet at its highest rocky horn. To verify this location, Jean-Michel Cousteau has spent weeks combing government maps and interviewing people knowledgeable about the Andes, including Mauricio de Romana, a guide who has made a career of organizing mountain expeditions and who will join the team.

Their preparations nearly complete, the Truck Team leaves Arequipa and heads north over a dusty mountain road that winds upward some seventy-five miles to the tiny village of Chivay, a cluster of adobe and stone buildings southeast of Mismi.

On May 18, Jean-Michel arrives in Chivay aboard *Papagallo* to join the team for the trek to Mismi. During the past week the younger Cousteau has shuttled from one Lima ministry to another securing final permissions for

Opposite, above:
The Cousteau Land Team's all-purpose truck—nicknamed *Amarillo*—shares a road in the Peruvian *altiplano* with a Quechua family and their llama herd. Bright tassles fastened to the animals' ears typify the Andean natives' flair for colorful decorations.

Opposite, below:
Two Quechua women weave a blanket outside a stone house visited by the Cousteau Land Team. Rock corrals offer protection from the wind to herds of llamas and sheep. Like their Inca ancestors, the Quechua use no mortar in their stonework.

each leg of the expedition, at the same time arranging for government assistance in the form of a Peruvian Air Force helicopter. His hope has been to use the helicopter to airlift the team to the base of Mismi, to provide medical transport in the event of an accident, and to fly Prezelin over the mountain to film the team's ascent. The filming flight presents no problems and the Air Force offers their assistance, but landing along Mismi's highest flanks is impossible. The helicopter could alight, but so thin is the high-altitude air that the chopper blades could not lift the aircraft up again, even if it were empty. The helicopter would simply become a permanent fixture of the mountain. The team will be obliged to drive as far as possible toward the base of the mountain in the six-wheel-drive truck, accompanied by a jeep supplied by de Romana. The last few miles will be crossed on foot.

That evening, Jean-Michel makes his first entry into a microcassette recorder which will serve as his journal during the days and months ahead:

"In four or five days we will set out for the ascent of Mt. Mismi, and as this challenge grows near I find myself wondering about the endurance levels of our team. Our friend Jacques Ertaud is the only Cousteau team member with any alpine experience. Yet Jacques, though slender and fit for his age, is fifty-seven years old; and the youngest among us is thirty-seven. More importantly, we are all sailors, people who have spent our lifetimes at sea level.

"Here along the altiplano of Peru, the high intermontane plane that winds among the spires of the Andes, the true altitude is deceptive. The peaks here rise from valley floors that are already 13,000 to 15,000 feet high—nearly three miles above sea level. The altitude of mountain summits does not *appear* dramatic, but is in fact extraordinary. The peak of Mt. Mismi seems tame in the distance, yet it is higher than any mountain in the forty-eight contiguous U.S. states, higher than Mt. Fuji or the Matterhorn or even Mont Blanc, the highest of the Alps.

"The climbing itself presents negligible hazards. By heading up the gentler north side of Mismi, we can count on a steep, icy, but manageable trek, demanding only crampons as special equipment. We will climb nearly 4,000 feet and risk treacherous slides if our footing gives way in the ice, but we can avoid the perils of snow cliffs, crevasses, or rock climbing.

"Mauricio tells us that a greater danger than the terrain is what the Andean people call *soroche* (altitude sickness). The lack of oxygen in high-mountain air works changes on the body, especially a body undergoing heavy exertion. Though the physiology of the condition is not completely understood, the symptoms and the ultimate dangers are well known: headaches, loss of appetite, mild nausea, and shortness of breath. As the effects become severe, a climber may undergo violent headaches, vomiting, and a sudden vertigo, followed by unconsciousness.

"*Soroche* is an uncommon affliction among the Quechua, who are an enormously hardy people. Along the dirt streets of Chivay we see llama herders walking barefoot despite the evening cold, which seems almost to plummet upon us like an invisible avalanche as soon as the afternoon sun drops behind the peaks rimming the valley. Within two hours the temperature falls forty-five degrees to below freezing, yet I have not seen any change in the footwear of the herders.

"More remarkable to us, however, is their respiratory stamina. Already we are finding ourselves winded by short walks, by the loading and unloading of our truck, simple tasks in New York City or Marseilles. Yet the Quechua people routinely climb up and down trails on steeply terraced hillsides and cross miles of rolling altiplano countryside in trips from their outlying subsistence farms to the marketplaces of the nearest villages. There is more than simple conditioning or acclimatization in this, we have learned. Residents of highland plains for centuries, the Incas and their descendants were driven even higher into the mountains in order to isolate themselves from the Spanish conquistadors who overwhelmed their society in the mid-sixteenth century. In their lofty retreats, the Quechua peoples seem to have evolved specialized mountain-survival bodies: capacious lungs, hearts 20 percent larger than average, and a circulatory system pumping about two quarts more blood than that of the average American or European. They are squat people, and even this physique seems a great advantage. Short arms and legs and a thick trunk mean a reduced demand on the circulatory efforts of the heart, and less exposed surface for heat loss.

"Tonight around the dinner table in a tiny Chivay restaurant we decided to spend a few more days becoming acclimated to the altitude before assaulting Mismi, and to become better acquainted with the Quechua people. They are the first humans to partake of the Amazon's bounty as it collects itself from glacial precipitation and heads downward to the jungle."

The team spends three more days in Chivay, then drives north to the 14,000-foot-high provincial capital of Cailloma, where a dirt road leads south to the base of Mismi. The village is large enough to support a few shops but has no gas station. The team stays here another two days, pacing their acclimatization and exploring the surroundings. Hotel accommodations, seldom plush in the Andes, are sobering in Cailloma: several wooden bunks in a thatched adobe stable. Hoping for a warm shower, the team confronts a single washbowl. To keep warm team members sleep in their cold-weather clothing inside sleeping bags.

It seems a bizarre prelude to a jungle expedition. The altiplano is a treeless gray expanse of wide valleys walled by gaunt mountains, bisected in places by deep gorges. Through the open terrain swirl columns of windblown sand. Against this stark leaden backdrop even pastel colors are accentuated, and shapes become apparitions. Rock spires resemble distant castles. Subtle pinks and reds streak the shadows along exposed ledges. A speck of crimson in the distance turns out to be a lone Quechua woman wearing a bright woolen poncho, carrying a baby.

The austerity, the extreme temperatures, and the thin air severely limit wildlife. The altiplano is the kingdom of the condor, a vulture, and four species of llamoids (llama, alpaca, vicuña, guanaco), all of them herbivores, camel relatives, ruminants which survive easily by grazing on the hard altiplano grass known as *paja*. By far the dominant member of the family is the llama, which has become so thoroughly assimilated into the rural Quechua economy that no wild herds exist any longer. The llama provides nearly everything a Quechua family needs: llama wool is sheared and woven, hides are tanned, about one tenth of a herd is slaughtered for food each year, llama fat supplies tallow for candles, and fecal pellets are burned in Quechua firepits.

Opposite, above left:
Quechua Indians, direct descendants of the Incas, walk cross-country from distant farms to sell vegetables in Cuzco. Their potatoes are one of seven hundred varieties grown in Peru, where the potato was first cultivated about the time of Christ.

Opposite, above right:
Built by Spanish conquerors on the ruins of the ancient capital of the Incas, Cuzco is believed to be the oldest continuously inhabited city in the Western Hemisphere.

Opposite, below:
From its strategic site, the Inca fortress of Sacsahuaman once stood guard over Cuzco. Stones from the fort—erected by twenty thousand Inca workers who labored thirty years—were removed by the Spanish to build the city's Catholic churches.

Llamas are also the principal Andean beasts of burden, though they willfully refuse to move if the load surpasses about one hundred pounds. Many Quechua families also herd alpacas, primarily for their wool. Lightweight and high in insulation value, alpaca wool is used in Peruvian coats, blankets, and sleeping bags—and once lined the robes of Inca royalty.

But many believe the finest wool of all comes from the smallest of the llama family, the vicuña, which remains wild. Vicuña hair is finer than that of any other animal—one seventh the thickness of human hair. Prized since Inca times, the silky red-gold fleece of the vicuña represents, when spun by mountain Indians, the most treasured wool in the world.

The last member of the family, the wild guanaco, may in fact be the first, since it has been suggested that llamas and alpacas may have been bred from wild guanacos by the predecessors of the Incas as early as 2000 B.C.

On a cloudless, frosty morning, the team sets out in *Amarillo* and the jeep over a rutted dirt road leading toward the base of Mt. Mismi. The route curves through boggy meadows soaked by mountainside springs that pool in small alpine lakes—cold, high oases. Approaching one lake, Cornu spots flecks of white moving in the distance. What could they be? It is too high for gulls, and the birds are too small and white for condors. While Cornu leaps out to film the flock, Murphy wanders along the edge of the lake, finding evidence from their tracks and droppings that they are altiplano geese.

Suddenly there is more movement and color near the lake, and the team is surprised by the arrival of pink flamingos, a sight they have previously witnessed only in warmer settings: the Nile, southern Europe, and the Caribbean.

The team's exhilaration, however, is quickly replaced by dejection. Attempting to drive *Amarillo* close to the flamingos, the men suddenly find themselves stuck in mud. Driver Gianfranco Guera, an Italian test driver loaned to the Cousteau expedition by the IVECO company, shifts into six-wheel drive and rocks the vehicle back and forth. But the altiplano muck beneath him, camouflaged by its mantle of *paja* grass, pulls *Amarillo* deeper into its clutches. En route to a mountain climb, the team abruptly finds itself bogged down in a desolate mountain valley, away from the heavy-duty machinery of civilization that could liberate the huge truck. For hours they try unsuccessfully the conventional methods of extrication: wedging rocks beneath the spinning wheels, then boards pulled from packing crates. They unload the truck. Each task, in the thin air, leaves them exhausted and short of breath. As the afternoon passes, it becomes clear that the chances of escaping the mud before nightfall are slim. The wheels are now deeply buried. De Romana leaves in the jeep to seek assistance from the manager of a silver mine several hours away. At 4 P.M., a camp is set up.

The evening passes quietly as the team warms, over a small camp stove, what they call "astronaut food," complete meals in foil packets, obtained by the expedition from a NASA supplier. The efforts to liberate the truck have taken their toll on energy levels. Most of the team still suffers from dysentery and mild altitude-caused headaches. Jouas is especially ill. Several of the men have bouts with bloody noses, and the dry air has already chapped hands and lips. Occasionally swallowing is difficult because dehydration causes the epiglottis to adhere to the larynx, or parts of the esophagus and

The Cousteau team arrives at the farthest source of the Amazon, the peak of Peru's Mt. Mismi. The group was only the third in modern times to reach the summit. *Pictured from left:* Cousteau, Ertaud, Golz.

Overleaf:
To turn their mountainous lands into productive farms, Incas built elaborate terraces like these near Chivay, which are still used by Quechua farmers.

trachea to stick together. If they stand up quickly, dizziness forces the men to sit down just as swiftly.

At dawn, as the men crawl from their tents, they see a frozen tableau about them—tiny brooks turned to solid ice, ghostly vapor dancing along the length of the stream, icicle daggers surrounding mountainside springs. The tents crackle with ice crystals; to Murphy and Jean-Michel, sharing a small tent, it sounds as if they are inside a potato-chip bag. Reaching up to touch the ceiling of the tent, they are showered with minute ice flakes, the frozen moisture from their breath.

The feeling of helplessness is renewed after breakfast. De Romana does not return. The truck won't budge. And from a small *wasi*—a Quechua adobe house—along the slope above them, an angry Indian farmer emerges and orders the team to depart. He has seen Cornu, Murphy, and Prezelin filming his llama herd and suspects they are out to harm the creatures. It becomes clear in a broken conversation with the man that he is not about to relent. Jean-Michel explains that they have no intention of bothering the herd, that in fact they are eager to leave but the truck carrying them is stuck. Jean-Michel points to *Amarillo*. The farmer stares blankly at the truck, then tells the men to leave anyway. The situation is explained once more, with the same effect, until Jean-Michel reaches into his pocket and hands the farmer a lemon cookie. Now the tone of the conversation begins to change, a tentative truce is struck, and the farmer walks home.

Since there is little to do until de Romana can find aid and return, the team simply waits all morning, reading or filming. Murphy takes water samples from a tiny stream to initiate the water studies he will carry out during the coming months, then wanders up to the house of the Quechua farmer. Sitting in the sun's rays before the *wasi* are two aged women weaving blankets. A teenager emerges from the house and invites the stranger inside.

Murphy enters a smoky darkness tainted by acrid odors—of unbathed bodies, of sheep and llama dung smoldering in an open-hearth fireplace made of loose stones. Quechua houses at this elevation have no windows; the only ventilation is provided by a single door that is left open during the day. There is no chimney either, so smoke lingers within the dark cubicle, interfering with breathing, irritating eyes and turning them bloodshot. On one side of the room there is a shoulder-high pile of blankets, and in a corner the family's only modern products, steel knives and metal pots, as well as their meager stores of food—corn, potatoes, some mutton freshly butchered.

Murphy is curious about day-to-day life and social customs. The water is too cold for frequent bathing, he learns. The family takes about two baths each year in Cailloma, where warm water is available. The men of the region have learned some Spanish, but the women in this family speak only Quechua. (It is the principal language of 90 percent of the people living in the southern Peruvian Andes, comprising some thirty dialects.) Murphy notices that the young man is chewing coca leaves and asks about their use. They are chewed with a few limey flakes of charcoal, he learns, which release a mild euphoriant effect. To provide a stimulus during the daily exertions of work or long travel on foot, and to quell their appetites, the Quechua have for centuries relied on the leaves of this native shrub, *Erythroxylon coca*, which grows on the cool slopes of the Andes down to the jungle's edge.

Above:
Workers from a nearby mine attempt to extract *Amarillo* from its boggy trap. The truck was mired here for three days before the miners and the Cousteau team succeeded in freeing it.

Opposite:
The enormous demand for vicuña hair—so fine that twelve fleeces are needed to weave a single yard of cloth—nearly condemned the creatures to extinction. Campaigns by Peruvian conservationists resulted in vicuña sanctuaries that have brought the country's herds back from 5,000 animals in 1970 to more than 60,000 today.

The stimulant is a pervasive aspect of Andean life, producing blackened teeth, dull misty-eyed gazes, and at the same time, temporary contentment in a world where survival demands a constant struggle. So integral has coca been in the Quechua life that distance between villages was once measured by the number of coca mouthfuls it took to walk the route.

"The life was dreary, it was dark, it was unrelentingly cold, it was surrounded by bleakness, it was extraordinarily simple in its elements of hard grass and heavy wool garments and llama droppings and raw meat and mud and rocks, and that was just it," writes Murphy later in his journal. "It was generally about as tough a life as I could imagine."

While Murphy is exploring highland Indian life, de Romana arrives with the manager of the silver mine and a dozen workers in a truck. The miners scramble about fastening a towline between the entrenched *Amarillo* and their truck, but when the operation of pulling the sixteen-ton vehicle out of deep mud begins, there is no movement at all. Every variation on the procedure proves fruitless. Jean-Michel sees little hope of extricating the giant machine without equipment unavailable in this remote valley.

He makes a decision. A small team will set out for Mismi from here so that the goal of the expedition is not jeopardized, and the remainder of the team will bivouac near the truck, guarding it and continuing the attempt to free it. Sumian, though valuable as a member of the climbing team, is also the strongest and most savvy problem-solver among them and therefore more useful with the truck. Driver Guera, soundman Jouas, and an Argentine team member, Ramon Avellaneda, will stay with Sumian. The climbing team will consist of Ertaud, Murphy, cameraman Cornu, Jean-Michel, and a Peruvian mountaineer, Paul Golz, who has been invited by de Romana to lead the ascent.

The next day proves disheartening. The team tries to procure pack animals to carry their heavy photographic and camping gear—as well as oxygen bottles to be used in the event of breathing difficulties—across the ten miles of foothills leading to the base of Mismi, but the Quechua farmer declines the rental offer. Then, after an hour of coaxing, he reluctantly agrees to accompany the men with a few llamas and a donkey as far as the snowline of the mountain. The group sets out, but a Peruvian Air Force helicopter, summoned earlier by Jean-Michel to fly the climbers toward Mismi, now arrives unexpectedly, swooping close to the team as it flies over the foothills, alarming the equipment-laden llamas. The spooked creatures bolt off across the hills, the Indian herder in angry pursuit. When he catches his animals, the farmer promptly unburdens them of their baggage and disappears, leaving the gear in a heap and the hapless *gringos* to fend for themselves.

The expedition shifts to the helicopter, which carries the team a few miles farther, landing when the pilot decides the air is growing too thin for a safe takeoff. It is early afternoon, so the men shoulder all they can carry—leaving the oxygen bottles behind—and begin a grueling four-hour walk to the snowline ahead. The pace slows as the trail leads higher and oxygen thins. Progress is interrupted every hundred yards by a pause so the men can catch their breath. Arriving at the snowline just before dusk, they hurriedly erect their tents and set about fixing a dinner of astronaut food. But the kerosene burner of their tiny portable stove cannot sustain a flame in the oxygen-poor air, so

Suspended hundreds of feet above some unnavigable stretches of the Apurímac, hanging bridges have been rebuilt annually by Quechuas since Inca times. As much as 22,000 feet of handspun bunchgrass is sometimes used in construction of a single bridge.

the frozen packets of food cannot be heated. Discouraged and weary, the men retire to their tents.

Murphy, whose ravenous appetite is a continuing source of amusement to the others, takes a packet of frozen food with him into his sleeping bag, calculating that the warmth between his legs will thaw the meal. When he awakens after two hours, the aluminum-foil packet has softened, providing him with aromatic, lukewarm salisbury steak. Jean-Michel and Cornu, his tentmates, protest that the odor of the food is making them nauseous, but Murphy downs the entire meal.

No one sleeps well this night, bothered by mild cases of *soroche*, hunger, and thirst. To while away the hours before dawn they write letters and record their thoughts on tape. Jean-Michel describes their feelings:

"The snow around us has begun to radiate the first dim hint of dawn, turning from gray to neon blue. Morning's arrival means the renewal of an agony that surprises us in its intensity. Every tiny movement requires an effort of will. We find ourselves winded by the act of bending and tying a shoelace. Our thoughts are drawn to the dull ache lingering in the temples and behind the eyes, which burn in the glare of dazzling snow and sun. The flexing of a hand means a sharp pain from skin cracked open by the dry air. It feels impossible to continue and impossible to stop now. The coming of daylight means returning to the terrible regime of walking, step by step by step, each stride a huge task that seems to accomplish nothing, since strength diminishes but the summit of the mountain seems to come no closer."

After a breakfast of chocolate bars and aspirin, the team sets out from their base camp to reach Mismi's peak. It is May 25, another open blue day along the Cordillera, warm in the unscreened sunlight, frigid in the shade. Headaches gradually pass, the fresh air and awakening spirits produce bursts of energy that Ertaud, calling on experience, reins in. "Walk evenly, slowly, conserving energy," he warns, "or you will run out of fuel too early."

The sunlight is troublesome. Cornu compensates with filters over his lenses and balances his exposures for the brilliant white and the rich blue of the cloudless sky above; and everyone must avoid its burning effect. The high-altitude air, less dense and clean of pollutants, does not filter the sun's ultraviolet rays as well as air above human settlements. Exposed skin can redden quickly. Because snow glare is also bright, one can receive a sunburn in unexpected places—under the chin, even inside the nose or on the roof of the mouth.

The exhausting trek continues for four hours. Constantly winded, the men stop every fifty yards to rest. With each halt, the task of setting out again becomes a test of determination. About five hundred yards from the summit, the team reaches a crest—the Continental Divide. The last leg of the climb follows a jagged ridge upward to the cornice that is the roof of Mt. Mismi. The team pauses to strap crampons on their boots for this passage, and then, in a final thirty minutes of effort, they push themselves to the top. They are only the third team in modern times to reach the top of Mismi.

It is an electrifying moment, and just as the last yards are crossed the men hear a whirring sound approaching: Prezelin in the Air Force helicopter, arriving above them with camera rolling at precisely the right moment, an unexpected blessing that crowns the moment of elation. A rabble of hoarse

Opposite, above:
The Cousteau team was forced to carry boats and equipment down boulder-strewn canyon walls, then up again when perilous whitewater forced the group to portage.

Opposite, middle:
A moment of near disaster: Dominique Sumian (*top*) has just been tossed from the raft as it lurches through a violent rapid. The veteran diver nearly succumbed to powerful cross currents and eddies, which swept him underwater seconds after the picture was taken and kept him submerged. Struggling to the surface for air, Sumian twice came up under the raft and was out of air when his third attempt to reach the surface was successful. Teammates pulled him to safety.

Opposite, below:
The team arrives to explore the Inca ruins at Tres Canyones on the Apurímac.

whoops erupts. From their packs, the team pulls a Cousteau Society banner and miniature flags representing the nationalities participating in the Amazon expedition—French, American, Canadian, Peruvian, Italian, Brazilian, Argentine. Exhilarated but drained of energy, the men attempt a reveling jig, moving in a slow-motion half-dance, arms and flags pumping up and down, feet stomping sluggishly.

Jean-Michel catches his breath and pulls out his cassette recorder. "Several times during the past two hours, I thought perhaps we had reached walls of exhaustion beyond which we could not go. I suspect each of us was silently dreaming of turning back. Yet here we are, sitting on a roof of the world in utter solitude.

"At a rounded shelf along the crest, we stop to carry out a symbolic act before Jean-Paul's camera. Ertaud, Murphy, and I hurl wedges of snow off either side of the ridge. The snow tossed down the precipitous southern slope will eventually reach the Pacific Ocean, only a hundred miles away. The snow tossed northward will join the cascade of waters heading toward the mighty Amazon and the distant jungle, waters that will roll all the way to the Atlantic."

Picking their way carefully down the icy slopes, the team completes the journey back to the base camp without incident, arriving just as night falls. They pass one more mealtime without hot food, chewing dry crackers and cold snow, and one more sleepless night.

Arriving back at the truck camp the next morning, they find *Amarillo* still entrenched, but there is a flicker of hope. Sumian and the manager of the silver mine have discovered sand underlying the mud, about two feet below the spinning wheels. Jean-Michel applies his architectural background to the problem. The sand, studded with rocks, could make a solid roadbase. The answer, though it involves backbreaking work, is to dig all the way to the layer of sand along two trenches extending fifty yards behind the truck wheels, imbed rocks in the sand, then construct a gradual incline by stacking a bed of wooden posts, arranged like railroad ties, over the rock-sand base. In effect, the only way to remove the truck from the mud is to build a long rampway out of it. The miners leave to fill the mine truck with rocks and wood planks. The Cousteau team sets about shoveling. When the mine truck returns the plan is carried out, and two hours later, with Guera gunning his truck in reverse, *Amarillo* backs up the ramp amid a chorus of loud cheers and a commotion of men rapidly scurrying around to shake one another's hands.

The team rests in Cailloma for a day, sitting all morning alongside the watchful townspeople in the central square, warming themselves, as Murphy observes, "like lizards in the sun."

In the afternoon, the men wander about the town, exchanging glances with people standing warily in doorways. After two weeks of mountain illness, Jouas, the team's inveterate prankster, is feeling better and spends some time inserting rubber spiders and snakes into unattended sleeping bags and burdening the backpack of Cornu, his favorite victim, with heavy stones. Sumian, the tireless organizer, prepares the equipment for the next leg of the trip—kayak and raft passages down the Apurímac. Cornu and Murphy range into the hillsides around town with their cameras. Murphy discovers an ancient graveyard that has been fenced to keep llama herds away. He is struck by the dense growth of grasses inside, which rise waist high. It is a revelation about the ecological dynamics of the altiplano. Where the herbivorous llamas cannot reach, the local bunchgrass is thick and tall, an indication of what the dusty habitat might produce if not thoroughly grazed by the ubiquitous llamas.

Jean-Michel studies maps and written records of the Apurímac and sketches out a route that will enable the team to ride the river for miles at a time, yet avoid rapids that have proven fatal in the past to more experienced river runners. The next day, May 28, *Amarillo*, three kayaks and an inflatable raft tied onto the top, pulls out of Cailloma, stopping at the village edge while Sumian scrambles onto the rear container and lifts the town's single power line as the high truck passes beneath.

Three experienced kayakers have joined the Cousteau team to escort them through the treacherous whitewater along this stretch of the Apurímac—Peruvians Alejandro (Chando) Gonzalez Choza and Talo Molinari Coello, and American David Ridley. The trip will pass through deep canyons and countless rapids. Below the village of Yauri lies a perilous stretch of the river called the Apurímac Gorge, which has never been navigated successfully. Two separate expeditions have resulted in one death each, and other adventurers have turned back as conditions became impossible.

The problems are many. Flowing some 750 miles before its name is changed, the Apurímac has the longest mountainous stretch of all Peru's rivers. It tumbles violently through deep gorges whose cliffs cannot be scaled should an accident occur. Rock falls threaten campers, as canyon walls cool and crack in the freezing night. And the steep descent of the river creates wildly cascading waters. The mountain Indians, unable to use the river for transportation, have long crossed over its gorges on high bridges they construct of *coyo*, a thick bunchgrass that is tightly woven into rope. The site of the most famous of these bridges is downstream along the Apurímac beyond Yauri. Its notoriety rests on a literary fiction, though an actual bridge once existed there. "On Friday noon, July the twentieth, 1714, the finest bridge in all Peru broke and precipitated five travelers into the gulf below," reads the opening sentence of a 1927 novel by Thornton Wilder. The hanging Quechua walkway over the Apurímac was *The Bridge of San Luis Rey*.

Two miles south of Cailloma, the Cousteau team unloads its river gear along the Apurímac's rock-strewn banks and sets out. The first few miles follow an easy course through a wide valley, and the team is exhilarated by the novelty of riding thundering waters. Jean-Michel waves directions, calls out to the men on the banks, and doubles over in laughter as Sumian bounces out of the boat and must hop along the rocky bank to catch up. About six miles downstream the smooth-flowing river enters a narrow canyon and the ride grows rougher. Electing to stop for a breather, Cousteau directs Sumian to grab hold of an approaching rock as they pass it. The muscular expedition leader does so, grasping it firmly and holding on. Unfortunately, the raft sails on without slowing down. Glancing over his shoulder, Jean-Michel finds himself alone in the boat and Sumian clinging to a rock midstream.

There are other mishaps, none serious. Twice the lurching raft crashes against boulders on top of which Cornu and Prezelin are poised with cameras running. Both men nearly plummet into the rushing water as they lose their footing momentarily.

Carved into the granite backbone of a mountain high above the Urubamba, an Amazon tributary that was the Incas' most sacred river, the citadel of Machu Picchu was an unassailable natural fortress covering five square miles of terraced construction linked by three thousand stone steps. Discovered in 1911, the ancient ruins beckon tourists from nearby Cuzco, who marvel at the ingenuity of Inca designers and at the mystery of their remote sanctuary, the purpose of which remains largely unexplained.

Some forty miles downstream, the team reaches a picturesque spot identified on their maps as Tres Canyones. Here two rivers—the Cayomani and the Cerritambo—join the Apurímac, all three pouring from gaping canyons. Noticing a difference in color between the Apurímac and the other rivers, Murphy suggests that the team stop and sample the water. As he will at countless sites downriver, Murphy measures for oxygen, nitrates, phosphates, pH, calcium, turbidity, and heavy-metal pollution.

The findings are disconcerting. Earlier, near the source, samples of Apurímac water have been clear and teeming with red copepods (the minute crustaceans abundant in zooplankton), but here the river is gray, devoid of plant life and copepods, and covered by a thin layer of green-brown scum. The water is one hundred times more turbid than in earlier measurements, ten times more turbid than the two rivers joining it, which are clean and lush in aquatic vegetation, animal plankton, and small fish. (A week later, exploring the roads winding above the Apurímac, the team finds an answer to the mystery: effluent from a mine is flowing untreated into the Apurímac, destroying its vitality for miles.)

On the west bank of the Apurímac, a mile farther downstream, the team makes out symmetrical rock formations—the ruins of an ancient Inca settlement. Carefully fitted mortarless rock walls connect circular stone rooms. Thatched roofs have long since disappeared, but the walls remain after hundreds of years.

"Inside this labyrinth of rock walls," Jean-Michel records, "we feel as if we are treading on history. This tiny village once drank from the Apurímac, which would now be risky because of pollution. To some modern engineers the river is a convenient sewage system, but to the people who lived within these walls, it was sacred. Listening to its torrents, they named it *Apu-Rimac*, 'Speaker of God,' believing that the river itself was a god of oracles.

"Last night, our friend Mauricio recounted the history of the Inca empire for us, and now, rubbing our fingers across the masonry work of these walls and imagining the days and nights spent within them hundreds of years ago, we are deeply moved. The people who huddled over their fires here, weaving fabrics as fine and colorful and complicated as any the world has known, eating their dried llama meat (which they called *charqui* and from which we derived our own word 'jerky'), drinking their *chica*, a corn liquor, must have taken for granted the immortality of their theocratic civilization. Their king, after all, who lived in Cuzco, which we will reach soon, was descended in a hereditary line of monarchs directly from the Sun, the supreme Inca god. This king (the 'Inca') ruled an area spanning 2,700 miles, and his subjects may have numbered 12 million. And the Inca had given his people modern improvements: one could journey about the empire on 10,000 miles of roadways; one could procure food through the Inca's welfare system if the local crops failed. The technological achievements under the Inca were themselves proof of an invincible power: metalworking processes such as smelting and alloying and casting, immense irrigation projects, agricultural terracing that created productive fields where only precipitous mountains had existed before.

"But the dwellers in these rock houses were unaware of the weaknesses of their Incan dominion. Strangely, despite their elaborate network of roadways, the Incas never invented the wheel. And for all the sophistication of

Above:
Displayed now in a Lima museum, this small gold statue was found atop Mt. Mismi by the first team to reach the Amazon's source. Inca tradition dictated that gifts—and sometimes human sacrifices—be left on mountain peaks, which were revered as gods.

Opposite:
The golden bird and monkey atop an Inca ceremonial staff reflect the mountain civilization's interest in the rain forest below them. Inca soldiers dreaded entering the dense jungle environment of heat, snakes, insects, and blowgun-wielding Indians. Though they traded for feathers and enslaved Indian bowmen, the Incas never expanded their rule into the jungle.

their society, they never developed a written language. To this day, the Quechua that remains as their linguistic legacy is only an oral language among the Andean Indians. Their great vulnerability, however, was the centralization of authority, which reposed ultimately in a single man, the Inca. When the Spaniard Francisco Pizarro arrived in 1532, he led a small force of only 180 men and 27 horses. Yet he overwhelmed an opposition army facing him across a valley in northern Peru that may have numbered as many as 30,000 to 80,000 soldiers. The trick was simple. He captured the Inca, Atahualpa, and the entire political structure of the empire dissolved in confusion."

For four days the men press down the Apurímac, camping some nights, leaving the river to spend other nights in a small hotel in Yauri. The rapids become more dangerous, forcing the team to portage on occasion. Frequently the men beach the raft and kayaks, then climb up a canyon wall to scout the rapids ahead. Chando Gonzalez estimates the levels of difficulty, using the numerical scale recognized internationally by kayakers. These "classes" of danger run from one to six—a Class One rapid being "very easy," a Class Six rapid being "very dangerous and just about impossible." At times the Cousteau team encounters Class Four and Class Five rapids on the Apurímac, electing to run some, avoiding others.

Chando and Talo, despite their expertise, each flip over in their kayaks once, and Talo, sucked underwater in a powerful eddy, fails to surface for nearly a minute. Helplessly, the Cousteau team watches his paddle and overturned kayak float nearly a hundred yards downstream before his helmeted head reappears. While running a rapid classified by Chando as a "low Five," Sumian is thrown from the raft as it crashes into a jumble of large boulders. He caroms from rock to rock, propelled forward too wildly to get a handhold on projecting boulders. He is finally tossed out of the roaring water chute into deeper water, but rushing currents pull him below the surface. When at last he fights his way back up for a breath, he emerges twice directly under the raft and is forced down again. Though capable of holding his breath for more than a minute and one of Cousteau's most experienced divers, Sumian nearly passes out, deprived of oxygen by the high-altitude air in his lungs. Struggling to the surface one more time, he grabs a paddle extended by Talo and is pulled to safety.

Just before midnight on May 31, the team pulls into Cuzco aboard *Amarillo*, stumbling with their backpacks, duffel bags, and camera equipment into the Dorado Hotel, where Anne-Marie Cousteau and Guy Gervais greet them. With hot running water, shiny tile floors, and stained glass windows, the Dorado seems an apparition of luxury after two weeks' camping in freezing, dusty mountains and dingy hotel rooms with only bowls for washing and without warm water.

Reaching Cuzco is, symbolically, like arriving at the core of the Andean spirit. When it was the home of the Inca and his nobility, Cuzco was the capital of the Empire; its name means "navel of the world."

The conquistador who broke the Inca dominion, Pizarro, was merely one of scores of Spanish explorers ranging through North, Central, and South America looking for the fabled El Dorado, the City of Gold. Pizarro found it, or at least an approximation of it, when he entered Cuzco. Peru was the last

Opposite, above:
Each year, Andean natives gather for a spectacular mountain festival called Qoyllur Rit'i, "Star Snow" in Quechua, at the base of Mt. Colquepunku, east of Cuzco. Ritual ceremonies reaffirm the sacred and interdependent nature of the entire ecosystem, celebrating man's place *within* it. In the Andean world, life-giving water is a magic fluid that rises from the jungle to settle on snowpeaks and then returns down mountain slopes, irrigating agriculture en route.

Opposite, below:
Vividly colored weavings have enriched life in the stark Andean environment for centuries. Hat styles among the Quechuas designate the wearer's place of origin and rank.

major Spanish discovery and the greatest treasure of all. Cuzco proved richer than any other place in the New World. Yet to the Incas, the metals that impassioned the strangers were merely esthetic materials used for ornaments and religious decorations. Gold was "the sweat of the sun," and silver "the tears of the moon." The empire's subjects needed no money—work or woven cloth represented the trading currency. Thus when Pizarro demanded as ransom for the release of Atahualpa enough gold to fill a sizable room, and twice that much silver, the Inca nobles obliged submissively.

The long history of a resourceful people dominated by invading armies and religions and cultures, of lost riches, of displacement into the least-productive highlands and the most adverse conditions for life, has left a lingering strain of distrust among the Quechua peoples. Near-absolute isolation only enforces their fear of the outside world. As one Peruvian writer notes, in Quechua minds "the Devil merges with the image of the stranger."

The caution and reserve show in the sullen eyes of the Indians in Cuzco. A few young men who hover around the marketplace and inspect the tourists passing through perhaps justify their attempts at petty thievery by comparing it to the exploitation of their world. Slashing a razor blade swiftly through a camera bag carried by Jean-Michel, an unseen arm tries to pluck out something of value before disappearing among the crowds of the market. Another cuts into Ertaud's shoulder bag. Hands reach out to grab the ankles of team members while other hands reach quickly into pants pockets. In the impoverished Andes, the crew realizes, desperation begets minor desperadoes. A Peruvian journalist tells the men that highlanders riding the train through the mountains south of Cuzco keep their belongings clasped to their chests. When the train passes through dark tunnels, thieves grab loose items and toss them through open windows to compatriots waiting alongside the tracks.

Remembering these Cuzco incidents, Murphy and Cornu grow alarmed when, a few days later, they realize that some eight Indians are quietly advancing toward a tent they have set up while filming in the mountains above Cuzco. Some of the Indians are shouting at them, a few are picking up stones. The two photographers recognize that to people barely scraping a living from scrabbled earth, they probably appear ludicrously wealthy. To avoid a confrontation, Cornu and Murphy quickly toss all of their gear into the jeep and drive away. Distressed by this episode of apparent hostility and perhaps near-violence, the two men soon come upon a festive crowd of Quechuas celebrating a wedding. Leery of stopping despite the photo opportunity, the men consider driving on. An Indian woman, however, beckons to them. They enter the party, are treated to food and *pisco* (the common Peruvian brandy), are embraced, are invited to photograph the bride and groom, and leave after three hours thoroughly charmed and confused about the Quechua attitude toward strangers.

On June 8, the Truck Team makes its first descent from the Andean highlands into the jungle. Jean-Michel has flown in *Papagallo* above the Apurímac Gorge the previous day and has pronounced it too dangerous for them to enter. The cold corridor has sheer walls rising nearly 4,000 feet to the Cordillera Vilcabamba, and the river itself, which looks from the air like a ropy green belt under the bellies of gray mountains, is in some places completely blocked by rocks.

Some Qoyllur Rit'i dancers dress as jungle Indians to enact ceremonially the connection between the highlands and the jungle lowlands where, it is believed, the ancient Inca ancestors now reside.

"To reach the jungle," Jean-Michel records later, "we would obviously have to drive around the Apurímac Gorge in *Amarillo*. My decision was to approach the low forest in two places, transporting a team led by Cornu and Murphy first to the Manú region east of Cuzco, one of Amazonia's most unique blocks of jungle, and then to send a team led by Sumian north to the Apurímac port of Luisiana. There, beyond the Apurímac Gorge, Dominique will oversee the assemblage of a large inflatable raft which we will eventually board for the next leg of our voyage down from the source.

"The seemingly easy exercise of driving from Cuzco to Manú has proven to be incredibly complicated. Because the mountain road is too narrow for vehicles to pass one another, the government has decreed it a one-way road. A schedule has been worked out so that traffic goes in one direction on Monday, the other way on Tuesday, and so on. The direction of the traffic switches each night at midnight.

"We leave Cuzco about 10:30 in the evening, after packing *Amarillo* and the jeep with enough supplies and equipment for a one-week expedition in the jungle. Things go well for about two hours as Gianfranco driving the truck and Murphy the jeep follow the thin dirt road along the steep slopes and then, suddenly, there is a tunnel ahead, a tiny tunnel. When we reach its mouth, it becomes obvious that *Amarillo* is too high to pass through it. There is no other route except through the impassable tunnel, which is not noted on maps and was never mentioned when we inquired in Cuzco about road conditions. We can't let the air out of the tires to lower the truck, nor can we remove the rear container, which is the obstruction. The ludicrous situation baffles us. I notice that everyone is shouting different directions to Gianfranco at the same time and waving him in opposite directions. We have no alternative but to back the truck up the narrow road looking for a site wide enough to turn around. Dominique and Murphy lead this strange entourage with flashlights and finally, about two miles back, Gianfranco is able to maneuver *Amarillo* around and point us back to Cuzco. Luckily, we meet no oncoming traffic before reaching the city. Now we must wait a day for the road to reopen and spend it removing the container from *Amarillo* and streamlining the truck for another attempt at the tunnel, which means a tiresome job of repacking everything once again. The task is further complicated by several cases of dysentery.

"This morning, just after midnight, we set out again and this time pass cleanly through the tunnel. The road climbs high into the mountains, through 15,000-foot passes, and starts to descend. By dawn the environment around us, nurtured by the moist jungle air, begins to soften. Mottled greens beard the mountainside, which is dominated by a resinous shrub named *tola*. We pass through colorful villages and the team's mood seems to improve the farther we descend toward the lush jungle. 'Down is good,' says Murphy, 'and flat is better.'

"Then a tire on the jeep blows out. We continue to the next village, where there is a gas station, but the owner says he can't fix tires. We spend two hours searching for someone who can, finding at last a man named Hernan, who says, 'I fix tires.' Hernan begins banging on the tire with a pick ax. When the tire and tube are off the rim, Hernan tells us, 'I have no patches.' We search the village again, locate a man with patches, and return to Hernan. When the tire is repaired, we are off again. But by now night is falling and we

The climactic moment of Qoyllur Rit'i comes as dancers dressed as bears ascend the mountain to gather sacred pieces of ice from a high glacier. Native beliefs and Christianity mingle as the dancers carry a cross.

are still far from our destination. When Murphy turns his jeep headlights on, nothing happens. No matter what we try—fuses, wires—nothing helps, the lights are dead. Now we have only a few hours to reach Manú, because at midnight the road direction changes and we would be stranded for two days.

"In order to continue, we must accelerate and Murphy must drive the jeep directly behind *Amarillo* as it races around hairpin curves and through unseen muddy potholes along a dark, curving road. A dense mist has arisen, meanwhile, to further obscure a road already hidden by the black Andean night. Concentrating intensely on the truck taillights, Murphy is reminded of arcade games in which one tries to steer around obstacles painted on a whirling drum. Blinded to all but the two tiny red lights ahead, Murphy and Cornu notice odd sounds from time to time, a dull thudding beneath their wheels. As they enter the jungle, it is warm enough to roll down the windows. They hear rushing water accompanying the curious thudding. Suddenly they realize that the occasional sounds were bridges. It is a chilling realization, since Andean bridges are often rickety assemblages of wooden planks.

"And here, where local people walk the roadway in the warm night, there is another peril. Amused by the sight of the strangers' yellow truck, adults and children wander into the road after it has passed, laughing and shouting, unaware of the dark jeep barreling along behind it. Murphy and Cornu spend a harrowing three hours honking and shouting to avoid a catastrophic accident.

"We make it before midnight and pull onto a grassy clearing near the village of Shintuya. The tents are set up, we ravenously down a stew prepared by Sumian, and we fall asleep quickly in the warm jungle night. As the dawn arrives and a flock of green parrots squawks overhead, we see about us for the first time a lush green palisade of trees and vines and suspended orchids. We feel warm air against our skin. I think of a similar moment described by the American William Herndon when he crossed the Andes in 1851. 'Before us lay this immense field,' he wrote, 'dressed in the robes of everlasting summer and embracing an area of thousands upon thousands of square miles on which the footfall of civilized man had never been heard. Behind us towered, in forbidding grandeur, the crests and peaked summits of the Andes, clad in the garb of eternal winter. The contrast was striking and the field inviting.' "

Above:
Bear dancers descend with ice chunks they will carry all the way to their home villages. The ice water will be stored carefully all year and dispensed gradually as a healing fluid supplied by a spiritual mountain.

Opposite:
A bear dancer passes among parading celebrants in a Cuzco street. Lightly touching the frozen burden, a young Quechua dancer illustrates the Andean belief in water as a source of magic—a source of life.

THE ENCHANTED RIVER

ABOARD "CALYPSO" | RIO AMAZONAS | BRAZIL

As *Calypso* pushes through the swirling currents of the main river en route from Belém to Manaus, the crew is kept on twenty-four-hour alert to sight hazards capable of disabling a small vessel. Through frequent storms and the black of night a headlight on the prow illuminates the water surface ahead so watch crews can spot jungle flotsam being swept toward the sea: hardwood logs that could bludgeon the ship's propellers, splayed tree trunks that could damage the pine hull planking, drifting islands of dense vegetation that could slide beneath the vessel and snarl the propellers.

The floating islands are a testament to the muddiness of the Amazon. So much silt clouds the water that grassy meadows chiseled from the banks by floodwaters can survive afloat for months, dangling their roots into the fertile soup of the river. The majority of this silt comes from Andean streams like those studied by the Cousteau Land Team in Peru. Sandbanks, sometimes eight feet in depth, are bulldozed along the bottom by strong currents, creating ripples of coarse sand that limit riverbed fauna and invalidate navigational maps. At its mouth, the Amazon discharges 900 million tons of sediment each year—the equivalent of every man, woman, and child on earth annually dumping a 450-pound bag of dirt into its waters.

Like all rivers, the Amazon rises and falls each year as the rainy season and dry season alternate. In such a massive water body draining such a vast area, the difference between low and high levels can be enormous, as much as sixty feet in some places and commonly thirty to forty feet. About January each year, the lower Amazon, swollen with rainwater, begins to surge over the rims of sediment built up like levees along its banks. Vast stretches of the jungle are engulfed by a sea poured from the river. This seasonal deluge creates the largest inundated forest area in the world, called the *varzea*, a wooded floodplain covering about 27,000 square miles in wide swaths along either side of the river. The mammoth swamping and then subsiding action

Sailing upriver between Belém and Manaus, *Calypso* sports a novel bowsprit, a Brazilian native sculpture called a *carranca*. Believed by *caboclos* of the São Francisco River to ward off evils, the wooden figureheads are mounted on canoes. Brazilian sculptor Davi Miranda created the oversized model on *Calypso*'s bow specifically for Cousteau's Amazon mission.

forces the jungle into an amphibious existence, surviving six months beneath the water and six months above.

As *Calypso* passes the mouth of the Madeira River, Cousteau decides to make his first trip into dense *varzea* and sends Braunbeck and Falco in the helicopter to scout along the banks for an entrance into the forest. At intervals they see glades opening into the jungle where boats can thread among the submerged trees. It is through these notches in the riverbank, called *furos*, that the high river gushes into the forest.

The watery scene below the two men is vaguely surreal. Where it penetrates the canopy of trees, the sun illuminates the flooded floor of the forest. The sea of water seems to flash and shimmer along the trees, a gold incandescence oozing through the dark jungle.

Passing over grassy meadows, Braunbeck and Falco are amazed as the mirrored glint of sunlight reveals water everywhere. The dense vegetation is in fact a verdant mat, a prairie floating atop the flood. Flying parallel to the river's edge, they come upon farmers' houses and entire villages invaded by brown water. Cattle and horses perch awkwardly on log rafts, vegetable gardens grow in wooden bins hanging from high poles, children wave at the helicopter as it blows water circlets about the dugout canoes that serve as their only playgrounds.

Returning toward *Calypso*, Braunbeck crosses an opening in the forest cover and Falco suddenly waves, directing the pilot to circle slowly. Something has caught his eye. Amid the trees they see an oddly shaped creature, as pink as a newborn infant, meandering gracefully among the inundated tree trunks: the pink dolphin of the forest. The creature's beak is abnormally long, javelin-like; from its back rises a low triangular bulge, more ridge than dorsal fin; its fins and flukes seem disproportionately large; from its head protrudes a rosy melon-size hump. Slowly but elegantly the dolphin twists its way through the trees, waving its beak as it hunts, sometimes contorting into gymnastic maneuvers as it weaves around branches or reverses direction. Neither Falco nor Braunbeck has ever seen such rubbery flexibility in an aquatic animal.

Back aboard *Calypso*, the two men report to Cousteau. "A dolphin in the trees," Falco smiles. "A pink dolphin that hunts through the woods with the dexterity of a jungle cat!" It is not the crew's first sighting of the Amazon's freshwater dolphins. Nearly every day they have seen glimpses of two dissimilar species rising to breathe along the river surface. One species looks nearly identical to marine dolphins and inhabits the main river, traveling in packs. Amazon settlers and fishermen call them *tucuxi* (too-coo-shee). The *Calypso* team refers to them as the "gray" dolphins, to distinguish them from the other species. The slower, larger, more solitary "pink" dolphins are commonly known in Brazil as *botos*.

Hoping to film the dolphin spotted in the forest, Cousteau and six others depart from *Calypso* in the hovercraft and a Zodiac. At the mouth of the Madeira they see two collapsing houses in the distance. Raymond Coll, who speaks Spanish and has acquired enough Portuguese to converse with river people, approaches first in the Zodiac. Two families have abandoned their wooden houses, one of which now dips into the river. The support posts seem to have given way, tilting the house precariously. A dog lies across a partially

Opposite, above:
During six months of each year, the Amazon's rainy season deluge causes the river to flood an area of forest nearly as large as Austria. In some places the dry jungle floor is turned into an eerie lake bottom fifty feet below the water surface.

Opposite, below:
The immense annual pulse of the river transfigures the surrounding jungle and determines the nature of human life at its edges. Settlers cope with a waterborne existence half the year, herding livestock on rafts, building hanging gardens, dependent upon their boats for mobility.

submerged table on the porch. Chickens perch on railings. A crowd of people, mostly children, have taken refuge in a ramshackle hut built upon a scrapped riverboat. They clamber over one another to peek at the Cousteau team.

Coll calls to a shirtless man who squats in a canoe, trying to shore up the support timbers of his house. The flood and the storm of the previous night have combined to do a little damage, he tells Coll. Perhaps it will take them two to three months to repair the houses.

"It happens nearly every year," he says stoically. "We keep the houseboat and move there for a time."

"How many are you?" Coll asks.

The man scratches his head, then calls out to his wife on the boat, "How many are we?"

The answer is "thirteen."

He adds, "We lost fifteen hens."

Watching from the Zodiac, Cousteau smiles and says to Falco, "A true farmer: he knows how many animals he has but not how many children."

The men set off again, skirting the forest's edge, and pass still more flooded homes. A fisherman beckons to them and they look inside his hut. He has unfurled a net across his submerged living-room floor. When he gathers it up, there is a fish in it.

Bebert laughs and tells Cousteau about the flooded church he has seen three days earlier. He docked the hovercraft at the entrance and walked across a slimy, water-covered floor to the altar, where perhaps two dozen bats suddenly emerged. A school of tiny fingerlings circled among the pews.

In an isolated clearing, the team spots a small hut that betrays no sign of life. When Falco approaches in the hovercraft, however, the sound disturbs a swarm of huge bees whose nest is lodged in the roof. They emerge in a buzzing cloud and Falco spins the hovercraft about as quickly as possible, narrowly escaping their attack. Sitting in the back seat of the vehicle, *Calypso* engineer Paul Martin sees three skeletal dogs in the hut, which is otherwise empty but for a foot of water. It is a pitiful scene, and Martin wonders: Is the owner away fishing? Has he abandoned his dogs and hut because of the flood? Or has he met with disaster, a victim of the storm, a disease, a venomous animal, a boating accident?

Occasionally the men pass farmers feeding their livestock. Confined to rafts or a small patch of high ground, cattle and horses are unable to graze, so their owners must carry the pasture to them. The team watches men fill boats with grass from floating meadows, then paddle to their small herds— usually one or two dozen animals—and loft the feed onto floating rafts or into shallow water.

J.-Y.C.—*I am struck by the curious life of these Amazon river people who are universally known here as* caboclos, *a term encompassing all of the subsistence farmers, miners, fishermen, rubber collectors, and hunters who live an impoverished existence in Amazonia and descend from a racial mixture of Indians, Europeans, and blacks. Their lives are water-dominated, determined by the vicissitudes of the perpetually changing river. They make decisions—about planting, building, raising livestock—with-*

Lights and cameras ready, two Cousteau divers prepare to descend into a flooded forest near Santarém. The *Calypso* team made the first extensive film documentation of underwater life in the inundated jungle.

out knowing if the river will reach up and obliterate their hard work, drown their gardens, swamp their houses, carry away their herds. They live with a fate that is unforeseeable, because the source of the floods is far away. The weather above their heads is not so important as the weather up tributaries hundreds of miles away, where heavy rains may start a deluge heading in their direction.

This vulnerability makes comprehensible the deep belief of caboclos in fearsome supernatural spirits, despite their widespread Catholicism. It is not so different from Andean tribes who worship the sun, their life-sustaining source of warmth in a fiercely cold environment. Here, dependent on the whims of an erratic river and the benevolence of a jungle filled with untamed creatures, the caboclos believe in river and forest spirits. These demons wreak havoc upon them as punishment for misdeeds, reward them for appropriate behavior, or simply play with them, sometimes maliciously.

Dr. Nigel Smith of the University of Florida, who has studied Amazon legends for a number of years, has identified countless supernatural creatures in the ontology of river people. Many believe in a giant water snake, perhaps a gargantuan cobra that is so large its slithering movements create channels in the flooded forest. Cobra grande can swallow a canoe-load of people and steal souls as it emerges from the river at night. Staring into its eyes, a person can become encantado, enchanted.

There is a tapir-nymph in the flooded forest that attacks people viciously or releases an insanity-inducing stench. There are ghosts haunting certain lakes—spirits of people whose violent deaths spilled blood into the water. So deeply do fishermen believe in these legends that they refrain from fishing in these lakes.

Some caboclos even believe that spirit villages exist at the bottom of the Amazon. Stories abound of river people who have heard beneath their canoes the sounds of netherworld settlements: chickens clucking, turkeys gobbling, dogs barking, goats bleating.

Perhaps the most engrossing Amazon legends, however, involve dolphins: how they sprout legs and walk away if caught, how they assume the form of a lovely woman and lure men to their river-bottom dwellings, how they deceive young women and, in the form of handsome men, sire children with them. Dolphins are blamed, for example, if a caboclo returns from a lengthy absence to find his wife pregnant. It is said that the eye of a dolphin can cure impotency, its tooth remedy a toothache. The stories tantalize us, heightening our curiosity about these unique freshwater dolphins.

We take a turn, at last, into a narrow channel that leads to peaceful waters from which project, as far as we can see, a bewildering assortment of trees—palms, figs, "kapok cotton" trees, rubber trees, and a mix of fruit and nut trees unique to the Amazon and known by exotic names such as cupuaçu, maracujá, açaí. It appears, despite the immersion, to be a robust, healthy forest. Yet how odd it all strikes me. The tree trunks would seem to be timber pilings for a monumental pier if they did not loom up and extend living umbrellas above us. We still our outboard motors and glide among these amphibious giants in awe.

Opposite, above:
A school of fingerling fish darts through a submerged forest. Countless species of fishes follow a seasonal existence—they feast in the swamped woods, then migrate up tributaries to spawn as the jungle drains during the dry season.

Opposite, below:
A Cousteau diver examines the foliage of a submerged tree in the flooded forest. Like animals of the river and forest, trees have evolved to survive an amphibious existence among rising and falling waters.

We have been told that the jungle is quiet during the midday heat. Yet I look at my watch—11:30 A.M.—and listen to a chorus of sounds penetrating the heavy air—birds, monkeys, crickets. Some calls seem to ricochet along the water surface and echo under the ceiling of leaves. I can only think of the ethereal music in a cathedral, haunting, wafting about like a cloud of sound.

I feel adrift in an anomaly of time and evolution. Here I am, a modern man, wearing a wristwatch, carrying in my shirt pocket a calculator, suddenly transported into an enduring scene of Creation. A green iguana appears in the water ahead of us, swinging its scaly reptilian head in a metronomic wigwag as it slithers through the flood. Suddenly, from an overhanging branch, diving objects hit the water around the iguana with loud plouffes! *Five identical green iguanas scatter through the water and trees like streaking torpedoes. It is a primeval moment, perhaps a miniature of scenes witnessed by our mammalian ancestors as gigantic iguanodons clashed during the Cretaceous period.*

Coll points to a bulbous brown nest attached like a tumor to a tree trunk. Cousteau carves a window into it with his penknife and a dozen termites scurry away. Workers will return to seal off this wound with bits of fecal cement and saliva, as millions of generations of termite workers have done for millions of years.

Mounier, studying the canopy for signs of life, spots a monkey about a hundred feet ahead and the team paddles toward it. Now they see not one but thirty or forty, many of them small, youngsters with parents they assume. As Mounier stands up in the Zodiac to train his zoom lens on the creatures, the adult monkeys begin to scream. The shrieks grow violent as the men approach, and now one adult comes screeching down toward Colin. For a moment he imagines the creature is going to leap into the Zodiac and wrest the offending camera from his hands. The monkey is beside himself with anger. But his compatriots quickly jump away above him, from tree to tree, and he soon retreats with them.

Now Falco spins around, his face beaming, and points quickly through the trees to the left. He cups his hand about his ear, signaling to Cousteau that he has heard something. The entire team sits in rapt attention. A moment later, the others hear it too—the gasp of a solitary swimmer somewhere behind the tree trunks in the distance. It is a freakish sound that breaks through the hum of insects and birds. Again, a minute later, this aberrant sigh and gulp of air repeats. It is an eerily human sound. With the next breath, they are able to catch a glimpse of the swimmer breaking the surface, puffing steamy air from its blowhole, humping up for an instant before plunging back underwater, its triangular pink back knifing through the surface. Though the wary pink dolphin disappears quickly, at times during the remainder of the day the men hear occasional gasps of respiration in the distance.

The glide through a primordial world continues. Scott Frier snaps shots of several khaki-brown birds resembling water rails, as they dive at crabs scuttling to and fro on overhanging limbs. A variety of nests hang like ornaments among the trees—red bees, honey bees, orchid bees, arboreal wasps. Ants file along branch after branch. Spiderwebs drip from some trees and cover

High-water marks clearly record the changing river levels, which can rise and fall the height of a four-story building. *From left:* J.-Y. Cousteau, Zlotnicka, Falco.

others like gossamer shawls. Blue morpho butterflies pass lightly by, as if on the impulse of the wind, scouting about for nectar. A ruby-colored butterfly alights on a canvas bag in the Zodiac and remains there a full five minutes, eliciting a smile of chagrin from Jacques Constans, the enthusiastic insect collector. He has not forgotten to bring along a butterfly net. It is inside the canvas bag.

J.-Y.C.—*The most enthralling enterprise is taking place below us. It is a phenomenon we heard about long before setting out for Amazonia, and this is our first opportunity to witness it closely. Falco has noticed the circles in the water beneath a flowering fruit tree. We drift close and watch in silence. A wine-red berry drops from a branch overhead, plopping into the water. Quickly a shadow darts through the murky water and the berry disappears before it can bob back to the surface. Falco reaches out to a low branch and shakes it, releasing a shower of fruit. As the red globules thud into the water, there is movement below. Suddenly the somber mood of the forest is shattered by splashes. Fish leap from the depths to gobble the floating berries and dash back into the darkness.*

During the long months of high water in the Amazon, many fish leave the river and emigrate into the flooded forest. Like flocks of underwater birds, they soar among the submerged branches to feast on the fruits, nuts, seeds, flowers, and insects of the rain forest. These "fish of the trees" surely have no true ecological parallel anywhere else in the world: they are aquatic harvesters of treetop produce.

We watch as a large oval fish with an olive-green back—a fish perhaps fifteen inches long—swims to and fro nearby, waiting. Generation upon generation of his species have cruised forest waters, no doubt, assembling a legacy of genetic information about tree barks and trunk shapes and sap fragrances. This individual knows instinctively to hover beneath this species of tree. "It is a tambaqui, *probably our most important commercial species," says our friend Dr. Assad José Darwich, a limnologist from Brazil's National Institute for Amazon Research (INPA) who is accompanying us from Belém to Manaus. "*Tambaqui *are related to piranhas, and they occasionally eat small fish and insects, mostly during the dry season, but their principal foods are fruits and seeds which they consume intensively during the high water." He motions to the tree overhead. "They seem to favor the seeds of rubber trees like this one," he says.*

The story he tells is one of phenomenal specialization. The tambaqui *have evolved strong jaws and broad, studded teeth that are perfect for crushing hard nuts. The seeds of rubber trees, abundant in the* varzea, *are high in protein, and the* tambaqui *gorge on them in the inundated forest for several months, building up reserves of fat. When the water begins to subside, the fish swim back into the river and migrate up tributaries, where they are believed to spawn. (There is still a great deal to be known about the behavior of these and most other Amazon fish species.) While the* tambaqui *are gone, and surviving on their stored fat, the forest is drying out. The rubber tree seeds that escaped the* tambaqui *lie on the forest floor. The purpose of specialized dentition in the* tambaqui *is evident in the hard, rough capsule that surrounds the seeds. This impermeable nut wall also*

makes the seeds buoyant, and during one or two months afloat, the capsules can be widely dispersed. So long as the fibers of the capsule wall are wet, the nut covering remains intact; but when the capsules are finally lodged on the drying forest floor, the fibers stiffen under the sun's heat and the capsules explode like tiny bombs. The rubber tree seeds are sent flying as far as thirty-five feet, ensuring that the seedlings will grow in scattered locations, a pervasive trick of the rain forest that limits pest damage by widely separating the individuals of a species.

Dr. Michael Goulding of INPA and the Goeldi Museum in Belém, who has studied the interplay between the creatures of the river and the varzea, *believes that the fishes of the Amazon and the flooded forest "have interacted to an extent unknown elsewhere on the planet." While the fish derive obvious benefits from the trees, they may perform some services for the forest, including dispersal of reproductive matter. Among the fruits and seeds they consume, some pass through their digestive tracts undamaged and descend to the forest floor.*

Though the water is too murky for good filming, we are curious to see beneath the surface of the flooded forest. Coll, Bebert, Arturo, Bertrand, and I suit up and then descend into the engulfed woods. As our lights flare through the burgundy-brown fluid around us, black shapes erupt with color. I drift downward past a dark tuft that turns into brilliant emerald leaves under my light. Reddened by the waters bathing them, buttressed tree trunks appear to be columns plunging into an infinite darkness below. I glide weightlessly through shady corridors streaked with shafts of iron-red sunlight. I have the impression of rambling dreamlike through a woods that has been transformed into a bewitched forest. I watch Arturo touch the bark of a palm tree; loose dust drifts upward rather than downward. Along the surface overhead a caterpillar flies. Rising to take a breath through my snorkel, I see in the dry branches above a flock of green parrots dining on berries, causing them to cascade down. Cherrylike fruits drift above me in the liquid breeze. I sink downward again. Strange markings on a submerged tree trunk catch my eye; I run my hand along ribbed scars produced during another season by a rubber collector's blade. I follow the tree to its base, perhaps thirty-five to forty feet below the water. A small fish dashes away upon my arrival, hiding behind the tree trunk. I peek around and the juvenile eyes me warily, moving to keep the barrier of the trunk between us as I gently circle the tree. Only when Raymond Coll arrives and switches on the underwater camera does the little creature dash away.

In the distance, once again, I hear the periodic inhalations of a pink dolphin, but my efforts to approach him underwater are to no avail. The creature knows we are here. The frail sonic bursts I hear are giving him an acoustic profile of the strangers intruding in his woods. I wonder if these odd-looking mammals might befriend us if we can find a way to swim at their sides for a period of time.

Suddenly there is a loud splash above, a diver entering the water. For an instant my mind is transported into the mythical world of the caboclos, *who believe that the tapir-nymph,* tapirê-iauara, *patrols the flooded forest to guard it from humans. It is the crashing sound of the beast's elephan-*

tine ears plopping on the water surface that warns people away. The eeri-
ness of the forest, swamped in blood-warm water and permeated with a
somber stillness, plays on my mind. I recall that caboclos *believe that a*
human who dies in water cannot be admitted to heaven. Rising from the
gloomy depths I crash into a bladelike palm frond, which slices my finger
open, a minor cut that nevertheless stings. As my head emerges into the
air, Falco calls out to me with a laugh, "Two brown water snakes just
zoomed past your snorkel!" I climb into the Zodiac, sucking on my bleed-
ing finger. Colin, camera focusing on the tiny wound, draws me back to
reality with a smile and jesting shrug. "La vie scientifique!" *he says.*

While the divers and the photographic crew explore the Amazon's edge,
Calypso's scientific team analyzes the waters of the main river. Their principal goal is to measure the amount of productivity—the volume of tiny aquatic
organisms sustained by the river, which provides the food base for larger
organisms. Through the day and night, marine biologist Phillip Dustan, Constans, and several Brazilian scientists supervise the raising and lowering of
equipment from *Calypso*'s decks, ranging from Niskin bottles, grabs, and
dredges to an expensive multiparameter probe instrument that continuously
carries out seven different measurements. Costing about $75,000, the probe
has been nicknamed "the Rolls Royce" by *Calypso*'s deck crew. The information recorded on the probe's cassette tapes is correlated with the ship's position and the time of day and then stored in computer diskettes. Though
chlorophyll content is of particular interest, the "stations" made by the scientific team also profile the Amazon's changing turbidity, pH, temperature, oxygen content, nutrients, conductivity, salinity, and light penetration. Water and
sediment samples are also collected for later analysis in laboratories. En
route to the rendezvous with Jean-Michel's Peruvian Land Team, the ship's
scientists will take about a thousand discrete measurements and samples.

What the river measurements reveal is an enormous paradox. So minimal
is the productivity of the Amazon's waters that one would expect a barren
liquid desert beneath the surface, nearly devoid of fish. Yet the river appears
to teem with fish. How is this possible?

The most important obstacle to life is the dense turbidity caused by the
nearly one billion tons of silt washing down from the Andes. Light-penetra-
tion measurements reveal that the photic zone, the depth at which at least one
percent of the surface light remains, is typically less than three to five feet.
Dustan believes that what phytoplankton there is may survive by "grabbing a
breath of light" as the turbulent river brings the tiny algal plants briefly to the
surface, then quickly mixes them downward into dark waters again.

Biological common sense dictates that the blockage of sunlight and corre-
sponding impoverishment of primary production should result in a dearth of
plankton-eating small fish and small-fish-eating larger fish. Yet when hydro-
phones are lowered into the muddy waters by Dustan, soundman Zlotnicka,
and Dr. René Guy Busnel, a bioacoustician who has studied dolphin communications on other *Calypso* voyages, the tape recordings reveal a steady,
widespread, and raucous murmur of fish "voices." Listening to the tapes in
the *carré*, Cousteau likens them to the cacophony of birds and insects in the
forest. There are periodic croaks and grunts, a fuzzy electrical hiss, doleful

cries like those of a human baby, rasps, and guttural belches. Laughing over this discovery, that "the fish of the Amazon talk all day," a sudden revelation strikes Cousteau: "The chattering fish are undoubtedly the source of the *caboclo* legends of spirit cities on the bottom of the river!"

Cousteau observes that the tapes provide evidence of two things: an abundance of fish, contrary to the measurable food support supplied by the river, and the evolution of highly developed acoustic behavior in fishes, presumably an adaptation to life in a dark environment where vision is of limited value in finding a mate, declaring territory, spreading an alarm, or discouraging the attack of a predator.

Dustan recalls reading in a book by Michael Goulding that scientist T. R. Roberts reported in 1972 the predominance of "ostariophysan" species in the Amazon, fish that have evolved a special sound-reception device: modified vertebrae that conduct noises from the amplifying swim bladder to the inner ear. Ostariophysan species may account for more than 75 percent of the fish in the Amazon, including catfishes, piranhas, *tambaqui*, carps, and electric eels. The team's hydrophone recordings thus seem compatible with the known taxonomy of Amazon fishes.

That taxonomy covers a freshwater fish fauna more diverse than that of any other river or lake on earth. Perhaps half of the fish species in the Amazon are still to be discovered and named. The estimated 2,500 to 3,000 fish species of the Amazon basin comprise four times as many species as those in the Zaire, eight times as many as in the Mississippi, ten times as many as found in the whole of Europe. Among the five hundred species of catfish—the most abundant species—there are tiny bloodsuckers only an inch long and behemoths that reach more than six feet and three hundred pounds. A tiny catfish, the *Candirus*, carries out a maneuver that frightens river people as much as the piranha, perhaps more so. About the size of matchsticks, *Candirus* enter the orifices of swimmers—not only nostrils but also anuses, vaginas, and urethras. There they lodge themselves by extending stiff spines attached to their gill covers. The pain on penetration is agonizing and the removal nearly impossible without surgery.

The Amazon is also home to archaic fish like the *pirarucu*, which can reach a length of ten feet and a weight of about four hundred pounds, perhaps the largest freshwater fish in the world. Confusion exists over its claim to the title because the largest specimens, intensively hunted by *caboclos*, may have disappeared now. There is a record more than a hundred years old of a *pirarucu* that measured nearly fifteen feet. In addition to gills, this biological relic also uses a primitive lung—adapted from its swim bladder—to breathe surface air in the oxygen-poor lakes it prefers.

Though piranhas have gotten the most press, there are other hazardous Amazon fish. An adult electric eel, whose battery-like tail organs discharge between five hundred and a thousand volts, can stun livestock and kill a human. Stingrays lie immobile on some sandy bottoms and defend themselves by injecting a venomous substance into the foot of an unsuspecting wader. Stingrays are one of the more than fifty species of oceanic fish found in the Amazon, which include bullsharks, herrings, anchovies, soles, puffers, and toadfish.

The extraordinary diversity of Amazonia's fishes is perhaps best illustrated

Opposite, above:
Rhaphidon vulpinus, called *peixe cachorro* (dog fish) in Brazil, uses its two enormous canine teeth to stab fish as large as half its own size; the victims are swallowed whole, head first. Amazon fishermen catch these efficient predators, which reach a length of two feet, as they pursue migrating fish schools upstream during the dry season.

Opposite, middle:
A young Ashaninca Indian shoulders his catch, one of the sizable catfishes found throughout Amazonia. Among the largest Amazon fish, catfish can reach nearly seven feet and 250 pounds.

Opposite, below:
In the still waters of the inundated jungle, *caboclo* fishermen shun hook and line for lance or bow and arrow to capture fish waiting near the surface for dropping fruits.

by the harmless beauties that thrive in its shallow tributaries: tiny tetras, which are captured and transported to home aquariums around the world, where their neon-rainbow colors entertain millions of people who are perhaps unaware that the flashy little buds of life darting about in their living rooms were once part of the legendary Amazon.

J.-Y.C.—*For several days we are absorbed in the mystery: how could such an extraordinary proliferation of fish, such a remarkably diverse collection of fish, thrive in a river of relatively sparse primary production? Eventually we find there are two answers to the riddle.*

Our first clue comes when we review our fish-sampling results during two weeks of casting nets along the course of the river between Belém and Manaus, then correlate these findings with what we know of the chemical nature of these waters. Scientists have identified three kinds of Amazon rivers, and caboclos *have anointed them with names: white rivers, black rivers, and clear rivers. Each river has characteristics that inhibit life. The "white" rivers, such as the main Amazon and the Madeira, are not really white but* café-au-lait, *muddied by the suspended Andean sediments that restrict light and therefore photosynthesis. Typically, the white rivers are neutral to slightly alkaline. The "black" rivers, such as the giant Rio Negro, are not really black but a cola-red color, stained by dissolved humic acids from the soils where they originate. Highly acidic and poor in inorganic ions, the black rivers are so barren of large fish that* caboclo *fishermen call them "hunger rivers." The Rio Negro has been measured at pH 3.2—closer to vinegar (pH 2) than pure water (pH 7). The "clear" rivers, such as the Tapajós and the Xingu, are not necessarily clear but often an olive green. Chemically they are similar to the black rivers. (To simplify a complicated matter, we have taken to referring to the latter two kinds of rivers as "black" rivers.)*

As we sail upriver, we see that the Andean-dirtied white rivers are cascading down from the west, while the black rivers generally converge from the north and south. Where these junctures occur, the two kinds of rivers mix, though in some places they travel side by side downriver for miles before the white river muddies and consumes the black river.

We notice an interesting thing: our scientific fish catch rises significantly at the conjunction of white and black rivers. Flying in Felix *above the meeting of the Amazon and the Tapajós, Jacques Constans saw blooms of algae near the line of convergence that he described as fluorescent green clouds feathered by the currents, resembling in places a living aurora borealis. The phenomena of phytoplankton and fish were compounded by the abundance of hunting dolphins at these meetings of white and black waters.*

Our conclusions are that a kind of aquatic alchemy takes place: when the waters mix, the white rivers add nutrients to the barren black rivers, while also neutralizing their acidity. At the same time, the black rivers dilute the turbidity of the white rivers, enabling sunlight to penetrate and photosynthesis to proceed. The answer is not a "miracle of loaves and fishes" in the Amazon but pockets of vitality that nourish fish along the points of black- and white-water confluence. Looking at a map, Phil Dustan points to the principal towns along the main river, most of them originally founded by fishermen—Santarém, Obidos, Manaus, Coari, Tefé. All are situated near a meeting of white and black rivers.

Yet the meeting of different waters seems to be only a partial solution to the puzzle of fish abundance. As we search for the answer, we again consult the studies of Dr. Michael Goulding, who has discovered an astounding fact: about 75 percent of the species caught commercially depend upon the flooded forest for their survival. Some fish eat fruits and seeds and insects directly, some prey upon these harvesters.

We confirm the fact when Calypso *docks in Manaus. At six A.M. Bebert and I roam the Mercado Municipalo fish market. As we walk from counter to counter, we ask the names of fish species. Tucunare, pirapitinga, jatauarana, pacu, tambaqui. Tambaqui!* Where were they caught? The answers vary geographically, but the pattern is clear. Most were captured in or near the flooded forest, or as they migrated to or from it.

The riddle of the fishes is found in the forests. The symmetry of nature's design is complete: the river spills its load of fresh Andean silt and nutrients into the adjacent forest, making it the most fertile land in Amazonia. The forest in turn sheds its nourishing produce into the river, providing an ecological welfare system that nurtures an immense and rich population of river fishes. When the floods withdraw through the furos *back into the river, they wash organic jungle matter into the impoverished Amazon. The photosynthesis that cannot take place in the dark or turbid river occurs in the sunlit canopy above, and then tumbles into the river.*

The river feeds the forest. The forest feeds the river.

Cousteau is curious about the fishermen who have learned to exploit the flooded forest. On June 15 he sends a team led by Coll to visit Isla Careiro, an island rising in the middle of the main river about twenty miles from Manaus. According to scientists from INPA, the flooded island is rich in commercial fish. Scouting about the island by Zodiac, Coll befriends a *caboclo* fisherman, Aldeberto Moreira, who volunteers to lead a diving and filming crew to his favorite fishing spots the next day. Since most of his fishing is done at night, the team is also welcome to wander with him through the flooded forest the following evening. When Coll asks Moreira what species to expect, the list is a long one, beginning with *tucunare* and *tambaqui,* ending with piranhas.

"Piranha famosa!" laughs Aldeberto.

When Coll relates the conversation to the rest of *Calypso's* crew over dinner, a few whistles erupt. There is some good-natured teasing of the divers who will make their first rendezvous the next day with the legendary Amazon predator; Xavier Desmier, Arturo Calvo, and Coll merely shrug their shoulders and grin.

Towing Aldeberto's canoe by Zodiac, the team follows his directions into a narrow canal that cuts through a dense carpet of floating water-hyacinth adjacent to the inundated woods. While the fisherman sets out a gill net near the hyacinth, the divers suit up and check the underwater cameras. Coll is the first to submerge. When he surfaces, the imperturbable veteran calmly warns Desmier to watch out for the piranhas, which are nipping at his flippers. The

Opposite, above:
So sharp are the triangular teeth of the piranha (*Serrasalmus*) that Indians use their razorlike edges as cutting tools. Though long characterized as the most lethal of predatory freshwater fish, not all of the piranha species—numbering about twenty—eat meat. Some consume fruits and nuts of the flooded forest.

Opposite, below:
Cousteau diver Bertrand Sion displays a piranha bite incurred when he attempted to remove the fish from a net. Powerful jaws enable predatory piranhas to clip out chunks of flesh, a formidable threat when they attack an injured animal en masse.

divers circle the net carefully, finding only a few fish, but among those whose gill covers are snagged, several show signs of ravaged fins. Piranhas are taking advantage of their immobility, diving to clip off and eat portions of their fins. With razor-sharp triangular teeth, the speedy predators can cut away chunks of fin as cleanly as if scissors were at work. As an experiment, Coll sticks his finger through the net, then quickly withdraws it as two small piranhas approach to investigate. It is the closest the divers come to danger.

Piranhas do not attack humans often. People living in the Amazon interior swim among them with indifference during most of the year, a fortunate situation since piranhas are found nearly everywhere in the river basin. However, there are circumstances that call for extreme caution. During low-water periods, the normally small schools of piranhas are sometimes concentrated within a shrunken habitat. The ferocity of the competition for food at such times creates great commotion, and river people, seeing the churning water, realize that they would be devoured along with the fish of the river. They stay on the banks. Piranhas also appear to attack wounded animals of almost any size, probably smelling their blood or sensing their vulnerability.

In this land of spirits and legends, the violence of the piranhas engenders tales of horror that range from the unlikely to the unimaginable. One legend has it that an entire army regiment was devoured while fording a deep stream on horseback. As the story goes, their flesh disappeared while their uniforms went undisturbed.

As with ocean sharks, however, the savage reputation of the piranha seems exaggerated and overly simplified. There are many piranha species, some scientists estimate twenty in the Amazon, and not all are meat-eaters. There are species that feed on the fruits, seeds, and leaves that fall in the river. There are also fin- and scale-eating piranhas that make their living stripping off and consuming rows of scales from passing fish, or snapping off chunks of caudal or anal fins. Since fishermen routinely bring up otherwise healthy fish missing portions of their fins, it seems that these foraging attacks of piranhas do not necessarily kill the victims.

At nightfall, Aldeberto sets a lance and trident into his canoe, ties a battery-powered lamp onto his head in the manner of a coal miner, and paddles noiselessly into the blackness of the water-engulfed jungle. Yves Zlotnicka sits in the rear of the canoe, holding out his microphone to capture the sounds of Aldeberto's hunt and of the enveloping forest. Coll and Mounier follow at a distance in the Zodiac, rowing quietly and doing without camera lights so the fishing will not be disrupted. Quickly disoriented in the darkened jungle, Coll and Mounier realize they would be lost without the tiny beacon of the fisherman's headlamp in the distance. Without a light of their own, they find themselves crashing from one low-hanging branch to another, bumping against wasps' nests and colonies of stinging ants as they try to pursue and film the fishing. The feeling is one of being lost in a dreamy maze, and it is both eerie and amusing. At one point Mounier asks Coll, "Do you see any branches ahead?" The answer comes back, "I don't know; I think you're in front."

Aldeberto, on the other hand, glides through the night forest cleanly, as if he knew the location of every tree. Occasionally he slows the canoe to a halt

Above:
As water levels subside, unsupported banks topple into the river, loosened by floodwater seeping downward, contributing to the Amazon's immense load of suspended sediments.

Opposite:
The extraordinary pink dolphin of the Amazon (*Inia geoffrensis*), known locally as the *boto vermelho*. In addition to its unusual appearance *Inia* exhibits greater dexterity than marine dolphins, twisting like rubber as it meanders through the flooded jungle.

Overleaf:
Seen from above, scalloped sands appear the color of embers through the cola-red waters of a strand of the Rio Negro. Humic acids leached from decomposing forest matter give the river its strange hue.

with his wide, heart-shaped paddle and stares fixedly at a tree trunk. The lamp on his forehead inevitably reveals a fish at the base of the tree, hovering motionlessly, stunned by the bright light or perhaps asleep. Instantly, and with extraordinary dexterity, the fisherman hurls his lance and pierces the fish. Aldeberto's skill with the weapon amazes the Cousteau team: throughout the night, he casts the lance time after time. Each time he retrieves the weapon, there is a fish on the end.

After an hour in the forest, the team realizes they are not the only interlopers come here to catch fish. Far off among the darkened trees they hear the distinctive sigh and gasp of a pink dolphin prowling the woods. They wonder what else is lurking here, aware that the flooded jungle is home to *jacarés* (the Amazon crocodilians known elsewhere as caimans), anacondas, poisonous spiders, and disease-carrying insects.

Aboard *Calypso*, Brazilian taxonomist Luis Portugal has told the crew of his experiences in the flooded forest. He was canoeing with another scientist one night in total darkness when suddenly, without warning, a salvo of flailing objects came rushing down upon them, tearing the other man's shirt, slashing into his side and back, drawing blood. They were huge iguanas, perhaps slipping from a tree overhead in panic, raining upon the horrified men, unintentionally wounding with their hard, sharp tails in their desperation to flee. Descending like demons of darkness, the lizardlike green creatures deeply frightened the two scientists.

To preface another story, Luis explains that many residents of the forest floor ascend trees as the flood season arrives, sustaining themselves in the treetops for months. Among the creatures leading this cyclical existence are fire ants. Rains and floodwaters take millions of casualties among fire ants, but some colonies gather on limbs, swarming in living balls. Occasionally these masses drop into the flood. Rather than dispersing, the ants continue to swarm and the living ball floats about the forest until it strikes a limb or trunk where the colony quickly streaks back up into the dry canopy.

Canoeing alone through the forest one night, Luis unintentionally struck such a drifting ball of fire ants with his oar. Instantly the swarm exploded in a frenzy of dashing insects that shot up the oar and into the boat. Momentarily stunned, and imbued with the natural curiosity of a scientist, Luis leaned forward on the rail of the boat to get a closer look at the chaotic scene. His forearm landed on a squadron of fire ants, and scores of the insects injected their stinging venom into his flesh. The welts rose quickly and the open sores that resulted did not heal for eight months. In such a situation the only solution, Luis explains, is to dive underwater and wait for the ants to disembark from your empty canoe and move onto a nearby tree.

For Coll, Mounier, and Zlotnicka, the night voyage through the forest proves no more than anxiety-inducing: no wounds, no horrors. When the dawn approaches, Aldeberto weaves back among the dense trees and the two boats emerge precisely where they originally entered the forest. In this way, explains Aldeberto, he catches ten tons of fish each year. Though impressed by this statistic, the Cousteau team finds more staggering his ability to pick his way perfectly through the ink-black forest and his nonchalance when explaining that he spends most of his nights alone in a shadowy jungle enveloped in haunting sounds and ominous possibilities.

Opposite, above left:
Like a temperate-zone youngster on a bicycle, a *caboclo* child rides a canoe about his principal playground, the cresting river. Amazon children learn at an early age to handle boats, which take them to school, to fishing grounds, to neighbors' houses.

Opposite, above right:
Exploring a water world as diverse as a coral reef—*from left:* Falco, Cousteau, unidentified team member (*behind*), Calvo.

Opposite, below:
Calypso divers Coll (*left*) and Desmier find underwater filming complicated amid the ubiquitous floating vegetation of the Amazon.

THE FOREST OF ILLUSIONS

LAND TEAM | MANÚ PARK | PERU

While seasonally flooded forests, such as those being investigated by *Calypso*'s crew, cover a mammoth area, they represent only about 2 percent of the entire Amazon basin. Most of Amazonia is characterized by woodlands that are humid but seldom if ever flooded: the *terra firme* forests. The Manú National Park in eastern Peru is one of the least-penetrated regions of the *terra firme*, an isolated pocket guarded to the west by the Andes and to the east by the absence of major rivers that could carry modern travelers into its luxuriance. Covering nearly 4 million acres, Manú's protected forest is the fourth-largest national park in South America. The few scientists and adventurers who enter it find an undisturbed world offering wildlife encounters that are increasingly rare in much of Amazonia.

Most of the Peruvian Land Team have driven downriver to the Apurímac port of Luisiana to prepare the rafting expedition that will rendezvous with *Calypso*, but at Jean-Michel's suggestion, Dick Murphy and Jean-Paul Cornu remain temporarily in Manú Park with two Peruvian scientists, ornithologist Deborah McLaughlin and ichthyologist Saoul Sanchez. The four spend several days canoeing along quiet meandering rivers, leaving the water occasionally to trek into the jungle.

Drifting down the reddish Manú River, Murphy and Cornu photograph caimans sunbathing on sandspits, turtles crowded together on floating logs, monkeys peering nervously from bankside trees, river otters bobbing their heads in and out of backwater streams to catch a periscope glimpse of the canoeists. Birds congregate along the water's edge in raffish abundance— tiger herons, boat-billed herons, horned screamers, sun bitterns. More than five hundred bird species have been identified in Manú, Deborah McLaughlin says. She points and raises binoculars to her eyes now and then: a toucan sits motionlessly in a treetop; dazzling hummingbirds pause and dart away.

Two Ashaninca girls wear the traditional sacklike garment, called a *cushma*, and facial decorations of red grease made from the seed pod of a small fruit tree (*Bixa orellana*) called *achiote* in Peru. Makeup designs are individualistic and change daily.

83

She identifies a strange musical call deep in the forest as a trumpeter bird. Macaws streak overhead, squawking hoarsely.

In the black warmth of the jungle night, Murphy dons a headband flashlight and follows a trail leading into the forest. Even at night in the *terra firme* forest he is struck by the pervasiveness of water. A mist hangs among the trees. Dewdrops cover every surface, dripping from leaves, streaking tree bark with glistening wormlike tracks. Stumbling against the trunk of a small chonta palm tree he is drenched by a dewy shower. His light reveals spider webs bejeweled by the vapory air, and along the floor he sees the pithy, liver-brown remains of decomposing tree trunks, miniature forests of fungi and lichens rising from them, a gloss of night moisture casting an eerie sheen over the mounds.

By day, along the same trail, the team looks for the layered structure of the rain forest proclaimed by classical forest science: an open understory of dead and living floor vegetation and shrubs, above that a layer of small-tree crowns, above that the interwoven and dense main canopy, and above that, at wide intervals, the crowns of a few forest giants that thrust their leafy heads through the canopy and spread out to soak up sunshine. From below, however, the team finds it impossible to see definitive divisions, though they know that within the tangle of lianas and branches life obeys a vertical distribution—species of birds, bats, mammals, and insects specially adapted to the foods and the shelter of each level.

To humans traversing the floor of the jungle, unable to see the biological business being carried out high above, the dominant form of life appears to be insects. On their arrival in Manú, the team was besieged by relentless swarms of biting flies along the river. The team continually spray themselves with insect repellent, which quickly washes away in perspiration. Their only sanctuary is the river. To fight the bugs they jump in and out of the water, trying to maintain a coating of moisture over their skins. The system is hardly practical as they attempt to film and to take biological samples. Now, after three days of jungle life, they are covered in bites. Ever the scientist, Murphy finds time to count his sores. Each consists of a tiny red dot with a white circle of skin around it. Murphy discovers 277 bites on his body.

Just before they leave Manú to rejoin the rest of the Land Team on the Apurímac, Murphy and Cornu hear a peculiar story from a park ranger. Occasionally the park staff has come upon the remains of tiny campsites, with smoldering firepits and rough palm-frond shelters. The primitive belongings scattered about do not resemble the gear of a hunting party from one of the tribes living in Manú's isolation. Finally the rangers encounter the campers: three naked Indian women living a lonely, wandering life, outfitted with only a blunt stone ax and a few arrows, speaking a language unlike that of any tribe in the park. They appear to be an aged mother with two teenage daughters. Seeing the rangers, they recoil in abject terror and flee into the woods. Their identity is a matter of conjecture: are they survivors of a tribal battle, ostracized offenders of a village code, victims of a mental or physical disease, or simply people who got lost and never found their way home through the faceless jungle? The ranger takes Murphy and Cornu to one of their abandoned campsites, where footprints, the cold ashes of their fires, and some debris from a cooked turtle remain.

Opposite, above:
Moments after it was christened by a champagne bottle, the raft dubbed *Pirarucu* set sail down the Apurímac toward an eventual rendezvous with *Calypso*.

Opposite, below:
The frigid Andes behind them, the Land Team relaxes on the warm, gentle Apurímac. *From left:* co-author Richards, Fabian Cousteau (Jean-Michel's son), Jouas, Ertaud, Parodi, guide Policarpo, Jean-Michel.

(Nearly a year later, a Cousteau team will return to Manú and find the three women. Though by then wearing dresses, they remain fearful as Louis Prezelin and Brazilian photographer Ayrton Camargo gently approach in a canoe. They do not run away, however, and permit the men to film. After about an hour, the sound of *Papagallo* rises in the distance, and the three women grow visibly tense. As Gervais sets the plane down on the river before them, the women cling tightly to Camargo and Prezelin. Before leaving, the men pass gifts around—blankets, fishhooks, knives—and the meeting ends in smiles all around. To the unknown language of the women three new words have been added, and they are called out repeatedly in farewell as the strangers depart: "Ayrton!" "Louis!" "Airplane!")

LAND TEAM | RIO APURÍMAC | PERU

The village of Luisiana is a tiny collection of low buildings a mile from the Rio Apurímac. It is dominated by a large plantation owned by a gregarious, mustachioed, sombrero-topped man named Pepe Parodi. In local parlance, Parodi is a *patrón*. His operation processes cacao into cocoa butter and chocolate and turns sugar cane into rum and a soft drink called Pepe Cola.

Adjacent to his sheds Parodi also runs a small vacation resort, which, though comfortable and decorated handsomely in tropical motif, is rarely visited by tourists. Parodi explains that his duties as a member of Peru's Chamber of Deputies in Lima—equivalent to the U.S. House of Representatives—prevent him from actively pursuing tourism. A workman on the plantation suggests another possibility: the growing guerrilla movement in the foothills to the west, which threatens to invade the sleepy Apurímac valley. When the Cousteau team settles into Parodi's hotel for two weeks, to build their river raft for the next stretch of the headwaters, they are warned not to venture beyond the gates of the compound. Guerrilla violence is the implied reason. (Though he pays little heed, Jean-Michel Cousteau has been told, at an embassy party in Lima weeks earlier, of a rumored terrorist plot to abduct him or his father.)

The now-gentle Apurímac and the rich greenery stretching in every direction from it, the comfortable hotel, the swimming pool, the fruit trees—all combine to soothe the tired muscles of the Land Team and dispatch any anxieties about political strife. When the Manú Park team lands on Parodi's grass airstrip in *Papagallo*, Jean-Michel greets them with a smile. "Welcome to Paradise," he says.

There is some exaggeration in this, because the team's work load has not diminished significantly. Dominique Sumian directs the assemblage of a 37-foot raft, a "Colorado-River-style" inflatable craft which has been carried aboard *Amarillo* from Lima, along with a ton of accessories designed and built for the expedition: watertight aluminum storage crates for cinema and science equipment, radios, canvas rain covers, jungle hammocks. When hand pumps have ballooned the raft's central donut and two side pontoons to the correct pressure, and the aluminum central platform is tightly bolted

Opposite, above left:
An Ashaninca woman prepares *masato*, the fermented drink found in Indian villages throughout western Amazonia. Manioc is chewed by the women, spit into pots, and mixed with yams for the purple color. Children drink fresh *masato*; adults down copious amounts of the beverage after two to three days of fermentation increases its alcoholic content.

Opposite, above right:
Ashaninca girls learn to weave baskets and prepare food while still very young, since many bear children and begin raising families by the age of twelve.

Opposite, below:
A young Ashaninca wife weaves cloth for a ceremonial *cushma* to be worn by her husband. Ashaninca women rarely don elaborate clothing.

together and packed with gear, the satellite "pinger" is transferred to the raft. Prezelin's guitar goes aboard, along with two bottles of Parodi's rum. The preparation is complete. Jean-Michel suggests a name for the ponderous raft: *Pirarucu*, after the largest Amazon fish.

At noon on June 29, christened by Mrs. Parodi with a bottle of champagne, the raft embarks. Standing near the bow, a local Indian named Policarpo signals directions to Sumian, who is aft steering the outboard motor. The first days of the trip are without incident as Sumian easily navigates two dozen rapids, then pulls up along sandy beaches at dusk, where the team erects camp. Throughout the day, settlers pass the raft in long rough-hewn wooden boats called "pecky-peckys," after the sound of their outboard motors. The team notices a resemblance between these river people and the Andean Quechuas. Deborah explains that the population pressures and altiplano hardships in the mountains have begun to drive highlanders down into the Peruvian jungle, which they call the "Selva."

Late on a July afternoon the team anchors on a barren spit of sand where the Rio Cutivereni joins the main river, now called the Ene. Immediately Indian children appear on the opposite riverbank, all wearing chocolate-brown *cushmas*, cotton gowns worn traditionally by the tribes of this region. Soon there are adults lining the rocky bank too. All are barefoot, some sport facial designs of a greasy red substance from a seedpod called *achiote*; one young man wears a headband. Deborah identifies them as Ashanincas, who are also known commonly in Peru as *campas*.

The Selva Indians have been classified into thirteen linguistic families living in more than a thousand identifiable communities. While some have peripheral commerce with the scattered towns of the Selva, most Indians have had little contact with any *civilizados*, except for an occasional missionary, miner, or settler.

On the plateau above, at the end of a long grass airstrip, is a Franciscan mission identified on the maps simply as Misión. The team is greeted by Father Mariano Gagnon, a robust, jovial man dressed in short pants, identifiable as a priest only by the gold cross bouncing against his bare chest. Father Gagnon is athletic and full of energy. Originally from New Hampshire, he has lived in the Peruvian jungle for thirty-two years.

The mission at Cutivereni is only ten years old, the third he has built. It took more than a year just to clear the airfield using machetes. About three hundred Ashaninca Indians live near the mission, but at least five thousand come here occasionally for fishhooks or matches or machetes from the mission dispensary and for medical help from the infirmary, which is run by five nuns. The area has one of the highest malaria rates in the world. Father Gagnon himself has the disease.

The Franciscan priest assures the team that they are welcome to stay at the mission and prepares a welcoming meal of fried *zungaro* (a large Amazon fish), *yuca* (a starchy root known elsewhere as manioc), and cold Peruvian beer.

Jean-Michel outlines for Gagnon his plans for an expedition from Misión through the jungle to SeWerd Falls, a spectacular, seldom-seen cascade. Gagnon believes he can help to arrange Indian guides and porters.

Gagnon is an impassioned protector of native tribes, among whom he has spent most of his adult life. Since 1979 waves of *colonos*—settlers from the highlands—have followed the rivers down to the Selva, where they are allowed to claim as much as one hundred square meters of riverfront land. The settlers quickly level most of their land claim and plant commercial crops of cacao, fruit, or, in many cases, coca, which can be sold to cocaine processors for a relatively high profit. Father Gagnon recognizes Peru's need for economic development and the desperate poverty that compels the settlers to seek new lives. The trouble is, he says, the settlers are ruining the lives of the natives. The tide of settlers is eroding Indian territory rapidly and compromising forest ecology. The river is suffering too, says Gagnon. Many of the settlers use dynamite to fish. Consequently, traditional Indian fishing is less and less productive.

The priest's primary goal at the mission on the Cutivereni is to create a practical school for Ashanincas. Gagnon wants to teach them not only reading and writing but also the growing of peanuts, cacao, *yuca*, bananas—so that families will survive as development encroaches on their homeland. An annual income would enable the natives to resist acculturation while at the same time they are gradually admitted to the Peruvian economy and society. At least, he believes, they could survive as a people and the shock of development would be softened. It would be unrealistic, he says sadly, to think that development will not eventually sweep this land.

As Gagnon speaks, Jean-Michel realizes that the fish they have consumed was a precious store in the mission kitchen. Fish are hard to come by in the river these days. This *zungaro*, a 155-pound giant, was caught two weeks ago, refrigerated, and saved for special occasions. It is sad how the life of the river has deteriorated, says Father Gagnon.

The next morning is spent filling up backpacks with supplies from the raft. To cool off in the heat, the team occasionally dive from the raft into the Cutivereni. Near them a young Indian boy catches a fish. Reaching down to remove it from his hook, he is bitten by the struggling creature. The boy comes to Sumian and shows him a badly slashed fingertip, which is quickly bandaged. Murphy recognizes the species of fish immediately: piranha. The team members spend little time digesting this interesting piece of information and leave the river.

Studying a map, Jean-Michel and Sumian calculate that the cross-country trek will cover about thirty-four miles to the falls and back, along the Rio Cutivereni and through dense jungle. They decide to fly the team, equipment, and porters to an airstrip near the native village of Comantavichi, and to set out on foot from there.

The "airport" at Comantavichi is merely a grass strip surrounded on all sides by forest, with a single thatched hut the size of a large tent at one end. "The terminal and gift shop," declares Jouas. The plane is greeted by a dozen Ashanincas, who are fascinated by the crew's bizarre equipment. They pick up the black rubber diving fins and laugh roundly.

From the airfield, the team walks about one mile through the forest to Comantavichi. They are invited into a large hut, where the men of the tribe are told by Father Gagnon the purpose of this visit. The chief is cooperative, but he imposes certain conditions. The strangers can stay the night in Comantavi-

Opposite, above:
Indian fishermen, helped here by the Cousteau team, barricade a spur of the main river, then spread *barbasco* in the dammed area.

Opposite, middle:
As the milky *barbasco* disperses, it interferes with fish respiration, killing some fish and driving others to the surface, where they are speared by lances or arrows.

Opposite, below:
Smaller fish caught during a *barbasco* poisoning will be used as bait; larger fish are sliced up and prepared in a stew.

chi (it is too late to set out). No problem. The villagers will guide them to the falls, as long as there is fair reimbursement (they need spools of fishing line, for example). No problem. If one of the strangers touches a village woman, they will cut off his penis with a machete. Jean-Michel asks Gagnon if the chief is kidding. He is not.

As a sign of hospitality, the men of the village then offer a drink of *masato*, the product of chewed *yuca* and saliva, a beerlike brew made daily by the women of the tribe, who spit the mash into bowls, add purple yams for color, and ferment the fluid in gourds. Seeing the team's reluctance, Father Gagnon points out that the drink is "no worse than a passion kiss."

Unfortunately it is dark when the men begin, for the first time on the expedition, to hang their mosquito-netted, canvas-roofed hammocks. The challenge of construction proceeds under winking flashlights and the rapt gaze of the villagers, who find this infinitely diverting. Guy Jouas proudly finishes before the others. As he tests his hammock for the first time, the metal ring at one end breaks and Jouas crashes loudly to the ground, to the delight of the Ashaninca audience.

The next day, the walk proves far more difficult and much longer than anticipated. The procession climbs up steep slopes, using exposed roots and stones as steps, over fallen tree trunks, across logs that bridge small streams and scummy pools. They pass through a cloud of flea-size white flies, like a buzzing ball of fog. Large wasps float about in their jittery way. Quickly the team's legs ache from the twists and shocks of the path—rocks slip away, mud slides, a vine snags a leg, a fallen tree limb rolls beneath a foot. Occasionally a team member reaches out to catch his balance only to discover he has grabbed a tree trunk covered in thorns. Orange mingles with the flecked greens about them: orange butterflies, orange roots snaking out of the forest floor, iron-orange rocks, orange mud, orange fungi clinging to dead trees, a centipede-like crawler with bright orange legs, orange *achiote*-smeared Indian faces. Hiking through the jungle understory they feel vaguely *inside* of something, an immense greenhouse perhaps, cool, moist, shady, filled with the humming of bees and wasps and the distant chatter of birds. When they emerge into the sunlight of a clearing or a stream, the impression is that of stepping *outside*. For four days the team pushes ahead over boulders, up vertical mud walls, hanging at one point from a limb in order to swing out forty feet above the river and drop to a narrow ledge of shale.

Nights are spent in small Indian villages, where the Cousteau crew's dinner of astronaut food cooks over the same fire with the Ashaninca soup of *yuca* and water. Like most Peruvian Indians of the jungle, the Ashaninca exist almost entirely on the starchy *yuca*, eating it at every meal, adding a fish stew or some fruit only to complement this staple. Their principal beverage, *masato*, is merely fermented *yuca*. Though they appear healthy, their diet is nutritionally barren, and the lack of old people in the village seems to indicate how vulnerable they are to diseases such as malaria and tuberculosis.

Though the walk is enormously tiring, there is solace in the teeming life about them. The team notices a fungus on dead logs that has the color and texture of human flesh; clinging to some logs there are what appear to be human ears, to others a nose or fingertip. Army ants caravan along the trail.

Opposite, above:
Two essential tools of the Ashaninca: a machete, with which trails are cleared, huts constructed, and animals dispatched; and a balsa raft, used by children and adults to ford rivers, to fish, and to travel short distances.

Opposite, below left:
While the fish catch is cleaned, Ashanincas often snack on fish lips, considered a delicacy.

Opposite, below right:
A young three-toed sloth (*Bradypus variegatus*) dines on leaves, moving in slow motion through high branches. Among Amazonia's most exotic creatures, these arboreal mammals spend nearly all their lives in the forest canopy, descending to the ground only to find another tree or to defecate, an act that occurs only every eight days because of a digestive system even slower than the creature's climbing motions. Once believed to stay in a single tree all their lives, sloths are now known to feed in nearly a hundred different species of trees.

Overleaf:
Though the swimming behavior of sloths had been witnessed, the creature's adeptness had never been so well documented before the Cousteau expedition. This sloth moved through water with greater speed than through the tree canopy.

Jean-Michel catches a flying red and green beetle the size of a small mouse. Butterflies dance in every direction. There are curious waterbirds, black with white heads, that play above the water and hop about on boulders. Sumian slaps a bug climbing his neck and a sweet perfume is released.

One afternoon, Cornu, Murphy, and Jean-Michel accompany the Ashaninca porters as they seek fish for the evening meal. They construct a temporary dam of logs, leaves, and soil, which corrals fish in a shallow offshoot of the Cutivereni. When the dam is complete, tangled brown roots gathered from the mountains are brought out. Several Indians pound the roots, releasing into the water a chemical called *barbasco* which interferes with fish respiration. Tiny fish struggle to the surface and the natives spear the flopping, stunned catch easily. That evening Jean-Michel describes the procedure into his tape recorder, then reflects:

"The Indians of the Selva regard their bounty carefully. They believe spirits reside in the trees of the forest and the water of the rivers. One spirit, the *Yacumama*, protects the flora and fauna of the jungle, punishing hunters who are greedy, rewarding those who take only what they need. They shake their heads in disdain when they see the *colonos* from the mountains urinate into a stream. Ashanincas avoid such acts religiously, as a symbol of respect for life-giving fresh water.

"The encroachment of less reverent settlers into the land of the Ashanincas is deeply regretted, but a stoicism born of their mythology seems to prevail. The current sadness in their lives—the arrival of *colonos*, loggers, miners, and drug buyers—the Selva natives explain as the destruction of the world by God, who occasionally recycles all of nature through a cataclysm, creating thereby a new world.

"Over dinner tonight we learned from Diego de Almenara, a young man from Lima who is a volunteer worker at Misión and has accompanied us as a translator, that the government is proposing to build three dams on the Rio Ene which would immerse nearly everything we have seen in the past few days—Father Gagnon's mission, many of the Ashaninca villages, including Comantavichi—beneath a lake ninety-three miles long. The hydroelectric output of the Paquitzapango project, named for the site of the dams at a narrow canyon on the Ene, would provide enough electrical energy for most of Peru, enough to export. Prior to construction, lumber companies would be authorized to clear the area of forests, so that vegetation would not interfere with the machinery of the dams.

"So it goes in the recycling world of the Ashanincas."

On the fourth morning, the team arrives at Sewerd Falls. Ribbons of white water drop nearly a thousand feet into a pool the size of a soccer field. About two hundred yards before the falls, the guides point to a flat floor of brick-red stone terraced into two levels. The water flowing across this natural patio has eroded it into perfectly symmetrical squares. The water cascades from one level to another, pouring through the slots between the "tiles" as if faucets had been placed there by landscape architects.

Jean-Michel, Sumian, and Murphy don their diving equipment and enter the cold pool. For about an hour they dive with underwater cameras. They find two species of fish, possibly three, and emerge beneath the velvety spray at the foot of the falls. They look from a distance like three black figurines beneath a milk shower. Perched on rocks about the pool, the Ashanincas follow the divers' every movement in puzzled admiration.

Jean-Michel decides the team will leave before dawn the next morning and attempt to make it all the way to Misión in one day—to make up precious expedition time lost en route and because food supplies are low. Rising a half-hour before dawn, Cousteau writer Mose Richards watches a bat skim and turn above the dark river, a vague flash of black wings and a tweeky sonar sound. Lighting a candle near his hammock, which has been stretched out on the ground, he sees a dozen sand spiders scurry away. He has spent the night sleeping among them without knowing it. When light comes, it brings ever-present yellow wasps, which have intensified their swarming as clothes and packs have grown more saturated with the salt of perspiration, which they crave. Sumian has warned the team to be careful with the wasps, which hover about their faces all day. Should someone accidentally inhale one into the mouth or nose, its sting could cause the throat or nasal passages to swell up and restrict breathing to the point of suffocation.

Leading the line of marchers, Jean-Michel sets a blistering pace, pushing to beat the darkness to Misión. Half an hour into the walk, thunder sounds and a light rain arrives. It is cool and refreshing, but the rocks grow slippery. Fifteen minutes later, Richards slips, wedging his right foot into a rock crevice, and falls at an awkward angle, badly wrenching his right knee. Each step from this point on shoots a burst of sharp pain through the knee. But there is no way to reach Misión except on foot, and Richards is not alone in his suffering. Nearly every team member struggles with a wound of some kind. Cameraman Cornu, who pushes ahead to film the expedition and the forest, then falls behind and must strain to pull ahead of everyone again, is feeling the constant pain of a broken rib, the result of a bad fall.

At 4:15, exhausted, soaked in sweat, in pain, the procession reaches Comantavichi and the nearby airfield, where it has been arranged that a plane will be waiting. There is no plane. Within minutes *Papagallo*, which cannot land in the high grass of this airstrip, arrives and drops a note. The plane that first carried them is unavailable. To reach Misión, they will have to go on foot another two or three hours. It is now only two hours before dark.

The seven team members and three guides set out. The pace has to be fast if they are to avoid solid darkness in the jungle. The prospect of reaching the mission for a cold beer and warm meal is exhilarating, however, and there is some whistling and joking. But the lightness drifts away as the trail grows difficult and the men feel the strains of the day. Gradually it becomes clear they are not going to beat the darkness to Misión.

With an hour or more of the trip to go, night falls. They have two reliable flashlights. The lead guide takes one of the flashlights; Sumian carries the other near the end of the line of walkers. The team walks as through an eerie dream. From time to time starlight casts a glow about the forest, but mostly the path leads through a fully roofed section of woods that is nearly a blind tunnel. Forest chatter is loud: insects, an occasional nightbird, other unknown sounds. It is not possible to see the trail with precision. They step onto short stumps, trip over low branches. At one point, a guide halts abruptly. There is a tapir crossing the trail ahead; the creature vanishes quickly into the green

Opposite, above:
A common egret (*Egretta alba*).

Opposite, middle:
A poor flier and an ungainly walker, the hoatzin (*Opisthocomus hoatzin*) is perhaps the strangest of all Amazon birds. It emits a strong musky odor, climbs awkwardly about trees using its wings like arms, and has a gullet fifty times larger than its stomach (used to help digest the mangrove leaves it consumes). The hoatzin's messy nest is built on branches overhanging water so that it can dive to the river when threatened and swim to safety.

Opposite, below:
Horned screamers (*Anhina cornuta*) add their loud call to the jungle bird and insect symphony.

gloom. Occasionally they pass through small Indian settlements of three or four huts, where drifts of smoke rise from dying campfires and a few brown-clothed figures sit cross-legged on the ground. Their arrivals are announced by yelping dogs, and the barking can be heard for five minutes after they have passed.

They come to a precarious "bridge," a tree trunk that crosses a slime-covered pool. The crossing is perhaps sixty feet long and they are forced to slide along the trunk in the darkness one at a time. "It is the last pain," says Fortunato, the lead guide. Fifteen minutes later they see an electric light in one of the mission storehouses.

When the team arrives at the mission headquarters, expecting a hot meal and a supply of cold beer, they learn that since no one believed they would enter the jungle at night, no meal has been prepared. There are only two bottles of cold beer in the refrigerator. "Welcome to Paradise," says Jean-Michel.

Treating raw feet, cut hands, and bitten legs at the end of this day, the Cousteau crew reflects on the experience. There is a feeling that they have been privileged travelers through a vanishing world of raw exuberance, shoulder to shoulder with a vanishing people. They cannot help but marvel at the stamina of the handsome people called Ashaninca, who thrive on the wretched jungle trails, gliding barefoot for miles with heavy burdens, who slip through their woods and over their rock-stubble riverbanks in this elegant way every day of their lives.

On July 13, the team shoves off from Misión, resuming the float down the river once called the Apurímac, now the Ene, soon to be the Tambo and then the Ucayali. Underway, a change comes over the crew after eleven days of strenuous work at Misión. The mood brightens, the practical jokes begin anew. They are sailors and they are sunnier when on the water and in motion.

The quiet hours on the river offer an opportunity to discuss the nature of the world they now have seen at close hand over several weeks. Sitting on aluminum crates at the aft end of the gliding raft, the team members compare observations and conclusions.

They are fascinated by the deceptiveness of the rain forest, which appears to be enormously luxuriant but betrays a curious hollowness upon close inspection—a soil so thin trees resort to buttresses and serpentine surface roots for stability, a relatively barren supply of ground vegetation, a scarcity of large creatures and herding animals, and human tribes suffering from nutritional deficiencies in the midst of apparent plenty.

Research indicates that one of the clues to the mystery is in the soil. During millions of years of rainfall, the soluble minerals of the ground surface have been thoroughly leached out, especially to the north and south of the main Amazon. But this leads to a paradox. Given the challenge to plants in a region of poor soil, how can one explain the tremendous diversity, density, and towering size of the Amazon jungle, the world's largest forest?

To the Cousteau team, the answer is more remarkable than the jungle's superficial statistics. The trees of the Amazon rain forest have "invented" elaborate schemes for prevailing in their battle against constant heat, rain, and undernourishment. Without the abundant tree food to be found in a rich

Opposite, above:
With only two hours of light left, the Land Team that trekked to Sewerd Falls sets out to beat the darkness back to Father Gagnon's mission.

Opposite, below left:
Cameraman Cornu leads the line of team members and Indians on the trip to Sewerd Falls. Indian trails switched back and forth between dense jungle and rugged streamside boulders.

Opposite, below right:
Dropping nearly a thousand feet, Seword Falls has been visited by few outsiders. Scientist Murphy found fossils of marine crinoids, starfish relatives, near the base of the falls—evidence that this area of the Andean foothills was beneath the sea about three hundred million years ago.

soil, the trees have "learned" to feed themselves. Their leaves fall more rapidly than those of temperate-zone trees, and on the ground they decompose more quickly, so that their nutrients can be recycled promptly back into the living trees around them. Lacelike nets of root hairs just below the soil surface act as filters, holding nutrients in place and capturing nitrogen and phosphorus for the trees. The root hairs are aided by fungi, which live in a tight association with the roots and through their fungal digestion (the process we call rotting) prepare the nutrients for quick absorption by the trees. This steady circulation keeps the vital food supply of the forest stored in its own foliage rather than in the soil, where it would be vulnerable to leaching and erosion. It keeps the jungle rich and the soil poor.

Another example of tree "cleverness" is the stratagem of coexistence among a multiplicity of species. There may be as many as a hundred tree species living within a single acre of Amazonian forest. Because each of these species makes its living in a slightly different way—with dissimilar food needs, root systems, shapes—the scarce nourishment is efficiently utilized. Nothing is wasted and competition seems to have reached a state of extraordinary balance. Moreover, because the members of each species are widely scattered, their insect and disease enemies are deterred from ever reaching epidemic proportions.

While these tricks of diversity enable the rain forest to flourish, they work against animal and human forest dwellers in some important ways. A large herd of herbivores must have access to abundant, easily cropped vegetation to support its numbers—such as the grassy African savanna or the western plains of America. But the Amazon forest floor is relatively dark and devoid of luxuriant vegetation, the principal reason there are no Amazon equivalents of elephants, antelopes, and buffaloes.

But there is another, infinitely more subtle limiting factor. The rain-forest vegetation, for all its opulence of color and shape and density, is for the most part a product of sunshine and water magically synthesized. The leaves and woody flesh of the jungle are actually deficient in vitamins and minerals, which forests elsewhere derive from fertile soils. This impoverishment cannot sustain large herds or great populations of humans. The lack of big jungle beasts, the preponderance of small Indian tribes, and the apparent undernourishment of peoples like the Ashanincas are easy to understand. The Amazon is, as American scientist Betty Meggers has characterized it, "a Counterfeit Paradise."

Jean-Michel recalls what the river pilot Manoel Araujo da Silva told him on the day he joined the expedition as captain of the *Anaconda*: "The Amazon is never exactly what it appears to be."

It is a maxim they will see proven time and again in the months to come.

LAND TEAM AND "CALYPSO" | RIO UCAYALI | PERU

The next few weeks, through August and into September, seem to pass quickly as the expedition teams take a break. *Calypso* reaches Iquitos, where most of the crew is dispatched home to France or the United States for a month-long rest. The vacations are mandated by French

maritime law, but they would be necessary regardless. Some crew members have had little time off since the ship departed from Norfolk, Virginia, for the Amazon on February 28.

The downriver journey of the Land Team aboard the raft *Pirarucu*, meanwhile, has taken longer than expected. A rendezvous with *Calypso* had been planned for July, but when the *Pirarucu* finally reaches Pucallpa, a bustling Ucayali port nearly four hundred miles upriver from Iquitos, vacation time is at hand. Under Sumian's direction, *Pirarucu* and her equipment are packed away for storage in Pucallpa and the six-wheel-drive *Amarillo* is loaded onto a barge for shipment downriver to Manaus.

By mid-September the teams have reassembled. *Calypso* and her riverboat *Anaconda*, looking like a youngster at the tail of its mother, set sail upriver. On September 18, at the confluence of the Marañon and the Ucayali, *Calypso* drops anchor. Soundings ahead reveal that further upstream there will be only a foot or two of clearance beneath the ship's keel. With the water level still dropping, Cousteau decides to avoid any risk of stranding. He radios *Pirarucu* with *Calypso*'s position. The Land Team aboard the raft has departed Pucallpa days earlier, and Guy Jouas calculates they will be in sight of *Calypso* within twenty-four hours.

At dusk this night, when the raft *Pirarucu* has been anchored to a boulder jutting from the sand of a low riverbank beach, Jean-Michel pulls from a storage crate a warm bottle of champagne. He has reserved it for this occasion—the last night together for the Peruvian Land Team after five months of shared exploits and camaraderie.

The evening passes in recollections and laughter: about the truck mired in altiplano mud, the dingy hotel rooms, the constant bouts with dysentery, Cornu and Murphy piling the jeep high with gear and racing to escape hostile highlanders. Sumian lists some of the pranks they have endured from Jouas: rubber snakes placed in front of tents during the night, clothespins (which, snapped from behind onto bare legs in the jungle, give the sudden impression that a snake has attacked), a ladder wedged under a hotel mattress which the exhausted sleeper never noticed. Along the Apurímac, Murphy put a strange green beetle on Mose Richards's face in order to establish the creature's size in a photo. The insect promptly stung Richards. The pain felt like a needle in his jaw. Jean-Michel remembers Murphy's response: "This is great! This is how we learn!"

The morning of the rendezvous is overcast but rainless. The raft team dons clean shirts saved for this moment and launches *Pirarucu* for its last sail, a ten-mile trip to *Calypso*, where it will be disassembled and stowed. Jouas pulls from his duffel bag a comic black tuxedo T-shirt, fixes the Land Team's pet macaw, Pepe, on his shoulder, and plants himself in mock solemnity near the bow of the raft, looking like nothing so much as a jungle butler.

As the raft approaches within five miles of *Calypso*, the team spots what appears to be an armada headed their way. From downriver, Captain Cousteau has dispatched nearly half his crew as a welcoming committee aboard Zodiacs, the ship's launch, the riverboat *Anaconda*, the hovercraft, and, buzzing overhead, both *Felix* and *Papagallo*. Waving and circling at full throttle, the *Calypso* team cuts figures around the slow Conestoga-like raft and accompanies it to the flanks of *Calypso*. Standing on the bow of the main

Opposite, above and below: Fungi along the forest floor, like these mushrooms, play a vital role in Amazon life. They quickly convert fallen trees and leaves into nutrients, particularly nitrogen and phosphorus, that can be taken up by the roots of plants, making possible luxurious vegetation in a world with poor soils.

ship, a small figure peering from beneath a straw hat commands everyone's attention. Braving the cameras, which she has resolutely shunned for most of the three decades she has lived aboard *Calypso*, Simone Cousteau stands with her husband to watch the reunion of their teams after completing the entire 4,000-mile course of the river. Waving to his mother, Jean-Michel is reminded of her response to a journalist many years before.

"How many sons do you have down there?" she was asked as Philippe Cousteau and four others were lowered to the bottom of the Mediterranean in an experimental habitat.

"They're all my sons," she answered.

J.-Y.C.—*When the tedious work of disassembling and stowing* Pirarucu *is complete, we all crowd into the* carré. *Bottles of Bordeaux are broken out, along with some* cachaça, *the Brazilian cane-sugar rum that is the vodka of the* caboclos. *I am reminded of other celebrations around this same old table—Christmas in Antarctica, our record anchorage in the middle of the Atlantic, the successful completion of our first Conshelf sea-floor colony. Some of the old friends are gone. Some faces are the same. Simone and I have noticed a few changes in the "family" during this expedition: some thinning and graying hair, some wrinkles, bulges around certain waists. They are honorable signs of experience and maturity, revealing to us the length of the enterprise we started so long ago and the continuing companionship of these good men, who have shared dangers and discoveries and, around this table, news from afar of marriages, divorces, births, deaths. I watch quietly as my friends embrace one another, and poke fun, and flaunt their sores and blisters, and brandish the souvenirs and pets they have accumulated. Jean-Marie France has a scarlet rash on much of his upper body, Raymond Amaddio a lesion the size of an apple on his leg, produced by some unseen insect. Dominique Sumian has fine, slender arrows made for him by an Ashaninca in exchange for a small carving knife. Jacques Constans has increased his beetle collection by several dozen, including a five-inch titanus, one of the world's largest coleopterans. Both Jean-Pierre Hervé, our chef, and Michel Treboz have adopted tiny marmosets as pets. Treboz's little friend scampers constantly about the electronician's shoulders and head; Hervé has fashioned a cage in the galley for his pet. Jean-Pierre shows Jean-Michel how the creature—a member of the smallest monkey species in the world—loves spaghetti and, horror of horrors to a French chef, Coca-Cola. Hervé says his pet weighs one third as much as an egg. He calls him "King Kong."*

While the revelry continues, Jean-Michel, Falco, Coll, Sumian, Constans, and I escape to my quarters to make assessments and plans. Overall, we are relieved by the lack of serious medical problems so far. There are no signs among our people as yet of malaria or other serious diseases. The insects are a nightmare, but their evening blitz seems to produce only a grouchy chaos as men rush to the cans of repellent. The scratching and flesh-slapping combine with the terrible sound of sizzling insects as they dive against an electronic bug-killer we have reluctantly set up in the carré. *The infernal machine bothers everyone. The incessant crackling as insects are electrocuted annoys the men as they sit at our long table, eat-*

Opposite, above:
Found in other rain forests of the world, the jelly fungi is used in oriental cooking, especially hot and sour soup.

Opposite, middle:
The mushroom *Podoscypha fulvonitens* grows only on wood and speeds up the process of breaking down cellulose and other substances into raw materials for absorption by living roots. Cousteau associates discovered a new species of Amazon fungus, which has been named *Rhabdomyces calypso.*

Opposite, below:
Though regarded as fungal plants, slime molds are capable of movement, oozing amoeba-like across the forest floor to ingest bacteria and decaying forest matter.

ing, chatting, smoking Gitanes or Tuscan cigars. They turn sometimes, occasionally shake their heads at the little clicks of death. These men are mostly gentle souls; the ultraviolet frying of insects is a procedure more crude than they would prefer.

The toll of noninsect wounds has been slight: Bertrand Sion was attacked by a piranha, but the incident occurred in a Zodiac as Sion was taking the fish off a hook, and the cut finger quickly healed. Humidity and contact lenses have caused an aggravating infection in Scott Frier's eyes, which was treated in Manaus. Otherwise nothing more serious than sores and heat rashes.

The damages sustained by Calypso have also been acceptable so far. Near the confluence of the Amazon and the Coari, the ship struck a hidden log, which slid beneath the hull and hit our starboard propeller. The impact was loud enough to bring everyone on deck, and we could feel a lurching that indicated something was stuck in the screw, but this passed quickly and left only a small upwelling of wood chips in our wake. Two days later Arturo and Xavier dived below the ship and straightened the bent prop with a sledgehammer.

The question I put to my friends around the small table in my quarters is the following: now that we have traveled the entire length of the Amazon, and have gained a general understanding of the biological machinery at work here, what shall we delve into more intimately during the remaining months of the expedition?

A consensus emerges quickly, summed up by Jean-Michel.

"Our role," he says, "should be to analyze how the Amazon is changing." Five issues in particular fascinate him. Three have been observed by his Peruvian Land Team: the plight of the surviving Indian peoples, the consequences of the exploding cocaine trade for the Amazon and its natives, and the impact of poaching, which takes many forms, on the balances of life in river and forest. Two more have been detailed in research by Paula and Silvio: the tremendous gold rush, and the influx of pioneers into the jungle, both occurring south of the main river in Brazil.

To these subjects we add the handful of grandiose development projects underway in Brazil, which have the potential of profoundly altering vast regions, and the fate of several animal species which we have as yet documented only negligibly. Falco wants to swim with river dolphins and otters. Sumian and Coll believe we could film jacarés and river snakes underwater. We know that our cameramen—Cornu, Mounier, and Frier—are eager to find undisturbed regions along remote tributaries where they can film wildlife.

To accomplish all of these objectives, we decide to organize several expeditionary teams with Coll and Sumian as leaders. Falco will oversee these operations and supervise the downriver journey of Calypso. Jean-Michel and I will shuttle between the missions in Papagallo and Felix.

Underway again this afternoon, Jean-Michel and I stand alone at the bow, watching the mottled forest wall as we ride the river down toward Iquitos. Our thoughts are on the future of this phenomenal world. Nowhere on earth have the same conditions prevailed on such a scale for such

a long time and created such an elaborate, awesome forest and river. Yet the intricate systems that enable it to survive also make it among the most fragile of all living systems.

I tell Jean-Michel what Phil Dustan has observed only days before on Calypso—*that the Amazon rain forest has some interesting similarities to a coral reef. Both are tropical, both survive in relatively nutrient-poor environments. Both cover immense territories but are inhabited by relatively small individual animals. They are among the oldest and most complex systems on earth, and within their communities dwell the most extraordinary, most colorful, most beautiful organisms on earth—the orchid and the anemone, the parrot and the parrot fish, the butterfly and the butterfly fish, the passion flower and the feather-duster worm, the harlequin beetle and the nudibranch, the slender liana and the delicate gorgonian, the sheltering coral head and the protective tree crown, the storm of color in a flock of scarlet ibises or in a school of iridescent jacks. The comparisons, like the living wonders of these two worlds, are infinite. But to us, the most profound similarity is in their parallel solutions to the problem of survival. Both involve many mutualistic relationships, both are highly productive and diverse, and both trap all of the nutrients available in a relatively poor supporting environment and intensively recycle these resources. The architects of the reef, the coral species, reach toward the sun from the bottom of the sea; the builders of the rain forest, the tree species, also reach upward, thrusting majestically to challenge, and to feed upon, the blazing equatorial sun.*

The simple removal of rain-forest trees—in order to plant crops or graze cattle or sell timber or mine the ground beneath them—eradicates the benevolent leaf ceiling that protects jungle vitality. The exposed soil is quickly baked by the tropical sun and washed away by thunderstorms. Without tree litter to provide nutrients, little can grow.

From either side of Calypso *we see settlers' thatched homes along the Amazon. Gaping holes in the forest surround each farmhouse and a low tangle of corn,* yuca, *young cacao trees, and coca shrubs have supplanted the native trees. We cannot help but wonder if these highlanders, yearning to improve their lives, have traded the cold sterility of the Andes for a bogus jungle fertility that will disappear under their saws and hoes, defeating their dreams. Children with sunny faces watch us pass by, laughing and leaping about and timidly returning our waves of "Hello." Where will they go when the plots beneath their dancing feet are as lifeless as the wretched highlands of their ancestors? Most of the world will never know their fate, here in this isolation. I am reminded sadly of Pope's line: "the world forgetting by the world forgot."*

Yet for now, the jungle remains robust and supreme. The thickening dusk is initiating the evening murmur of the forest. The static of living organisms surges into the gray air about us. Calypso's *few lights are enough to cast a sheen on the barrier of trees alongside us, heightening the sense of mysteries beyond, reminding us how privileged we are to be here while the throbbing Amazon remains bounteous with living secrets. Perhaps it will always endure. I remember an Amazon Indian proverb: "Man and the river always keep going. Only the forest remains."*

EYES IN THE JUNGLE

"CALYPSO" | RIO | AMAZONAS | PERU

From the air at midnight, when the evening flight from Miami arrives, the Peruvian jungle capital of Iquitos looks like bits of silver in an endless black sea. The grid of lights suggests a human oasis, but most of the tourists crowded aboard the 707 have come here to see not a pocket of civilization, but what lurks out beyond in the uncivilized vegetation.

They are bound for one of the new "explorer" lodges on the outskirts of the city, where they will follow marked trails with the help of guides and guidebooks. If they come with a dream of anacondas draping the trees and pumas slinking about, however, they are likely to be disappointed. The same seductive fascination with jungle creatures that draws an increasing tide of tourists to Amazon vacations also encourages local hunters to kill or capture and to sell the exotic animals the vacationers come to see. Except for an occasional fleeing monkey or passing parrot along a hotel trail, the most likely spot to see wildlife is at the Iquitos zoo.

From Pucallpa downriver to Iquitos—and on to Leticia, Manaus, and Belém—the major cities of Amazonia are collection points for a commerce in living and dead animals that turns the colorful creatures of the rain forest into cash. The international network that eventually produces chic reptile handbags, pet macaws, alligator shoes, and much more actually begins with the *caboclos* and Indians living up Amazon tributaries, the adroit hunters who know how to find the creatures of the jungle and river.

To Amazon Indian tribes, the exotic animals moving about the surrounding jungle are a source of protein in a nutritionally limited world. They are wild livestock. But although tribes have hunted in Amazonia for centuries, the impact upon wild populations has been minimal because Indians have never represented a great population themselves and hunting parties take no more than needed for village consumption. As the tide of settlers entering the Amazon increases, however, the demand for wild food and for the cash obtained by selling wild creatures expands. Buyers roam the tributaries in motorboats, purchasing wildlife and skins, then pack their bounty off to dealers in the major cities.

At the southern extremity of Amazonia in the region known as the Pantanal (swamp), two wood storks (*Mycteria americana*) survey a water-engulfed world below their nest, where abundant fish represent food, and crocodiles offer the prospect of sudden death.

Alarmed by the prospect of a depleted animal stock in coming decades, most Amazon nations—including Brazil, Peru, and Colombia—have enacted strict laws against the procurement, sale, and transport of species. Brazil has also quadrupled its wildlife-reserve acreage in recent years. But despite good intentions, the smuggling and even the open sale of animals continues to be a flourishing industry. The Amazon is too large to police, for one thing, and the suffering economies of South American governments have left little money available to run enforcement operations. The casualty counts are impossible to reckon, since so little is known about what once lived here, or what would be living here today without human intervention. The official tonnage of dead and living creatures being shipped out of the jungle is hardly a reliable indicator, since most of the traffic moves surreptitiously.

Walking through the marketplace of Iquitos during shopping trips for *Calypso*, chef Jean-Pierre Hervé sees the meat of river turtles for sale, the shells overturned to display as many as fifty eggs inside and about ten pounds of meat, which, he is told, should be served with boiled bananas. A young girl nearby is cooking turtle soup with onions and tomatoes. All of this despite the fact that Amazon turtles are seriously endangered and protected by law.

Jean-Pierre also confronts mounds of meat, much of it salted and dried in the sun. The vendors avoid awkward questions by labeling the mixed cuts "jungle meat," whatever their origin. A young woman tells him the next counter is loaded with dried monkey, a favorite among jungle peoples. When Jean-Pierre points out that Peru's flora and fauna legislation makes such sales illegal, she explains that while hunting for profit is illegal, hunting for personal needs is usually allowed. To make extra money, settlers come to Iquitos with surplus monkey meat, mix it with other cuts of flesh, and sell it without interference. It is probable that professional hunters use the loophole to kill thousands of monkeys. The meat of woolly monkeys and red howler monkeys, both endangered species in western Amazonia, is a common favorite in the Iquitos market.

Another disappearing creature that continues to be sold for its meat is the *pirarucu*, the giant fish known in Peru as *paiche*. Their bountiful and tasty flesh has made them an unparalleled target of Amazon fishermen for centuries, so that now their numbers, while unknown, are dramatically diminished, as evidenced by the growing difficulty in locating them. Despite their scarcity, *paiche* meat is available in virtually every market along the river.

In a lagoon of the Pacaya wildlife reservation southwest of Iquitos, an expedition team in the riverboat *Anaconda*, led by Jacques Constans, watches an old man in a canoe catch one of the once abundant, immense creatures which have been called "the kings of the river." The capture is dramatic. The old fisherman sits motionless in his canoe, a harpoon across his lap, listening for the distinctive sound of an air-breathing *paiche* gulping at the surface. As Mounier films from a Zodiac, the fisherman suddenly rises and hurls the harpoon toward a dark underwater shadow which flees as it is pierced, unwinding a reel of nylon line in the canoe. The giant fish fights for thirty minutes, while the fisherman calmly pulls in slack. Then, in a burst of seeming defiance, the creature swims rashly at the canoe. It is the opportunity the fisherman has been waiting for, and he repeatedly strikes the head of the *paiche* with the blunt side of a machete blade.

The old man is reserved but jubilant, Constans notices, rinsing his mouth

Above:
A baby Maguri stork (*Euxenura maguari*) awaits the return of its mother, now away from the nest scouring shallow Pantanal streams for fish, frogs, and insects. Like other species of young birds here, it will soon face a flight for survival: if the fledgling attempt is unsuccessful, the juvenile could fall among hungry caimans waiting below.

Opposite, above:
A Cocoi heron (*Ardea cocoi*) swoops low over Pantanal waters.

Opposite, below:
A family of Roseate spoonbills (*Ajaia ajaja*): the adult is at left.

with river water and disdainfully spitting it back over the side of his canoe. It is a revealing gesture; in Amazonia, nature and the wild animals it offers up are still forces to overcome heroically, or so it seems to river people.

"All of these *gringos* around him, with their movie cameras and scientific instruments, may have impressed the old man," Constans says. "But the look on his face was an expression of victory. Alone like Hemingway's old man in a tiny boat, he, Antonio, had successfully stood up to the great *paiches* of the Amazon."

There is an even greater river creature in Amazonia, the largest of all Amazon land or water animals, and like the *paiche/pirarucu* it is in danger of vanishing as a result of centuries of hunting. The gentle, vegetarian manatee—known in Brazil as the *peixe-bois* (cow fish)—is an aquatic mammal that weighs as much as 1,300 pounds and reaches a length of ten feet. These slow swimmers have long been a staple food of *caboclos*, who harpoon the creatures at night, then suffocate them by stuffing wooden plugs into their nostrils when the exhausted animals surface to breathe. The *caboclos* are not the sole reason manatees are endangered. Commercial exploitation began in the sixteenth century with the arrival of Europeans, who fried manatee meat in its blubber and shipped it home. The taste was compared to ham. Early in this century a tanning process was invented for manatee hides, which are so thick and strong that the leather was used for such industrial products as machinery belting and high-pressure gaskets. By 1967 the population was deemed sufficiently imperiled that Brazil halted all hunting and proclaimed the manatee an endangered species. Peru and Colombia soon joined the ban.

At INPA in Manaus, Paula DiPerna introduces Jean-Michel to Robin Best, a young Canadian zoologist who has begun a quiet crusade to save Amazonia's manatees. In tanks nestled among the uncut rain-forest trees that shade the research agency compound, Best shows Jean-Michel fifteen manatees being analyzed by his laboratory staff.

Though Best has been involved in "pure" manatee research for seven years, he appears most proud of an ingenious program he has developed with his assistants as a means of preserving the creatures and exploiting them at the same time. Best explains to Jean-Michel how he employs *caboclo* fishermen to capture manatees. He then arranges shipment of the creatures to a man-made reservoir near Santarém, Lake Curua-Una, the product of a major hydroelectric project built by the Brazilian power company Eletronorte. The engineers who designed the dam were faced with an unanticipated problem: dense mats of floating grass and hyacinth had gradually taken over the lake surface. The vegetation increases evaporation rates and seriously depletes the lake of oxygen as it rots and ferments. The anaerobic waters host a bacterium that produces poisonous hydrogen sulfide, which attacks the blades of turbines like acid, causing the generating equipment to wear out in half the normal time. Eradicating the prolific vegetation would mean a costly chemical spraying operation that would also pollute the lake with herbicides.

Best proposed a novel solution: introduction of manatees as living lake-cleaners. Each of the peace-loving creatures can consume nearly a hundred pounds of hyacinth and grasses per day. A sufficient population of manatee custodians, Best reasoned, would not only provide a long-term end to the

Opposite, above left:
The Cousteau team came across these possums clinging to a Pantanal fence post.

Opposite, above right:
Spotted-breasted woodpeckers (*Chrysoptilus punctigula*) excavate for an insect meal in a dead Pantanal tree.

Opposite, below:
Adroit at catching fish, giant otters (*Pteronura brasiliensis*) are also ravenous fish consumers. A pair of otters may eat three tons of fish in a year's time. In their shallow tributary haunts, the creatures are considered competitors by *caboclo* fishermen, who attack them occasionally with machetes or rifles.

overgrowth of vegetation but would also return as much as half of the ingested matter to the lake as fertilizer, stimulating plankton growth and increasing fish populations.

The final benefit, perhaps incidental to the hydroelectric project, was paramount to Best: manatees in the employ of the dam would not be subject to hunting. The idea offered a potential sanctuary, not only for the manatees in Curua-Una, but for countless others if Brazil's plans for a series of dams were to be carried out. Eletronorte agreed to an experiment, and Best went into action.

In 1980 the INPA team released twenty females and twenty-two males into the reservoir. Each animal was fitted with a radio transmitter belt so that the behavior and movements of the herd could be followed. Best calculated that the population could grow to two hundred in a decade through reproduction and additional animal transfers, and the herd would then consume more than a thousand tons of plants each month.

In a shallow lagoon near Lake Amanã, about halfway between Manaus and the western border of Brazil, Best shows Jean-Michel twelve manatees recently captured by *caboclos*. Within a month these, too, will be carried in slings to a barge, then shipped to Lake Curua-Una. "The program is proving to be a harmonious blend of economics and ecology," Best says. "The importance of conserving manatees in Brazil goes far beyond simply preserving a heritage or an odd, interesting creature. The manatee is the largest herbivore consumer in the Amazonian aquatic ecosystem, and as such is an integral component. The fertilizing service they provide to Amazon lakes may equal the effect of the hippopotamus in the lakes of Africa."

"We are encouraged by the foresight of Robin Best and his INPA colleagues," Jean-Michel records later in his taped journal. "But despite glimmers of hope, it often seems that illegal animal traffic will outpace wise management, since research is a slow process and poachers are everywhere.

"In the hold of a riverboat moored in Manaus, I saw racks of plastic trays filled with aquarium fish taken from a tributary of the Rio Negro. About half of the fish were dead. Silvio, Mose, and I prowled about among the lumber and beverage crates in the hold. We found two huge river turtles, each nearly three feet across. Their legs were bound, but their heads were free to move about pathetically. The boat owner, carrying lumber out a door at the far end of the dark hold, was using one of the turtles as a step, roughly stumbling onto his head at times. I asked why he had the turtles and he responded with a friendly shrug. Silvio believed they were probably destined to become soup bowls at a party among the Manaus elite. I can believe this; I noticed four jaguar skins in the home of a foreign consul in Manaus.

"When our raft *Pirarucu* pulled into Pucallpa en route to our rendezvous with *Calypso*, we struck up a conversation with a *caboclo* in a nearby boat. We were interested in the macaw on his shoulder—it was 'Pepe,' who joined our crew that very day—but it soon became evident that his boat contained illicit goods. There was little reticence on his part to show us a boa skin he had taken, or to regale us with stories about his methods. He ties a monkey on a line and tosses it in the path of a swimming boa. When the snake has attacked and swallowed the helpless monkey, the man pulls the line in and kills the boa with a machete. The skin is sold for belt leather.

Above:
A caiman and a boa constrictor battle in the swamps of the Pantanal.

Opposite:
Though known as the spectacled owl (*Pulsatrix perspicillata*) because of the plumage about its eyes, this predator is more commonly called the knocking owl by Brazilians because its call resembles the pounding sound of woodpeckers.

"When we questioned him further, he admitted having a jaguar pelt in the boat. 'It is for selling, not for seeing,' he said when we asked to view the skin. Reluctantly, after an hour of discussion, he produced the pelt and marveled with us at its beauty. 'It can eat a calf,' he said. 'Something like that must be killed.'

"He was not a vicious or heartless man, but a father whose children swarmed about his little boat and drove him to hunt wildlife in order to supplement a meager income from rice farming. He was just a man in the wilderness, perhaps a little braver than some, and the wild harvest he took did not look so terrible. A skin here, a skin there. But of course we knew that perhaps half or more of the boats crowded into Pucallpa harbor probably carried a few skins each and a turtle or two, and new arrivals streamed in hourly, and this was only one of the river's many ports."

FLYING TEAM | THE PANTANAL | BRAZIL

On September 25, Captain Cousteau dispatches cameraman Cornu and diver Desmier by commercial flight from Iquitos to Manaus, where they meet assistant cameraman Philippe Morice. Two days later this threesome takes a flight to Cuiabá, a Brazilian town along the southern fringes of the jungle. There they are joined by a fourth team member, Brazilian naturalist and photographer Haroldo Palo, who has spent years studying the wildlife south of Cuiabá in the Pantanal, a swampy stretch of wilderness larger than Kansas.

The decision to create a Pantanal team is based on reports that the most intensive poaching operations in South America may be taking place in this virgin marshland. Brazilian wildlife authorities estimate that at least half a million animals may be illegally caught or killed here annually, most of them crocodiles (*jacarés*). Cousteau cautions his team to be alert to danger themselves; poachers have been known to use their guns against interfering humans as well as animals. Led by Cornu, the team leaves Cuiabá in an equipment-laden jeep on October 1, following the Transpantanera highway south to Porto Jofre.

The animal life that has eluded their cameras behind jungle trees in the north is suddenly abundant and exposed here in the open bogs of the Pantanal ("swamp" in Portuguese). Cornu and Palo quickly accumulate film of the region's ubiquitous birds (herons, wood storks, ibis, roseate spoonbills, and giant jabiru storks), capybara families, and *jacarés*.

On October 7, while exploring marshes north of Porto Jofre, the men see a vivid white tree on an island in the distance. Though nearly a mile away, the image is arresting—thick, snowy boughs surrounded by steamy swamp. "Our hearts were in our throats," Cornu later writes in his diary, "but we waded into the *jacaré*-infested waters nevertheless in order to reach the island and see this mysterious white tree. To drive the *jacarés* away, we shouted and slapped the water as we went. It took nearly an hour of hard going in mud and swamp to solve the mystery." Not until they are within a few hundred yards of the island do they realize that the tree is covered solidly by tiers of white herons and storks.

Water birds flock in immense numbers to this region in order to rear their young. The marsh is deep enough to be abundant in fish, yet not so deep that it prevents the wading birds from fishing. After catching a meal, parents return to nests built in trees looming up from the dry island. The fish are disgorged to feed the chicks, which are safe as long as they remain nestled high in the trees. The drama arises as the fledglings begin to stir from the nests and to take their first adolescent stabs at flying. Below, waiting motionlessly amid the camouflage of water hyacinth, are thousands of *jacarés*.

"While we are filming this extraordinary nursery grounds," Cornu writes, "a tiny spoonbill falls from its nest and lands clumsily on the water hyacinth around us, only yards away. It stumbles about awkwardly, trying to sort out its new predicament. Suddenly, as we watch, it disappears in an explosion of splashes. Moments later we see a *jacaré* munching what remains of the spoonbill. None of us had seen the *jacaré* approach. It had risen beneath the bird and snapped it downward into the water. To us, the scene was chilling: the drama had taken place precisely where we had just been wading!

"Hardly have we recuperated from this shock when a young stork tumbles from its nest and quickly meets the same fate. But now the *jacarés* have spotted us and they appear wary. When another stork falls to the ground, they circle but resist rushing to it while we are present. What follows is a four-hour session in which the stunned bird runs to and fro along the edge of the water, unable to find a way back to its nest and too immature to fly, and the *jacarés* remain within striking distance, eager to catch this vulnerable youngster but uncertain of us. It is an agonizing period. We are caught in the dilemma of wanting to film the violence of a capture, yet rooting all the while for the little bird, tempted to whisk it up and deposit it safely in a tree, yet not wanting to interfere with a natural act. There is no right and wrong in nature. This is a matter of hunger and survival. We content ourselves that our presence is buying time for the doomed chick. But the inevitable finally comes, a *coup de grâce* that is over in a fraction of a second. Xavier, who has been poised near the bird for hours, is saddened by the kill, and when another young stork falls a few moments later, he dashes over, scoops it up, and returns the chick to its nest. This is heartening, yet it is ultimately an empty gesture since other youngsters all around us are rapidly disappearing into the jaws of *jacarés*."

During the next ten days the team explores farther south into the Pantanal. The roads become increasingly difficult, exhausting and depressing the team. At one point the jeep is mired in mud for five days before a team of oxen is found to pull it out.

Furthermore, the wildlife seems to be diminishing, a puzzling phenomenon finally explained by a guide the team encounters and quickly hires. Alipio, a gaunt, ageless man who has spent his life in the Pantanal, explains that the gauchos who drive cattle through the swamp are probably responsible. They wear pistols on their hips like cowboys in the old American West and entertain themselves by shooting at anything that moves.

On October 18, along the Rio Taquari near Corumba, a village on the Brazilian border with Bolivia, the team makes contact with poachers. Though at first reluctant to cooperate, the men eventually agree to let the team accompany them on a hunt. During the discussion, Alipio admits that he is a poacher himself, that he has personally killed nearly 200,000 *jacarés*.

The hunt takes place that night, and the Cousteau team's Zodiac follows the hunters' small swamp canoe, called a *chalana*. The tools are strikingly simple: a flashlight, a .22 calibre rifle, a lance, and a sharp machete. Slipping through the pitch-black swamp, the rifleman trains his gun-barrel-mounted flashlight on the water plants lining navigable channels. Floating amid the dense cover of vegetation, *jacarés* would be impossible to detect in the green darkness but for the betrayal of their eyes. When the flashlight beam passes across the reptiles' heads, their ruby-red eyes glow like reflectors. The hunter has a perfect target: the space between the two fiery jewels in the ray of his light. Blinded and confused, the *jacarés* remain motionless, relying on camouflage for protection. When the shot strikes, the wounded creature instinctively dives. The boat closes in quickly and the hunter harpoons the *jacaré* in the shallows, then slices its neck open with a machete.

When the filming is completed this night, Cornu asks Alipio how many *jacarés* can be taken by a single poacher.

"Some men can take twelve in an hour, one hundred before daybreak."

"How many poachers prowl the Pantanal?" Cornu wonders.

"The authorities claim there are about three thousand," Alipio says. "It is impossible to say. Any man in the Pantanal who has no other job may be a *jacaré* poacher."

At dawn the hunters show the Cousteau team how they unload their take of *jacarés* onto dry land, then cut away only a narrow strip of skin along each flank. Since nothing else is of value to the poachers, the entire carcass is flung to piranhas in the river. The flank skins are sold to dealers and eventually tanned in Europe for shoes. It takes four *jacaré* kills to produce enough leather for a single pair of shoes. Each skin brings about $1 to the poachers. Since the hunting is illegal in Brazil, the skins are smuggled to Corumba and across the border in small planes to Bolivia and Paraguay, where export controls are lax or nonexistent. The traffickers take precautions to mislabel the skins so that international buyers have no qualms about purchasing them. The volume of traffic and the difficulty in determining every species in a mixed shipment makes it nearly impossible to police the operations.

Estimates of the *jacaré* kill range from 240,000 per year to 2 million, and the value of the skins, after exchanging hands a few times, may reach $26 million. In Cuiabá, Dr. Paulo Benedite de Siguiera, regional director of Brazil's Federal Forest Service, shows the Cousteau team a shipment of 550 Pantanal ocelot skins his agency has recently confiscated. The problem, Siguiera explains, is that the high profit in illicit animal products has created a kind of "mafia" of *contrabanidistas* who are heavily armed and well outfitted and who cavalierly shuttle across the porous borders.

"The poachers and smugglers have fast hydrofoils and machine guns," Siguiera says, "while our men have old-fashioned outboards and revolvers." Siguiera has eighteen men to patrol the entire Pantanal. The only effective program would have to involve cooperation on the part of Bolivia and Paraguay, he explains, but so far both governments have declined. Although Siguiera refuses to express an opinion, he acknowledges that there are abundant rumors of participation in the animal trade by corrupt government officials.

"Worst of all," Siguiera says, "the ecological balance is being upset. The Pantanal has never suffered plunder on such a scale before." The decline in

Opposite, above left:
Near Lake Amanã scientist Robin Best (*second from left*) oversees the transfer of a manatee—captured by local hunters—to a barge that will carry it to Best's manatee relocation project near Santarém.

Opposite, above right:
Largest of all Amazon animals, manatees require a formidable effort when moved overland, as revealed in the face of Cousteau pilot Guy Gervais (*with glasses at rear*).

Opposite, below left:
Assisted by the Cousteau team, Best's crew transported twelve manatees more than a thousand miles in this barge, which was flooded to keep the aquatic mammals wet.

Opposite, below right:
Captain Cousteau and two divers film a transplanted manatee in its new home at Lake Curua-Una.

the population of *jacarés*, which feed heavily on fish, is causing a proliferation of piranhas. The unchecked swarms of these predators are now attacking livestock that stand in the swamp to feed. A vicious circle is established, because poor farmers who lose their cattle and horses may be compelled to poach *jacarés* in order to make ends meet, further distorting the balance.

"CALYPSO" | RIO AMAZONAS | LETICIA, COLOMBIA

While Cornu and his team are documenting the southernmost tip of the Amazon basin, *Calypso* and *Anaconda* leave Iquitos for a slow journey downriver marked by frequent daylong anchorages for scientific work. The dry season has begun in western Amazonia, providing an opportunity for the team to profile the river's characteristics as waters subside and to compare these data with measurements taken during the flood-season trip upriver.

On September 30, the two vessels reach Leticia, the port situated at the tip of a narrow land corridor that establishes Amazon frontage along the southeastern border of Colombia. The city is known informally as the drug and illicit-animal capital of the upper river. "There is hardly another reason for the city to exist," a Peruvian journalist has told *Calypso*'s crew. "You can sit in a restaurant of this otherwise impoverished city and watch dealers cruise about town in fabulous sports cars, despite the fact the streets are unpaved dirt and are not long enough for the drivers to shift out of second gear."

For some twenty years, Leticia was the headquarters of an animal-export business run by American Mike Tsalickis, who owned a hotel and snake farm, ran hunting safaris, and achieved fame as the *gringo* jungle man pictured wrestling anacondas and caimans in *National Geographic* and other magazines. In fact, most of the animals were procured by hundreds of Indian hunters employed by Tsalickis, and his principal markets were the world's zoos and medical laboratories. When author Alex Shoumatoff visited Tsalickis in the late 1970s, the entrepreneur claimed that until 1974, when Colombia banned the export of any animals or parts thereof, he was shipping some eight thousand monkeys a year to medical researchers studying cancer, malaria, viruses, hepatitis, and heart transplants. (Though Tsalickis's business is defunct, a government-sponsored primate laboratory visited by Raymond Coll in Iquitos continues to ship live monkeys from Peru to biomedical researchers abroad, while conducting censuses of wild monkey populations and experimenting with captive breeding.)

Tsalickis now spends most of his time in his native Florida, but the hotel and its small tourist zoo remain in Leticia. While doing preliminary logistics research in advance of *Calypso*, Silvio Barros learns that the dilapidated zoo still holds a young male giant otter. He telexes Captain Cousteau, who has flown to a European scientific conference, suggesting that the expedition might be able to acquire the animal, keep it aboard *Calypso* on the downriver voyage—to film and to study it—then locate a more humane home for it before leaving Amazonia. Cousteau is interested and directs Barros and Falco to visit the zoo. The two men find the otter pacing about a small circular

Cousteau diver Xavier Desmier and a young manatee friend.

cage with a concrete floor. It is a pathetic scene and the animal's distress seems pointless—there are few tourists to see it. Barros speaks with the manager of the property and arranges to purchase the creature.

When the two Cousteau team members return to *Calypso*, Falco immediately commandeers a crew to help him construct a home for the otter on the ship. Wire fencing is erected to form a wide corral on the foredeck. Within this enclosure the men build a wood frame to support a plastic pool. Two days later, with the pool in place and river water pumped into it, Falco returns to the zoo and claims the new crew member.

They name it "Cacha"—a derivative of the French term for "hide-and-seek"—and the entire process of familiarization and friendship takes less than twenty-four hours. At first reluctant to venture out of the traveling cage that carried it to the ship, the otter seems to relax completely when it is finally coaxed into the pool.

Falco notes later in his diary, "We understand why Indians sometimes take otters as pets. Cacha has an endearing 'personality' and a ceaseless curiosity. When he rubs the water from his coat after a swim, pulling his paws over his eyes to dry his face, he resembles a sleepy infant.

"And how beautiful he is! His thick fur is a dark brown when dry, but when wet he becomes a shiny figurine of black chocolate. He appears awkwardly hunched over when scampering about on all fours, constantly bobbing up and down, but underwater he is graceful and sleek. When we toss a living fish into the pool, Cacha plays with it, swimming circles around it and batting it into the air with his paws before finally carrying it onto the deck to eat it. The method of eating is always the same. Cacha grips the fish in both webbed 'hands' and chews his way gradually from head to tail, humming as he chews. The sound is unusual, a cross between low moans of ecstasy and cooing.

"We are surprised by the strength of Cacha's vocalizations. He barks like a terrier, purrs like a Siamese cat, snorts like a pony, and squeaks like a dolphin. Sometimes he makes a little snapping utterance and then turns to explore in a different direction, as if expressing his disgust at the boring fixtures of our human world."

The most commonly reported trait of the giant otter is its fearless exuberance, even in the presence of humans. Early Amazon explorers claimed their canoes were sometimes surrounded by a dozen barking giant otters. Unfortunately, this jauntiness has nearly doomed the creatures. Because they hunt and frolic by day (other freshwater otter species are nocturnal), all the while chattering loudly, giant otter families are relatively easy to locate and to kill. Hunters coveting their extremely fine and valuable fur have left them nearly extinct in Amazonia—the only place they are found. In 1971 they were declared a protected species, but by then they were restricted to the most remote areas, beyond easy access to the hunters. Scientist Nicole Duplaix, who has done one of the few studies of these creatures, places them among the twenty-three most endangered mammals.

Humans seem to represent the chief danger in the world of the giant otter. They appear to have no other relentless predator stalking them, although there is evidence they occasionally fall victim to a jaguar, puma, anaconda, or perhaps piranhas. Living in groups as large as twenty individuals, they

Opposite, above:
A capybara flees a Cousteau photographer in the Pantanal.

Opposite, below:
Cousteau divers with *tambaqui* (*Colossoma macropomum*), a species intensely fished by Amazonians. *Tambaqui* commonly eat fruits and seeds in the flooded forest. The team visited Peruvian experimental aquaculture farms where *tambaqui* and other species may be raised commercially in the future.

travel widely along tributaries, sleeping at night in dens tunneled into the riverbank and spending the days diving beneath floating vegetation to snatch fish.

On October 7, *Calypso* leaves Leticia and heads toward Manaus. For nineteen days the ship alternates short passages with anchorages to set out fish-specimen nets, to lower her complement of scientific instruments, and to explore tributaries by Zodiac.

In their evening gatherings before a tape recorder, Falco, Constans, Mounier, Coll, and others list the more unusual encounters of the trip: the arrival of a bat in the *carré* at 5:00 A.M. one morning during coffee time, the en masse landing of a storm of butterflies that descended upon *Calypso* in mid-river, a collision with another submerged tree trunk that moved the propeller shaft about four inches but did not badly impair the propeller. Their curiosity is drawn to the changes around them now that the dry season has arrived. Near Tefé, Coll, Amaddio, and the photo team revisit the flooded forest where they first succeeded in obtaining underwater shots of trees, fish eating fruits, and the pink dolphin hunting. Now the water has disappeared but for a trickling brook. Butterflies flit about where *tambaqui* once swam. Ship's doctor Darnault climbs up a buttressed tree trunk—the same one Coll remembers swimming around and filming—and locates the high-water mark among limbs thirty feet above the ground.

On October 25, near the mouth of the Purus River, the team witnesses a scene that dramatically illustrates the hazards for shipping in the annual rise and fall of the river. A huge freighter, the *Amazonas*, sits aground amid fresh grass on an island in the river. Several of the men recall this vessel: it sailed past *Calypso* on the trip upriver. Sion remembers waving to its crew. On her return downstream, however, a miscalculation was apparently made about the depth of the subsiding river. Mounier and Jim Standard, a Canadian helicopter pilot temporarily relieving Braunbeck, survey the ship from *Felix* and report a mud rut trailing behind it like a frozen wake. Under full sail, the *Amazonas* slid onto the hidden sandbank, slicing a track in the ground behind her. When the crew later visits the ship, they learn that the *Amazonas* has been stuck since early September and will not budge again before December, when the river begins to rise.

The next day, *Calypso* pulls into Manaus. Waiting on the dock, after an overnight flight from Paris, is Captain Cousteau.

J.-Y.C.—Bebert, Martin, Sumian, and Vidal take me by the arm and lead me to the foredeck to judge their pool-building handiwork and to meet their little companion, Cacha. Seeing the grin on Bebert's face I am reminded of two other temporary crew members that roamed Calypso*'s decks—Pepito and Cristobal, two sea lions that joined us near the Cape of Good Hope in 1968 and remained aboard* Calypso *for seven months, becoming so involved with us that they were diving buddies.*

Cacha now prowls the entire ship, invading every quarter and rambling over tables, telex machines, sidescan sonar, sniffing faces and dinner plates, rolling on his back to solicit some help from human hands in rubbing his fur.

The young otter's irresistible charm is matched by an extraordinary grace in the water. He propels himself with supple waves of his body and his long, flat tail, like a living tremor of energy. When Bebert tosses a fish into the water, Cacha swivels abruptly, shoots across the pool with a flex of his body, seizes the fish in his mouth, tumbles playfully underwater for a few moments, and then dashes up the ramp. All of this has the appearance of a single flowing movement. Our friend Susan Schiefelbein, an American writer who is visiting the expedition for two weeks, describes this sight eloquently, "Cacha is as fluid as the river," she says.

Our joy at befriending this rare wild creature is mixed with melancholy, however, because his jovial good nature merely reminds us of the precarious future that lies before him and perhaps all of his species. Poachers and subsistence hunters are visible threats to Amazonia's irreplaceable creatures, but the most sinister and most invincible menace is the almost imperceptible erosion of forest habitat as humans enter the jungle. There is no mystery in this: when wild food and shelter are removed, animal populations that depend upon them disappear.

Bebert tells me that between Tefé and Manaus the men could see fires at night far into the forest and great trussed assemblages of cut timber being pulled by boats to sawmills. Colin and Standard filmed patches of naked ground wispy with smoke, marked by the black and gray stubble of scorched trunks. Much of this clearing is taking place among the trees of the temporarily dry flooded forest, the varzea. What will happen to the fisheries when life-sustaining fruits and seeds are gone with the trees that bear them? What will happen to the remaining otters like Cacha, which depend almost exclusively on fish that feed for part of the year in the flooded forest?

Paula reads me a line quoted in Nicole Duplaix's otter study and it sinks like a cold blade into my soul. To illustrate the value of a creature and the connections of nature, the Shaw Karen Indians of Thailand have a proverb: "If you shoot a gibbon, you leave seven lonely rivers." In Amazonia, one could change "gibbon" to otter, or manatee, or woolly monkey.

Sitting with Simone tonight in the electronics room as she types out a letter, I reflect on the images and sensations of the day. From dawn to dusk Manaus perspires under a white sun. The faces of the men carrying fish and boxes of vegetables on their heads are shiny with sweat. The caboclos trudge ahead in the heat, fueled by a quiet determination to overcome, to rise, to reap profits. In the afternoon, claps of tropical thunder ricochet across the city's rooftops, and a suddenly slate-colored sky sprays warm rain. Water drops down the backs of yellow Volkswagen taxis onto black asphalt as shiny as the back of a jacaré.

When the swelter of day turns to the dark heat of night, a fragile breeze pushes smoke across the city from fires smoldering in the surrounding jungle. It is a dismal reminder of changes already manifest, and changes to come. Dogs have replaced tapirs along the edge of Manaus. The roar of autos has driven away the thunder of howler monkeys. The musty gray odor of cremated trees has flooded air once streaked with plumes of perfume from frangipani and cedar and cinnamon trees.

The fires of man spread like an epidemic in Amazonia, restlessly radiating out from every settlement and city and cleared roadway, rings of growth for human enterprise and surrender for other kingdoms.

Opposite, above:
Though at first reluctant, a Pucallpa poacher eventually displayed the pelt of a jaguar he had killed to Gervais (*left*) and Cousteau.

Opposite, middle:
In Cuiabá, Desmier inspects part of a confiscated shipment of 550 poached ocelot skins. Brazilian conservation agents face extreme dangers when trying to arrest well armed and better equipped poachers in the vast Pantanal region.

Opposite, below:
Near the town of Benjamin Constant, *caboclos* attack and kill a large *jacaré* found swimming nearby. To most Amazonians, wildlife remains a threat to overcome or a resource to use. In analyzing the creature's stomach contents later, a Cousteau scientist found a three-foot-long *jacaré*, the remains of fish and kingfishers, and a can. The animal was nearly fourteen feet long and weighed about eight hundred pounds.

RED HIGHWAYS, GREEN VILLAGES: I

TRUCK TEAM | MANAUS | BRAZIL

They sit around a lunch table on the roof terrace of the Hotel Monaco—Captain Cousteau, Jean-Michel, Coll, Mounier, Zlotnicka, DiPerna, Barros—eating fried *tucunare*, sipping Brahma Chop beer or Brazilian coffee. Through the high wrought-iron railing that encircles the open-air Restaurant Gabriela they can see the sprawl of Manaus's stucco buildings for miles, until the city disappears into distant jungle that shimmers through the hot air. Along the city waterfront they can make out the tip of *Calypso*'s flying bridge among the masts at the floating docks. Beyond, under the noonday sun, slow riverboats and long motorized canoes, called "motors," move like dark blades through the glinting surface of the Rio Negro. The city seems bathed in a tropical dreaminess.

Behind the bar, a waiter twists the knobs of a radio and into the listless afternoon comes Frank Sinatra singing "New York, New York." A flashy discharge from one cultural atmosphere pierces the moist quiet of another.

The intrusion is symbolic. It comes as the team is discussing the truck mission they are about to undertake through areas of southern Amazonia that are rippling with social turbulence—where territory trod only by scattered and small Indian tribes for centuries is being penetrated by modern homesteaders from the industrialized south of Brazil and by immense public and multinational development projects which are prelude to overwhelming change.

Or are they?

The enduring question about Amazonia is whether human enterprise on a mammoth scale can ever tame the jungle and harvest its resources. More than any other Amazon nation, Brazil is banking heavily on a future flow of wealth from its northern rain-forest lands—minerals, timber, agricultural products—to reduce a prodigious international debt approaching $100 billion, the world's largest.

Reminder of a bygone era of opulence, the famed Manaus opera house, Teatro do Amazonas, has been restored to appear as it did when Enrico Caruso and Jenny Lind performed before rubber barons. Some 66,000 blue and gold tiles were imported from Alsace to gild the dome.

For all the machinations of bureaucracy and economics, the direction of Amazonia's future may come down to a single acid test: the success of the highway system that has begun to plunge through it. For the outside world to infiltrate the marketplace of Manaus, as it has, with Rolling Stones T-shirts and Sony Walkmans required only an expansion of commercial shipping routes. But it is another thing to build a permanent network of all-weather truck-bearing roads through thick stands of hardwood trees stretching across an area nearly as large as Europe, over terrain that turns to mud under the perpetual deluge of tropical thundershowers and among clouds of insects that attack construction gangs with debilitating, often fatal diseases.

Nevertheless, in 1960 the first Amazon highway was completed between Belém and Brasília, and since then roads have been bulldozed through rain forest to link Manaus, Santarém, and Belém with the south. To open up the jungle, Brazilian planners chose highways as conduits rather than the existing river system, which flowed in the wrong direction, away from the southern industrial centers. The availability of cheap foreign oil and the worldwide shift toward automotive transportation made highways appear more attractive than railroads. It was a decision many planners probably regret today, since the surge in oil prices that began unexpectedly in 1974 has been a major factor in the colossal foreign debt of oil-poor, highway-dependent Brazil.

In 1970 a new governmental push into Amazonia began with construction of an east-west "TransAmazon" highway coupled with ambitious plans to relocate impoverished Brazilian families in small cluster villages to spring up at intervals along the road. The president of Brazil announced that one hundred thousand families would settle along the TransAmazon within three years. Thirteen years later, only about eight thousand families remain; the highway is subject to massive erosion; and unbridled optimism about Amazonia's future, though not extinguished, has been profoundly sobered.

As the Cousteau team has seen, the massive highway program, whatever its measure of success or failure, has irreversibly changed the lives of the people who were already settled successfully within the rain forest, the Amazon Indians. The road builders have sliced through hunting territories, pushed tribes off traditional lands, and introduced diseases for which the Indians have neither immunological defenses nor appropriate medicines in their rain-forest herbal pharmacopoeia. There have also been incidents of murder, rape, and retribution between "whites" and Indians.

J.-Y.C.—*While Jean-Michel and I have been away from the expedition, Raymond Coll, Colin Mounier, and Yves Zlotnicka have flown in* Papagallo *to visit a tribe known as the Matis, who have been forced to relocate from their ancient homeland to a small territory between the Ituí and Itacuai rivers south of Benjamin Constant, a Brazilian port on the Rio Javari along the Peruvian border. In fact, it has been a return trip for our men, who first contacted the tribe during* Calypso's *voyage upriver in July. Representatives of Brazil's Indian Agency, known as FUNAI, originally alerted us to the plight of the Matis, who seem to us afflicted with most of the tragedies now spreading through nearly all Amazon tribes. When our men arrived, they were only the seventh, eighth, and ninth outsiders the Matis had ever met. Now, as we share lunch at the Hotel Monaco, Jean-Michel*

126

and I listen intently to their stories. They provide a valuable prologue as our Truck Team sets out on the highways that have caused the deterioration of Indian peoples.

It is obvious that our men have developed an affection for the Matis. Colin tells how, during their first visit, the Indians asked him through a translater to remove his glasses so they could get to know him better. When the team returned, the tribe hailed them and called them by name.

Colin imitates them: "Here is Yves with his tape recorder!" they would say, "Here is Colin with his camera!"

"They have a droll humor," he says. "They make fun of one another constantly, and of us, too, in a kindly manner. When they wanted our attention, they called us with kisses, as you might summon your dog."

As Colin speaks I am reminded of two stories that illustrate the innocence of some Amazon tribes. A FUNAI agent told us how, when one of their teams landed near an uncontacted tribe in a small plane, the Indians swarmed about the aircraft, the first they had ever seen on the ground. They were trying to determine if it was a male or a female. Our new friend Manoel Araujo da Silva, who has served as a river pilot most of his life and now commands Anaconda, *told me another story. On one of his trips up a remote tributary, Manoel's boat was surrounded by a suspicious tribe. The Indians hauled Manoel and his companions onto the bank and spent most of an hour hotly debating a course of action, or so it appeared to Manoel. Finally, perhaps as a kind of test or as an exhibition of strength, the chief confronted Manoel, staring deeply into his eyes. Suddenly, with dramatic flare, the Indian violently plucked from his ears two long ornamental wooden pegs, presenting Manoel with a personal challenge. Manoel reached into his mouth and jerked out his false teeth. The Indian was stunned by this act of courage and magic, and he accepted Manoel immediately.*

"Mostly," Yves says, "we were impressed by their continued suffering from disease—influenza especially. Since our first visit four separate Matis groups had combined together in one village, principally because this made it easier for FUNAI doctors to treat their ill. In 1978, when they were first contacted by FUNAI, there were 184 Matis. Now only 84 are left; 32 died from a single outbreak of flu."

Obviously, the Matis are dying out inexorably, victims of diseases transmitted to them by only a handful of outsiders. The vanquishing blow, however, was a government decision in 1978 to construct a highway between Benjamin Constant and Cruzeiro do Sul, a route that creates an incision through their territory. FUNAI convinced the Matis to move, and now they occupy a relatively small area. Unfortunately they were compelled to settle along a river in order to facilitate their vital medical assistance from FUNAI. It was a radical change for the Matis, whose entire history has been that of a remote-forest people, a terra firme *tribe. Our team describes how they struggle now to master canoes and to fish in water deeper than their forest brooks. Mosquitoes plague them along the river, as do biting gnats called* pions, *which leave drops of blood on the skin and cause horrible itching.*

Despite their illnesses and their struggles with river life, the Matis dis-

Opposite, above:
The experimental amphibious truck—dubbed *Jacaré*—sails an Amazon lake, taking the team to a diving spot quickly and eliminating the need to transfer to a boat. The truck makes 60 mph on land, seven knots in water.

Opposite, below:
The six-wheel-drive expedition truck *Amarillo* pulled many Brazilian vehicles from the highway's muddy grip.

played a wealth of knowledge about jungle animals and plants and an extraordinary sense of direction whenever they ventured into the forest. Matis hunters showed our men how to hunt with blowguns. These infamous weapons are between twelve and eighteen feet long and have two parts: the barrel, a long, blackened, rectilinear tube of wood, and a mouthpiece, like that of a trumpet only larger, which is made of another wood. The barrel and mouthpiece are joined by clay overlaid with snail nacre. The sight is made of two capybara claws. The whole thing weighs about five pounds. The darts are slivers of bamboo; the tips are coated with deadly curare; the other end is wrapped with a little cotton wool as a propulsive surface and caked with bits of clay for weight. The hunter fits the dart into the mouthpiece, aims, and blows easily. The dart shoots straight out for about fifty feet, silently picking off a monkey or bird without alarming its neighbors. More than once, the team saw Matis hunters return with eight or ten monkeys at a time.

Like the Ashaninca of Peru and many other Amazon tribes, the Matis use root and herbal poisons to stun or kill fish in shallow rivers. While Colin was filming a fishing expedition, he was summoned by two Matis to see a small snake no longer than his boot sole. It was a drab-looking fellow the color of tree bark and Colin was not very interested until he noticed that whenever the snake moved slightly the Indians leaped backward. They called it a jaracará and told Colin it was one of the few snakes capable of jumping. Why were they so quick to keep their distance? Colin wondered. The venom of the nearly invisible creature, he was told, could kill within two hours.

The forest knowledge of the Matis is recorded only in their brains, and as they die off it may disappear. Attacks of influenza have eliminated most of the elders already, including the tribal chief. His daugher, Nanoï, now serves as the leader of the tribe. She is the only Matis with gray hair, and though less than fifty years of age, she is the oldest person still living.

Nanoï told Coll the history of her tribe. Long ago, she said, a huge pheasant called a Moto bird found an empty house in the forest and laid two eggs in it. Two Matis hatched from the eggs, a male and a female, and they begat the Matis nation. They revered forest creatures. They pierced their noses and chins with permanent wooden needles, which looked like the whiskers of the jaguars they admired. When they killed a tapir, they waited until dark to butcher it, out of respect, believing that to expose the animal's intestines to daylight would chagrin its spirit.

Life was not perfect. There were wars with other tribes occasionally. There were snake bites, there were periods of too much rain or not enough. There was usually sufficient corn and manioc, some fruit, meat regularly, fish that could be dried. There is a memory of the first sighting of white men, probably rubber collectors, which Nanoï says occurred around 1910. Her concept of time is vague. The date matters little. The important aspect of the memory is that the Matis chief deliberated over a course of action for some time before deciding not to kill the whites.

Nanoï stresses this fact heavily because not long after the chief's decision a white man killed three Matis men with a rifle and raped a Matis woman. In revenge, the tribe killed two white women and two white chil-

dren. There have been no killings lately. Nanoï thinks that is because there is a FUNAI agent living permanently with the tribe. But the Matis territory is situated among good timber that is much sought after by ma-deireiros (wood merchants) from Benjamin Constant and is laced with rivers sufficiently deep to transport logs. Nanoï believes that the caboclos who work for the madeireiros will kill the Matis if FUNAI ever abandons the tribe.

Raymond later asked the FUNAI agent, Omar Santos, what the future holds for the Matis.

"For a long time," said Omar, "the policy regarding indigenous people in Brazil has been solely one of hope. There is nothing concrete to solve these development problems. The policy of the Matis themselves consists only of hopes. They hope the disease will abate. They hope the white people will stop bringing devastation. They hope the Matis will survive. These are only hopes."

The highway system is merely the latest in a series of jungle-exploitation schemes that began with the discovery of the Amazon by the Spaniard Francisco de Orellana in 1541. The conquistador had been sent eastward from Quito by a brother of Pizarro, not in search of a beautiful wilderness but rather to find valuable cinnamon and gold. The most famous invasion of Amazonia, however, came in the nineteenth century. The elegant iron framework embellishing many of the older buildings in Manaus is a reminder of a time of phenomenal opulence and ambition, when this city was considered one of the richest in the world.

It had begun with the great French scientist Charles Marie de la Condamine. While traveling in Amazonia in 1743, de la Condamine discovered a curious elastic fluid oozing from many trees and he took samples back to Paris. This latex, or rubber, was principally a curiosity until the invention of the automobile and the pneumatic tire. Suddenly the outside world descended upon Amazonia, the only source of rubber, centering operations in Manaus, and set about collecting the milky fluid of *Hevea brasiliensis*.

The rubber barons of Manaus at the turn of the century can be compared only with the oil sheikhs of today. They turned a once-sleepy jungle trading post into a European-style city. The designer of the most famous Paris landmark, Alexandre Eiffel, came here to create an elegant complex of buildings—with elaborate finger-thin iron railings and stained-glass gables—that still serves as the city's Mercado Municipalo. A lavish opera house was built of Italian stone in a Florentine design and outfitted with chandeliers from Venice, pillars of Carrara marble, tall vases of Sèvres porcelain. The city elite paid Enrico Caruso, Jenny Lind, and the Comédie Française to journey up the Amazon and perform in their ornate opera house before crowds dressed in the latest European fashions. The conveniences of twentieth-century life suddenly appeared in the middle of the jungle: electricity (only two cities in the western hemisphere had electricity before Manaus), telephones, trolley lines, fashionable shops. *Le Matin* was sold on corner newsstands. Imported butter arrived from Denmark, sauerkraut from Germany, potatoes from Portugal.

But the boom collapsed even more suddenly than it had begun. Amazo-

nian *Hevea* seeds were smuggled to Malaysia, Java, Ceylon, and Sumatra and planted in orderly rows. By 1910 the production from these plantations had begun to overwhelm the Amazon wild-rubber industry. Within a decade most of the rubber barons had disappeared, leaving behind crumbling Victorian mansions, ghostly reminders that most large-scale human enterprises have failed in the attempt at converting the Amazon to gold.

TRUCK TEAM | HIGHWAY BR-364 | BRAZIL

On October 28, the Truck Team, led by Coll, is loaded aboard a ferry to cross the Rio Negro and the Amazon, then sets out on the roadway leading south in three vehicles: a jeep, the six-wheel-drive *Amarillo*, and a new amphibious truck called *Jacaré*. The two trucks have been provided to the expedition by IVECO.

The 7,000-mile route of the team will take them south to the Mato Grosso region, then north as far as Santarém, then eastward along the TransAmazon, hooking north finally to arrive at Belém. There are some worries about the long mission, which will last several months. To begin with, the rainy season is about to arrive in the Mato Grosso, presenting the possibility that the team could find itself mired in mud.

The team Raymond Coll supervises is an unusual mélange of nationalities and talents. Among the permanent members, Coll, Cornu, Jouas, and Sion are French. Cameramen Prezelin and Henri Alliet, also French, will join the mission periodically. The team's two truck drivers, Ugo Lamprati and Gianfranco Guera, are Italian test drivers employed by IVECO. Still photographer Ayrton Camargo is a Brazilian from Rio de Janeiro. The jeep driver and logistics manager is Tim Trabon, an American friend of the Cousteaus' who has volunteered to take leave of his printing business in Kansas City to assist with the Amazon expedition.

The first obstacle encountered by the team has nothing to do with the hazards of the road. It is an amusing matter of communication. Team leader Coll is fluent in French and Spanish, neither of which is comprehensible to his English-speaking jeep driver and "money manager," Trabon, who also does not understand much Portuguese, the only language of the local Brazilians with whom he must bargain for accommodations, fuel, and repairs. More important, no one on the team is fluent in Italian, and neither of the two Italian drivers speaks either French or English.

When, weeks later, Trabon describes the problem to Jean-Michel, he offers as an example the daily decision-making process concerning the route of the trucks.

"The decisions were arrived at in French, after which the route was conveyed to the Italian drivers in Spanish and Portuguese. Comprehending none of this, I decided simply to follow the others. When we got to the trucks, Raymond Coll pointed to me behind the wheel of the jeep and said, 'You lead.' I did this by keeping one eye on the rear-view mirror to see if the other two trucks were still behind me."

Within a few days the team develops a lexicon of the road, involving common words, hand signals, and facial expressions. As communications improve, however, road conditions deteriorate. The paved highway ends a day out of Manaus at Pôrto Velho. The red dirt road that continues southward to Cuiabá can be crossed in three days under ideal dry conditions, which seldom exist. During the rainy season the same trip can take six weeks.

The Cousteau team steers their heavily burdened vehicles over a rutted red-clay road that when dry relentlessly jolts the wheels, as an interminable cattle guard might, and when wet turns to a patchwork of spongy soil and standing or careening orange water. If a truck drifts too far away from the hardened tracks, wheels can sink quickly into mud the consistency of cake frosting. During one of their first five-hour entrapments in a mudhole, on a side trip west of Pôrto Velho, the team conceives the idea of securing the winch cable of *Jacaré* to a huge tree and pulling themselves out of the pasty morass. What follows is a dramatic lesson about the thinness of Amazon soils. The 100-foot hardwood giant immediately topples over, its roots unfastened by the winch from their delicate surface clutch of the shallow soil layer.

Even the miseries of highway travel are superseded by a more troublesome, and potentially dangerous, situation. The Truck Team has entered a region plagued by clouds of mosquitoes and other species of biting insects. Along the Manaus–Cuiabá highway (BR-364), malaria has reached nearly epidemic proportions as arriving farmers and miners expand existing settlements, providing the disease-carrying *Anopheles* mosquitoes with a greater pool of infected persons to tap and victims to contaminate. Development compounds the problem: birds and bats, the natural predators of mosquitoes, decrease in number as humans arrive, and forest cutting increases the acreage available for mosquito breeding grounds.

Ironically, though it is now the most widespread disease in Amazonia, malaria is a foreign invader, transported to South America nearly a century and a half ago aboard African slave ships. The principal symptom of malaria is a debilitating cyclical fever that can recur for the rest of a victim's life as the injected parasite attacks red blood cells. There are several species of *Anopheles* mosquitoes and several strains of the disease. Modern medicines can prevent or lessen the discomfort of most types of malaria, but these drugs are not abundantly available in remote areas and remain suspect among many Amazonians. There are also strains of malaria that have developed resistance to all known drugs and are often fatal.

The team encounters a dramatic illustration of the Amazon's insect menace when they visit two railroad sheds, one of which has been converted to a museum, only blocks from Pôrto Velho's central square. The tranquility of the odd little museum nearly camouflages the immensity of human failure and suffering to which it pays tribute—the Madeira–Mamoré Railroad.

It has been called "the first great contest between modern man and the Amazon jungle," an engineering project first tackled in 1872. The idea: to cut through the rain forest from the Bolivian border to Pôrto Velho and to install a railroad, thereby providing Bolivia with a rubber-transport route to navigable stretches of the Madeira River and beyond to the Amazon and the sea. American and European construction engineers foresaw nothing remarkable in laying a mere 230 miles of track, less than a tenth the distance covered by

Opposite, above:
Gold from the bottom of the Madeira River being weighed in a gold-buying office near Pôrto Velho.

Opposite, middle:
Hoses from Madeira barges carry gold-bearing bottom sediment to sluice boxes.

Opposite, below:
Suction hoses are directed along the river bottom by divers unable to see more than a few inches through the muddy Madeira.

the U.S. transcontinental railroad completed three years earlier. But in their "contest" with the jungle, they were beaten convincingly. So great was the loss of life among construction gangs, most of whom were imported from as far away as Europe, that the abandoned railway is still referred to as the "Railroad of the Dead." More people died attempting to build the Madeira–Mamoré than in any other construction project in modern times, including the Panama Canal. Old-timers in Pôrto Velho still repeat the slogan generated by the disaster: "Under each cross tie a human skull." In fact, the total body count will never be known because reliable records were not kept; but no one disputes the estimate that perhaps ten thousand people died.

The primary killers were diseases, especially malaria and yellow fever, along with amoebic dysentery, beriberi, and typhoid. When the project began, medical science had not yet connected malaria and yellow fever with mosquitoes, yet so great were the swarms of insects that the death toll would probably have soared even with better medical preparation. Termites ate clothing, ticks and blowflies left workers covered with welts and infections, sweat bees were so relentless that an engineer assigned two men to swat them away from the eyes of a third so that he could carry on with his surveying.

Moreover, the progress of the railroad did not seem to justify the miseries. When the second set of contractors gave up after five years (the project was interrupted several times as companies abandoned it), only five miles of track were in place and only forty more had been surveyed. Besides the insects, the Amazon jungle offered up its own engineering nightmares. The rain forest was so dense that surveyors were as helpless as sailors in a soupy fog, able to measure off only a few feet at a time. Paths were often abandoned and begun again when the track struck an unpassable hill that had been camouflaged by jungle. The rainy season swamped finished roadbeds and shifting rivers carried them away.

So dispirited were thousands of workers that they fled in small boats or rafts, often meeting up with new catastrophes in their attempts to escape the project. Seventy-five Italian workmen departed for Bolivia and none was ever heard from again.

The ultimate tragedy, however, may be that the loss of life was a horrible waste. The very year that the rail line was finally completed saw the peak of the Amazon rubber boom. When trains were at last running on the Railroad of the Dead, rubber from the Orient quickly extinguished the demand for their freight and the rail traffic soon halted. Brush, trees, and vines quickly covered rusting locomotives and cars.

The dream that brings newcomers to Pôrto Velho these days, and victimizes many of them, is not gold-producing rubber or construction, but pure gold itself. Some sixty miles up the Madeira River from Pôrto Velho, at a site called Jirau, the Truck Team spends several days observing a remarkable "gold rush," thousands of people combing the bottom of one of the Amazon's largest tributaries to dredge up gold flecks carried down from the Bolivian Andes.

So extraordinary is the mining operation that Coll and Jouas radio *Calypso* with details, and a day later Jean-Michel arrives in *Papagallo*. What the team sees is a wide belt of brown river congested with some 460 canvas-roofed barges, each trailing behind it thick hoses. Some 1,500 divers—called *palombares*—descend into the muddy river daily, fed by surface air lines and tethered by ropes, blindly directing the vacuum hoses along the riverbed in hopes that the muck carried up to the barges will contain placer gold. Usually it does. One barge owner interviewed by the team has produced a kilo of gold (about $15,000) in only three days. Divers average about $13,000 each per month. The stakes are high and the competition is intense. In his taped diary, Jean-Michel describes the operation he sees:

"The Madeira is deep here, sixty feet in some places. Lone divers spend three hours along the bottom before being relieved by another man. Working in a swirl of muddy water, combating six-knot currents, the *palombares* can be tragically caught in invisible hazards along the bottom, such as sunken tree trunks. The death rate from embolisms is high among these inexperienced divers. Worse, when word spreads that a barge has located a rich area, competing divers are said to arrive with knives, trying to drive away other miners by cutting their air lines to the surface. Entire barges are sometimes lost when their anchors are cut and the river carries them several miles to rapids that quickly break them up.

"Nowhere in the world have we seen such cavalier attitudes toward diving safety nor such a peculiar acceptance of violent death. We met a man who had given up all of his gold to the owners of another barge in order to purchase the exoneration of his brother, who had killed one of their workers. Neither he nor the other prospectors seemed deeply bothered by the transaction, since the river bottom still held countless fortunes and the ethics of the moment were as loose as the gold flakes washing down the Madeira.

"In addition, the malaria rate is skyrocketing, the settlement lacks sanitation except for an open communal defecation area, and the new town that has sprung up a few miles away is largely a collection of exploiting shop and bar owners. Prostitutes collect their fees in gold: ten grams ($150).

"Yet we also sense a human anomaly. The prodigious wealth recoverable from the river engenders a kind of breezy friendliness that is a curious counterpoint to the violence. It is as if we were in a bizarre and temporary world in which only extremes of human behavior are possible."

The hospitable side of the Jirau mining community is illustrated by a story Tim Trabon tells. While the film team was at work in midriver one afternoon, Trabon set out alone to get lunch. Passing a score of hastily built bars, restaurants, and shack homes—all of which looked alike and presented no identifying signboards—Trabon turned and entered the open door of a tiny cafe. Seeing no menu, he simply pointed to the food he wanted on the shelves and sat down at a table. Twenty minutes later he was served without comment by the cook, a young woman of about thirty. Finishing the meal, Trabon stood up and pointed to his wallet.

"There is no charge," said the woman in the kitchen. Mistakenly, Trabon had walked into a home and ordered lunch. Without any discussion it was served, and with no thought of recompense the stranger was bid farewell.

As the team wanders about Jirau filming, Jean-Michel grows curious about the gold-extraction process, and in studying it, he discovers a sobering aspect of life in the gold camp. Radioing *Calypso*, he summons Jacques Constans and visiting Johns Hopkins University scientist Dennis Powers to the site aboard *Papagallo*. The two men spend several days taking samples of water and fish from the Madeira in order to determine whether or not Jean-Michel's suspicions are correct: that potentially dangerous mercury poisoning may be taking place.

Mercury is commonly employed in gold production because it forms amalgams with most metals, including silver and gold. This bonding action effectively extracts fine gold flakes from ores or river sands. When the mercury is then burned away, pure gold remains.

Jean-Michel notices that the men working over the burning amalgam, as well as the children flocking about the work site, are breathing mercury vapor. The ashes, as well as mercury waste and spillage, are dumped into the Madeira. So extensive is this pollution that Jean-Michel wonders if the danger may not be similar to that resulting from the infamous mercury disaster in Minamata—the Japanese port city where thousands of people suffered crippling or fatal poisoning after eating fish contaminated with mercury wastes flushed into Minamata harbor by a chemical company. The team accompanies Constans and Powers downriver to Cachoeira do Teotonio, the site of rippling cataracts and a fishery that exploits the fish schools blocked by the rapids. The Cousteau team reasons that most of these fish may have been exposed to mercury pollution in the river. Constans and Powers purchase fish directly from the nets of local fishermen and seal them in containers for detailed analysis later by Powers.

On November 10 the trucks set out again on BR-364 toward the next focal point of the mission, the village of Vilhena. Pôrto Velho and Vilhena mark the northern and southern borders of Rondônia, Brazil's newest state, promoted from the status of "territory" in 1982. It is named after Colonel Candido Mariano da Silva Rondon, who was part Indian and one of Amazonia's most famous explorers and Indian defenders. Rondônia is to Brazil what Oregon was to the United States during the nineteenth century—a frontier expanse open for settlement by impoverished families and young men looking for a fresh start. Convinced that Rondônia's soils can support more agriculture than the acidic, leached, nutrient-limited soils that characterize much of Amazonia, the Brazilian government initiated a homesteading program in the state in the early seventies, upon completion of BR-364.

To encourage migrants, the government builds access roads, schools, banks, hospitals, and issues land titles to qualifying citizens. If a family is approved at the Vilhena checkpoint, they are added to a long waiting list, eventually to receive title to a 50-hectare (124-acre) plot. Between 1978 and 1982 nearly a quarter-million people from southern Brazil passed through the immigration checkpoint.

The tide of immigrants has been so great that surveying teams and geologists trying to demarcate landholdings with promising soils have been unable to keep ahead of the incoming families. The vast majority of the immigrants are compelled to squat on public lands or to occupy the limited supply of public housing while awaiting their land titles—sometimes for years.

On the morning of November 12, through billowing clouds of highway dust, the Truck Team can make out low wooden buildings in the distance.

Opposite, above:
Diving miners risk being carried away in six-knot currents; they suffer frequent embolisms; and they vie with competitors who sometimes cut the air hoses of divers who have found a rich site.

Opposite, middle:
Despite frequent fatalities, miners eagerly dive for the Madeira's placer gold riches. Divers average about $13,000 each per month.

Opposite, below:
A miner at Jirau heats an amalgam of gold and mercury, releasing toxic mercury vapors. The Cousteau team discovered significant amounts of mercury in the river and in the bodies of miners and their families.

What they see about them as they drive into Vilhena is spellbinding: a town that seems to have popped through a time warp from the American Old West, collecting some modern trappings along the way. Men in cowboy hats line the facades of one-story wooden hotels and bars. They stand over pool tables in dark rooms, sit on barber chairs. The town is covered in red dust, its streets patchworks of gummy mud.

Yet Vilhena is a twentieth-century frontier town. Stereo shops butt against stores selling rifles, shovels, and saddles; some men sport high gaucho boots but others are wearing Adidas sneakers; people pass on horseback and in horse-drawn carts, but more commonly they rumble by in Volkswagens, Fords, and Mercedes diesel trucks.

At the Hotel Mirage, a new brick and stucco building near the center of Vilhena, the Truck Team meets Angela Elias, an energetic woman of thirty-five who built the hotel and talks tirelessly of Vilhena's future. Angela says that she was the twenty-seventh person to arrive in Vilhena. Today the population exceeds fifteen thousand. As characterized by Angela, the town is not a wild outpost but a nascent community of families struggling to build a city with civility, with dignity. She takes the team to a public housing site. Rows of one-room wooden houses without running water are crowded close together, but they are neat, unlittered, and bordered by picket fences.

Back in the lobby of her hotel, Angela says that many of the settlers in Vilhena are of European stock, especially German, and that they come from the state of Parana, south of São Paulo. As she talks, a television set in a corner of the lobby flickers with programs relayed from urbanized southern Brazil. A commercial invites viewers to join other Brazilians in the new land of opportunity, Rondônia. On a wall not far away there is a map of Rondônia that illustrates graphically the bountiful optimism of the settlement program. The map includes a table of distances from Vilhena to the capitals of the world—New York, London, Paris—but it omits the mileage from Vilhena to the next town, Colorado.

On a Sunday morning, Angela takes the Cousteau team to meet *migrantes* who are already working on homesteads. As the trucks leave Vilhena and head west on an access road, the team suddenly finds the road blocked by several hundred head of Brahma cattle herded by six cowboys on horseback. The scene could be a cattle drive on the Chisholm Trail. The *vaqueiros*, wiry men in leather chaps and wide-brimmed wrangler hats, have slept the night before in bedrolls around a campfire. One trails behind the herd, a newborn calf draped over his saddle. Another rides in front of the procession blowing continuously on a curved bull's horn, leading the cattle with a plaintive, monotonous call. Soundman Jouas records the rich sounds of the cattle drive as it wends past the trucks: the low wail of the horn mingling hypnotically with the dull thud of hooves, the shrill whistles of the *vaqueiros*, and the sporadic moans of complaint from shuffling cows.

Thirty minutes later, Angela signals the drivers to halt at an unmarked spot in the road, which she identifies as Linha São Rogue. About a dozen families live within walking distance. Angela leads Coll, Cornu, Jouas, Sion, and Camargo up a steep embankment to a cleared plot. There is a rough wooden house, a pigpen, chickens and ducks, and three dogs leashed to stakes. The windows of the house are covered by black plastic sheets.

Opposite, left:
Symbolic of the futility of conserving only fragments of the rain forest, the towering Brazil nut tree (*Bertholletia excelsa*) is protected by Brazilian law. But when the surrounding forest is cleared, the giant trees succumb anyway, blown over by unimpeded winds and bereft of the vital support systems of the rich forest biota. "You can never do just one thing," say ecologists.

Opposite, above right:
Caboclo children clean fish adeptly at an age when youngsters elsewhere are forbidden to play with knives. These fish caught at Cachoeira do Teotônio, downriver from Jirau, were analyzed by the Cousteau team for possible mercury contamination as a result of mining practices. The results showed no cause for alarm yet, but a serious situation to be closely monitored.

Opposite, below right:
Blond-haired, tan-skinned children from a homesteading family embody the racial mixture of many settlers from southern Brazil, whose ancestry includes European lineage.

Almiro Junques drops a handsaw and greets the visitors. His wife, Regina, emerges from the house and children seem to appear everywhere. As Angela interprets, Almiro describes their life to Raymond Coll. They are the newest arrivals at this spot along the road. They came from the state of Santa Catarina only four months ago. The first *migrante* to arrive here claimed thirty thousand acres and hired gunmen to drive the other settlers away, but government agents came to their aid and the dispute was quelled. Angela says Rondônia has been plagued by such fights over land titles.

Almiro says he borrows a chain saw to cut the timber on the land, leaves the logs where they fall because there is no way to haul them off, and plants rice, potatoes, corn, beans, manioc, and pineapple in the sunny patches between the logs. He has built a coop for the chickens because an ocelot was taking too many.

Coll asks if Almiro is happy. He thinks for a moment and then says that he would return to Santa Catarina if he could, but he has no choice. He has to keep at it now. The problem is the malaria. In only four months in the jungle it has struck the entire family—two adults and six children.

It is a difficult life, he says. The family survives on a diet of beans, rice, and manioc. On Sundays they kill one chicken for dinner and slice up one pineapple for dessert.

At another farm, owned by Jośe and Anna de Lima, the story is repeated. The parents and their three children all suffer periodic bouts with malaria. José tells Coll of other problems the settlers face. Although a weekly bus now carries them to Vilhena, it is only a recent development. Before the bus, settlers here had to walk to town, more than thirty miles, for provisions, tools, and medical help. He tells the story of a neighbor woman who began to deliver a breech birth. Four men on foot carried her in a hammock for six hours, all the way to Vilhena.

There is also the matter of profiteering traders who come on horseback with goods from Vilhena and barter with the farmers. To purchase a single container of dried milk for their children, a farmer may have to give up a fifty-pound sack of dried beans from his fields.

What is exploitation to some is unlimited opportunity to others. Paula DiPerna, who has scouted Rondônia ahead of the Truck Team, tells about an interview she had with Carlos Almeida da Silva, an official of Brazil's land reform agency, INCRA.

"Carlos told the story of a man who came to Colorado with one metal first-aid kit and began selling medicine to farmers. Now he owns a pharmacy and is running for election to the National Assembly. Another man started a business with a pickup truck, carrying goods from Colorado to Vilhena twice a week. Now he runs a supermarket."

DiPerna notices another aspect of life here. "Few people I met in Rondônia," she says, "talked about the jungle as a living system. To most of those who live in it, the jungle is simply in the way of other things they need or want."

The next day, the team drives south from Vilhena to investigate the immigration office through which new arrivals must pass. Of the four agents at the "Dispersal Center," only one appears to be more than twenty-five years of

age. It is a surfeit of young people and an escalating birth rate, in fact, that have compelled authorities to initiate the settlement program. When the project began, the average number of children per married woman in rural Brazil was 7.6. As these youngsters grow up, they set out for São Paulo, Rio, and Belo Horizonte. Amazonia was perceived as a giant relief valve for the unemployed masses reaching maturity and a reversal of the migratory pattern from countryside to city. The government correctly perceived an urgent situation. United Nations experts project a population of 26 million for São Paulo by the year 2000.

To process the incoming *migrantes*, the Vilhena Dispersal Center remains open 24 hours a day, 365 days a year. All immigrants are interviewed and inoculated for yellow fever. Families that qualify for land but have no money are given meal tickets to eat in local restaurants for three days. This day, November 15, traffic through the center is light. It is the first election day in Brazil in eighteen years. Since Brazilians are compelled to vote or suffer such consequences as prohibition from government employment, migrating families have halted for the day to vote at villages along BR-364.

The quiet Center has the feel of a place in the heart of an empty continent. Standing in front of it, the Truck Team can look down the straight, jungle-lined red highway for five miles, then turn and see five miles in the other direction. Occasionally a speck forms at the vanishing point of the road, gradually grows to a tuft of orange dust, then becomes the metal cheeks of a flatbed truck. Four or five people crowd the cab; children cling to the stakes behind it. Sometimes they wave a thumbs-up signal—the ubiquitous Brazilian gesture of salutation. The dust cloud passes by and diminishes in the distance. Then it is quiet again.

That evening the team sits on Angela's hotel porch, chatting about what they have seen. Trabon and Mose Richards, who is accompanying the Truck Team in Rondônia, remain after the others have retired, listening to a steady percussion of rain, talking about the endless work and the loneliness of a long expedition. A polite Brazilian boy of eight climbs onto the couch next to Richards, asking his name. He is typical of the golden children of southern Brazil, with straw-colored hair from European ancestors and an almond-brown complexion from native stock. The Truck Team has evoked his curiosity. The two talk in a loose Portuguese. His father works in the hotel. His mother is dead. It is just his father and he. About the yellow trucks: why is one both a truck and a boat? How soon are they leaving, why, for where? His lively eyes are riveted on Richards. They seem full of yearning, eager to discover something more remarkable than the squalor and monotony of continuing privation, like every soul that has descended upon Rondônia. Why, where, when, how?

Richards tells him the men are going to Cuiabá and Santarém and Belém, to the Rio Xingu and the great Rio Amazonas, and then even far beyond those places, none of which strikes a familiar chord in him.

Where, why, when, how?

The men have a large ship, a *barco grande*, which is now on the Rio Negro. The trucks are nothing to that ship. Richards is flying to it in three days, then a few weeks later to the *Estados Unidos*. The boy listens intently, and when the list of faraway places is finished his response is immediate.

"I will go with you," he says.

RED HIGHWAYS, GREEN VILLAGES: II

TRUCK TEAM | CUIABÁ–SANTARÉM HIGHWAY | BRAZIL

By the time the Truck Team reaches Cuiabá, at the southernmost tip of the Amazon basin, the rainy season is descending quickly. The plan is to spend several days in Cuiabá, cleaning equipment, repairing and tuning up the trucks. But there are reports of gathering storms and the team fears that impassable roads could disrupt expedition timetables.

The decision is made to press on northward immediately. On November 26, the three trucks set out on the Cuiabá–Santarém Highway, an unpaved corridor cutting through rain forest for 1,500 miles before reaching the Amazon River. To the amazement of Lamprati, Guera, and Trabon, road conditions are even worse than those of the past month on BR-364. Cameramen Cornu and Prezelin spend three days filming the truck drivers' efforts to negotiate dusty washboard roads that are transformed into pools of orange water and mudbars at the onset of a cloudburst.

The team passes dozens of heavily loaded trucks buried in mud to the top of the wheel rims. A bus leaning awkwardly off the shoulder of the highway has been stuck for two days. A farmer sits glumly on a sinking tractor in a slush pond five feet deep. The tractor had been summoned to pull out a truck.

Over dinner at night, the team wonders about the future of the Amazon highway system. Where landfills cross deep ravines, the roadbed is often severed by eroded gullies. The entire landfill must soon be rebuilt. Blacktop would help, but even with a top layer of asphalt the foundation of the road would probably continue to slip away until the pavement above cracked and collapsed.

Occasionally the road narrows to pass over frail and battered wooden bridges. At each the team scrambles out, leaving the drivers on their own. Coll inspects the shaky timber trestles and the fractured planks that serve as wheel paths, then directs the drivers with hand signals. Frequently cracks of breaking wood are heard and the team skitters about shouting in four languages, but none of the perilous bridges gives way.

Txukahaméi ceremonial headdresses are made of feathers from egrets, parrots, and oropendolas (common Amazon birds that build hanging nests and whose call sounds like gurgling water).

145

About four hundred miles north of Cuiabá, the trucks turn east onto an arterial road called BR-080. Built in 1971 as a shortcut between Brasília and the frontier, BR-080 became a symbol of the government's attitude toward Indian tribes. The national constitution ensures that lands occupied by tribes shall belong to them. To simplify obvious problems of demarcation, Brazil has created nearly two dozen Indian Parks under the direction of FUNAI, prohibiting the intrusion of outsiders within park boundaries. Yet when the need for BR-080 was determined, the rights of Indians were circumvented and the highway was routed directly through the most celebrated of these parks, Xingu National Park, which was created in 1961 and encompasses the headwaters of the Xingu River. Indian defenders organized public protests, but the roadwork never abated and some three thousand square miles of the park were declassified from their protected status.

At the Xingu River, the entire team transfers to the amphibious *Jacaré* and sails upstream to visit a tribe known as the Txukahamẽi, a branch of the Cayapo nation. FUNAI agents have acceded to the visit, but warned the team that the tribe can be dangerous despite their "civilized" appearance.

In Cuiabá the team has heard immigrants voice their anxieties about Indians. The fears seemed wildly exaggerated, since the only pure Indian the team had met between Manaus and Cuiabá was an old-timer in Vilhena. Marciano Zonoece had lived in the frontier outpost for sixty-one years, arriving to work on the first telegraph line. Among the flood of Portuguese-speaking newcomers, Zonoece seemed embarrassed by his Indian blood. The Cousteau team concluded that settlers passing through Cuiabá had seen too many "bangy-bangys," the Brazilian term for Hollywood westerns.

The Cuiabá–Santarém highway, however, skirts the edge of Xingu Park, where nearly twenty tribes maintain most of their traditions and greet the advance of "white" people into their Israel-sized tract with differing degrees of hostility. These are the indigenous people settlers have seen in the glossy magazines of São Paulo, with feather headdresses and dyes smeared on their bodies and disks planted in their lips. With bows and arrows, and blowguns, and clubs. They may one day hide in the darkness of a shack like Marciano Zonoece, but not yet.

When the *Jacaré* crawls up the riverbank near their village, two dozen Txukahamẽi appear. They are young people mostly and they surround the curious yellow truck that drives on water, touching its wheels and the enamel Calypso maiden painted on its hood. The chief, Rauní, greets Raymond Coll with a solid handshake and asks him, in Portuguese mangled by the plate in his lower lip, about the strange vehicle. Coll's answers and gentle smile satisfy Rauní, and the team is invited to the village.

Before BR-080 severed Xingu Park, the Txukahamẽi lived farther north, in the region annexed for the highway. They had been contacted years before by three Brazilian brothers who have become legendary figures in Amazonia: Orlando, Claudio, and Leonardo Villas Boas. First arriving in the Xingu region in 1946, the Villas Boas brothers recognized the Indian slaughter to come as Brazil penetrated its northern interior. They conceived a policy of Indian protectionism and of gradual integration of the natives into the society that would inevitably overwhelm them. Their stubborn battles with government bureaucracy and their courageous efforts to contact endangered tribes set the tone for Brazilian programs that continue today. It was the Villas Boas brothers who created Xingu Park, and it was their initiatives that set the stage for the creation of FUNAI six years later. Though nominated for a Nobel prize because of their work, the Villas Boas brothers are still considered controversial. Critics charge that their approach, creating Indian Parks and cushioning natives from outside influences, condemns indigenous people to a primitive life and to isolation in "human zoos."

The Txukahamēi tribe was split into two factions when the highway builders arrived. One group wanted to fight. In the ensuing battles seven Indians were killed. Rauní led his group of about 120 people, at the Villas Boas brothers' urging, southward into the park. An uneasy peace, interrupted by sporadic violence, has prevailed for more than a decade. Part of the tension is caused by a drawback in the park concept. Previously, a tribe hunted through and defended areas covering hundreds of thousands of acres. The scarcity of game made such expanses necessary. Often the tribes beyond these hunting grounds were mortal enemies. With the introduction of parks, tribes harboring old enmities were often crowded close together in greatly reduced hunting territories. The Txukahamēi now live near their ancient enemies, the Kréen-Akaróre. Their old territory is now checkered with cattle ranches.

The Truck Team spends five days with the Txukahamēi, filming both their traditional ways of life and their adaptations to the outside. Forming long lines, the Txukahamēi perform a "turtle dance," during which, as custom dictates, names are mystically conceived for each infant in the village. There are tours of the tribe's palm-thatched huts, demonstrations of basket weaving. But after this prologue of traditionalism, a transformation takes place. The time has come to resume work. The men of the tribe don Levis, T-shirts, and baseball caps, start the village tractor, and set to work in a rice field they are cultivating on ground only recently cleared of trees.

Chopping the soil with hoes and disking with the tractor, they look like farmers anywhere in the world, set apart only by the extended lips jutting out beneath some baseball caps. One man rolls a cigarette, another sticks a Bic pen above his ear. There are wristwatches and transistor radios. Rauní explains that some members of this and other tribes cross the boundaries of the park to work for farmers or rubber collectors. Sometimes they are paid in cash, and it is spent on "white man's" items; sometimes they work in trade for fish hooks, nets, or radios.

The most impressive and treasured possession of the Txukahamēi is their red tractor. Seeing it, Cornu is reminded of a story told by Captain Cousteau after meeting with an officer of Brazil's Ministry of the Interior. Discussing the plight of the country's Amazon tribes, the ministerial assistant said, "I want the Indians to keep their cultures, their languages, their identities. I ask only that they learn to do one thing: learn to drive tractors."

The tractor, wristwatches, and jeans engender an image of the Txukahamēi enveloped by white culture, conditioned to accept its work ethic and its materialism, sporting their feather hats and their three-foot hunting clubs in a hollow reenactment of a former identity. Or so it seems.

On the last day of their stay in the village, Coll, Cornu, Sion, Camargo, and Jouas enter a *caboclo*-style hut in which a young woman from FUNAI teaches

Opposite, above:
Economic hard times have left Brazil unable to maintain much of its Amazon highway network. The result: erosion and crumbling bridges. Scenes like this are not uncommon on *main* Amazon highways.

Opposite, below:
Jacaré pulls out of the Xingu River before curious Txukahamēis (choo-kah-HAHM-eyes) who marvelled at "the truck that swims."

147

Portuguese to the next Txukahamëi generation. One of the children has composed a paragraph on the blackboard. Camargo reads it in stunned silence and then translates it for the others.

Indians have killed white people with their bows and arrows because white people have stolen their land. It is the duty of Indians to kill white people.

The paragraph is dated November 26, six days before. It has been only a month, the teacher tells Camargo, since the Txukahamëi clubbed twelve settlers to death.

The odyssey through the muds of the Cuiabá–Santarém Highway resumes. Clothing that left Manaus white or beige is now indelibly stained orange. Tires battered by the corduroy roads begin to go flat. A mechanic in a small village discovers mud *inside* the differential of the jeep. Constantly drenched and weary, the team's moods swing from tension and bursts of temper to levity born of exhaustion. When Trabon skids off the road one day in the jeep, straight into a neat pile of watermelons stacked before a settler's house, the team quickly buys the shattered fruit and then breaks into gales of laughter. Slightly shaken, Trabon lights a cigarette, which promptly explodes—a prank successfully carried out by Jouas scores of times on the chain-smoking American.

On December 5, the convoy turns left onto the TransAmazon Highway, the most important east–west artery of the Amazon road network, and arrrives some fifty miles later at the Tapajós River, a sparkling blue, 800-mile tributary that rises just north of Cuiabá and empties into the Amazon at Santarém. The next day *Papagallo* arrives, makes three passes over the trucks, and sets down smoothly on the Tapajós. Jean-Michel tosses his bags into the *Jacaré* and climbs in for the team's entry into the bustling town of Itaituba.

Once a sleepy Tapajós fishing village, Itaituba was picked in 1970 as one of the handful of villages to be intensively developed during the first phase of Brazil's Amazon settlement program. It would serve as a mother city to rural farms and villages clustered around it—a key part of the territorial expansion celebrated by then-President Emílio Garrastazú Médici's declaration that Amazonia would become "a land with no men for men with no land." There was a rush to Itaituba—the population multiplied fivefold in a decade—but poor soil quickly doused the excitement and Itaituba languished. The population might have decreased had it not been for a sudden burst of excitement. Significant gold discoveries were made fifty miles up the Tapajós—it became a popular idea, in fact, that all of the Tapajós tributaries were swollen with gold—and Itaituba metamorphosed into a major gold town.

The flood of *garimpeiros* (gold seekers), shop owners, mechanics, gold buyers, soldiers of fortune, and prostitutes that descended upon Itaituba overwhelmed its municipal systems. There was little piped water and less sanitation. Garbage was strewn in the streets, where it subsidized a population explosion of rats and flies.

At Jean-Michel's suggestion, the team takes a circuitous route to Itaituba. They enter the Tapajós in the *Jacaré* and sail upstream to test the vehicle against a formidable current, and to inspect the river mining that fuels Itaitu-

Opposite, above right: Despite the traditional appearance suggested by ceremonial garb, young Txukahamëis attend a village school taught by a teacher from the Brazilian Indian Agency.

Opposite, above left: Increasingly, nudity and facial paint are reserved for Txukahamëi ceremonies. When the festivities are over, this young mother may don a Western dress obtained from white merchants.

Opposite, below: Txukahamëi men blacken their bodies with the juice of a fruit called *genipap* for hunts, war parties, and ceremonies.

ba's boom. After an hour of sailing, the team spots a lone *garimpeiro* digging along the bank. The man identifies himself as Pascual Rabelo de Carvalho. He has a home and family in Itaituba, but he spends three to six months at a time camped along the riverbank, panning the alluvial sands at the river's edge. When he has enough gold, he returns to Itaituba and sells it. From his pack, Pascual plucks a leather pouch swollen with gold dust accumulated during the past two months.

When Jean-Michel explains that the team is headed for Itaituba and invites Pascual along, he accepts immediately. Five minutes later, his few belongings jammed in the backpack, he is ready to leave.

In Itaituba, the team passes store after store emblazoned with the same sign: *Compra-se Ouro* (We Buy Gold). Pascual directs Lamprati to a bleak storefront with counter and scale and a door leading to a money room at the back. Pascual intently watches every step of the evaluation process, nervously perspiring as the proceeds from two months of work are assayed not only for weight but for purity.

The man behind the counter writes his findings and his offer on a slip of paper and shoves it before Pascual. The gold weighs nearly 750 grams and it is of good quality. When his calculations are complete, the gold buyer opens his safe and places before Pascual a huge stack of bills, amounting to about $11,250. For the first time all day, Pascual smiles.

From the gold shop, Pascual accompanies the team on a tour of Itaituba. On the outskirts of town, he points to an orphanage. "The bad side of this business," he says softly. There are 270 children in the orphanage. Most are the offspring of prostitutes who relinquish custody to the orphanage, and of *garimpeiros* who are either unaware of their parentage, too consumed with gold fever to care, or simply gone without a trace.

When classes let out for the day, the team watches youngsters of every complexion race about playing soccer. A challenge is issued and the Cousteau team joins the game. Coll, Prezelin, Guera, Lamprati, Sion, and Cousteau soon find that their ages and the broiling heat do not make them quite the overpowering force they had expected. The match lasts forty-five minutes. Score: Gold Kids 14, *Calypso* Stars, 0.

The team spends one more day wandering through the squalor of Itaituba. They are now less than two hundred miles from Santarém, which they will reach by December 14, in time to fly home for Christmas with their families.

Trabon stops at a tiny post office and sends a letter he has written a week earlier to the New York staff of The Cousteau Society. It is an attempt in his own style to summarize the experiences of the Truck Team to date:

Dear Friends:

Things I have broken:

1 headlight	1 tent
1 taillight	1 camera
1 luggage rack	1 chicken (live)
2 rims	2 tires
1 set of windshield wipers	1 briefcase
1 Toyota roof	1 hammock
2 sets of Toyota suspension	12 watermelons
1 set of expensive sunglasses	

Things I have lost:

1 spare tire	1 license plate
1 reserve gas container (full)	2 pairs of pants
2 girlfriends	Most of my socks
2 pairs of shoes	My health
5 shirts	My temper (3 times)
400 feet of rope	

Things I have received:

300,000+ mosquito bites	Motion sickness
145,000 unidentified bites	Diarrhea
637 cuts and abrasions	Stomach cramps
1 severe anxiety attack due to hostile Indians	At least one chewing-out from everyone on the team
47 minor anxiety attacks due to unidentified *large* insects	

Things I used to like but don't now:

Anything green
Rice
Jeeps

Having a wonderful time.
Trabon

FLYING TEAM | NORTH OF THE RIO NEGRO | BRAZIL

W hile the truck team has been struggling over the highways of the south, *Calypso* has headed north from Manaus up the cola-colored Rio Negro. Four times the size of the Mississippi, the Negro and its tributaries descend from the southern slopes of the Guiana shield. It contains some of the purest waters on earth and meanders through a New-England-sized swath of jungle that so far has been spared the intrusions of the outside world that are opening up the southern Amazon.

By mid-November, a consensus is reached among the expedition leaders aboard *Calypso*—both Cousteaus, Falco, and Sumian—that a Flying Team should be dispatched to some corner of Amazonia completely untouched by the influences of modern civilization, where Cousteau cameras can capture raw rain-forest life. Jean-Michel suggests that a team be deposited in a remote location and left there for two weeks. Silvio Barros believes that an area in the northernmost reaches of the Brazilian Amazon, close to the Venezuelan border, is one of the most virgin tracts in all of Amazonia, and he knows an Indian guide who could lead a team to its wildest part.

Within a week, Tatunca Nara and his wife Anita are aboard *Calypso* to help plan the mission. Tatunca suggests that a camp be established on the upper Rio Padauari, a serpentine tributary of the Negro that issues from slopes in the Serra Tapirapecó Mountains, which straddle the Brazil-Venezuela border. The range has blocked the advance of settlers from the north, and the remoteness from Brazil's major cities has discouraged all but the most reclusive pioneers from the south.

Opposite, above:
Dancing and feasting occur frequently among the Txukahamëis as part of Turtle Festivals held to name village infants. The celebration includes a meal of turtle meat baked in shells over hot stones.

Opposite, below:
Coll and Jouas are given headdresses by Chief Rauní. Txukahamëi lip discs, like that worn by the chief, are rapidly disappearing among younger tribe members. Jouas holds a hardwood club, traditional weapon of the tribe.

Overleaf:
Sunset along the Tapajós River near Itaituba.

Captain Cousteau says the selection of the site should rest with Tatunca, but he makes one adamant qualification. He does not want to risk any contact with Indians, nor to intrude upon Indian territory without a tribe's knowledge and permission.

Tatunca nods and declares that he knows every twist in the Padauari. Trained in Rondônia as a FUNAI *sertanista* (jungle Indian contact man), he was assigned in the early 1970s to travel about the northern reaches of Brazil and to prepare tribes for the Perimetal Norte Highway, which would sweep westward just below the Venezuelan border to link Macapá on the Atlantic with the northwest corner of Amazonia, before turning south to Benjamin Constant. Conceived during the heady period when everything seemed possible, the highway remains unbuilt today.

Tatunca and Anita spent eight years living in the jungle, while Tatunca journeyed by canoe from their home on the Padauari to contact tribes. When the highway plans were shelved, they moved south to a Rio Negro village called Barcelos.

Captain Cousteau is curious about Tatunca's past, since the guide speaks not only Indian dialects and Portuguese but German as well. Tatunca is reticent, but Anita tells his story over a dinner on the ship. His mother was a German nurse. While on a tour of the Amazon, she and a female companion were captured by Indians. The companion was killed and Tatunca's mother became the wife of the tribal chief, Tatunca's father. The boy was raised with a dual education—instructed in the ways of the tribe by his father and grounded in European culture by his mother. When the Amazon highway system forced the tribe to migrate hundreds of miles north to the Padauari region, Tatunca joined FUNAI. While in training he met Anita, a Brazilian girl from Pôrto Alegre whose parents were both German immigrants.

In 1972, Tatunca and Anita, who was pregnant, set out from Barcelos in a six-meter canoe to settle on the Padauari. The trip took twenty-five days. They stopped at an impassable rapid called Boa Branca Falls and Tatunca built a *tapiri*, a hut made of palm fronds. Within forty-five days Anita had contracted malaria and had lost the child. Anita was fearful of Indians in the beginning. They were the first outsiders to enter the region since the early 1940s, when a surveying commission was sent to determine the border lines between Venezuela and Brazil. The survey party was attacked by Indians and seven men were slaughtered. Eventually Tatunca and Anita befriended scores of Indians and Anita became convinced that they were more trustworthy than whites.

She remembers life on the Padauari as a great adventure. Anita bore two blond-haired children, who grew up frolicking in the falls when they needed a bath and learning about the jungle from their father. Because Anita had spent one year in a college medical course, the few *caboclos* living to the south considered her a qualified doctor, a role she shirked but found unavoidable. One evening a seventy-two-year-old man on the edge of death was brought to her by canoe. His belly was gaping open, the flesh gnawed away by piranhas. Lighting two kerosene lanterns, Anita operated with her only surgical tool, a razor blade, while the old *caboclo* lay unanesthetized on a bare kitchen table. The man is still alive, she says proudly.

With Tatunca's help, Cousteau outlines a plan for the Flying Team. Tatunca's home village of Barcelos will be used as a staging area. From here, Gervais in *Papagallo* will carry men and supplies to Boa Branca Falls, the last site on the shallow Padauari where an amphibious plane can set down on water. They designate this Camp One. From the Falls, Standard in the two-seat helicopter *Felix* will shuttle the team to a site upstream, Camp Two, to be selected by Tatunca. Jean-Michel and Sumian will act as team leaders, with Mounier as cameraman, Zlotnicka as soundman, and Frier as still photographer. It is essential to keep the team small, Tatunca says.

In contrast to the new boom towns encountered by Coll's Truck Team in southern Amazonia, Barcelos is an aging jungle village overgrown with vegetation. The only signs of former glory are a decaying mission founded in 1728 by Carmelite monks and the concrete streets poured when it was briefly a rubber-gathering center. The concrete has turned cinder-gray under the leaching tropical rains, and grass bunches up through its yawning fractures. The people of Barcelos are darkened by Indian blood and they live in weathered wooden houses on stilts. Bare-chested men sit on porches or lean from open windows, whiling the time away. The town might have disappeared but for its location along the Rio Negro. Passing riverboats stop for fuel, unloading passengers and freight from Manaus before continuing upriver. About three thousand people live in Barcelos, Anita tells the team. There are ten cars, one telephone, no hot water, no glass windows, and one flight in and out of the local airport three times a week. Barcelos seems cloaked in stillness. Occasionally a small boat putters by on the river, the dull pops of its motor drifting to shore like muffled beats of a bass drum.

The team checks into the Hotel Oasis, owned by Anita's parents, Werner and Elfriede Katz. Despite the name, Hotel Oasis is just a home, really, perched on a high bank above the Rio Negro. There are two rooms and an open veranda with three dining tables. Werner and Tatunca built the hotel by hand when the Katzes sold an office supply store in Pôrto Alegre and retired to the jungle. The pole skeleton of the building is made of *louro*, a beautiful dark hardwood, the walls of brick and white stucco. Elfriede cooks three immense meals each day for guests—fresh *tucunare* from the river, local fruits like *goiaba* and papaya, rice, black beans. She apologizes for her current lack of meat. She ordered a side of beef two weeks ago from Manaus, but, she explains in haphazard English, "I received no meat because the ship drowned."

Werner lends his bicycle to the team and they take solo tours of Barcelos. The smell of cook-stove smoke drifts through the streets, mingling with the cloying smell of discarded fruit rotting under houses. Walking among the dim booths of the small city Mercado, the men are jolted by the dark odors of aging meat and fish. The market is nearly empty; so are the streets. A few children pass carrying baskets of bread or vegetables on their heads. Old men stagger out of dark bars, their eyes bleary and red. Pigs wander aimlessly through the streets alongside emaciated dogs.

Barcelos is caught between the human compulsion for order and the lush disorder of tropical-rain-forest civilization. The former has pasted concrete streets onto the soil, planted street lights, and laid out, recently, a small park along the river. The latter has left the streets in disrepair because ten cars are hardly enough motivation to spend money on street repairs, and the street

In an Itaituba grocery store, a *garimpeiro* presents his shopping list and payment in pure gold to a clerk.

lights that do not work are not fixed while the ones that do work are left on twenty-four hours a day for some reason that is probably rooted in a passive disdain for civilized gadgets. No one uses the park because it is not near the part of the waterfront where people always gathered and always will.

After a brief visit to both Camp One and Camp Two in *Felix*, Captain Cousteau approves the sites and the two expedition aircraft begin shuttling the team into the interior. Often the two pilots are alone above an infinity of treetops stretching hundreds of miles in every direction. Once, on a flight lasting more than three hours, Gervais counts only five solitary thatched huts below him. During a half-hour period on each of his flights between Camps One and Two, Standard in *Felix* is out of radio contact with the world. He wears a U.S. Air Force survival vest. Packed in its pockets are first-aid gear, reflector mirrors, flares, cigarette lighter, pocket knife. The helicopter carries two plastic cases with food to sustain two people for six days. There is a sheathed machete on the floor. Standard jokes about the situation, but everyone recognizes that locating without coordinates a plane lost in the dense mottled canopy of the jungle would be a formidable if not impossible task.

Following rivers to avoid disorientation over the trackless forest, the two pilots see the Rio Negro and the Padauari during their driest periods. (The equator, which slices between Barcelos and Camp One, determines alternating seasons in Amazonia; while the Truck Team in the south is experiencing the beginning of the rainy season, the Padauari Team sees the height of the northern dry season.) Along the Negro, white sandbars loom up from black-red water. Where these bars slope beneath the surface, scalloping currents carve stunning patterns into the pale bottom. Some of the sand designs look from above like red brains in the river, knotted organs, intestines.

The Padauari, by contrast, is a "white" river, in fact turned glassy green by turbidity, its winding shape a narrow corridor twisting like uncoiling cable through the tree mat.

Camp Two lies at one of the meanders in the river and is manned during the Padauari mission by the *Anaconda*'s captain, Manoel Araujo da Silva, and a friend, Raimundo do Serrão. They have carried barrels of aviation fuel to the camp in a small boat, and now they wait to be of further help, sleeping at night in an abandoned hut built by seasonal manioc harvesters.

When Mose Richards is en route to join the Padauari team at Camp Two, he spends a night with the two Brazilians, sharing a meal of sardines and *farinha*, the gritty, bland manioc flour that is a staple of nearly every Amazon meal. Manoel and Raimondo sleep in hammocks hung from the rafters of the hut, Richards on a bare table. In the middle of the night, the American is awakened by a flicker of movement near his bare ankles. A flashlight reveals nothing, so he slips his sneakers on and lies down again. Moments later there is a rush of cool air across his legs; Richards begins to recall reading about vampire bats in Amazonia. Suddenly, something with the mass of a small bird strikes the toe of his sneaker and glances off. Nothing more happens and Richards convinces himself that his imagination has been inflated by the tropical heat.

At dawn, Manoel hobbles in to wake Richards up. The Brazilian's eyes are flashing and he points to his toe, which is covered in blood. Raimondo arrives with a similar wound. "Vampiro!" they shout in unison.

The next morning, limping along a path near the hut, Manoel suddenly freezes. Alongside his foot sits a coiled cobra, called *surucucu* in Brazil. Manoel knows of a man who died within twelve hours of being bitten by a *surucucu*. As the terrified man watches, perspiring profusely, unable to swat away the red sweat bees settling on his brow and his ears, the snake withdraws into the brush. "My heart is beating like the heart of a *beija-flor*," he says "a humming bird."

Camp Two, at the edge of the mountains along the border, is cooler and nearly free of biting insects. It consists of six tiny tents and a palm-thatch lean-to built by Tatunca and Sumian. There is a seductive serenity to life in the deep jungle. There are elements of risk in being beyond direct radio contact with *Calypso*, in being perhaps twelve to eighteen hours from a medical facility, but the beauty of the river and the leafy green opulence of the forest are a tableau of tranquility.

Each morning Mounier, Zlotnicka, and Tatunça, often accompanied by Sumian, glide for miles downriver, the outboard motor of their Zodiac stilled. Mounier films river otters, turtles, water snakes, *jacarés*, and capybaras. Zlotnicka, all the while, records the curious sounds of these creatures and the steady barrage of noises that emanates from the hidden recesses behind the wall of trees bordering the river.

Jean-Michel orchestrates the day's work, sending the men out from dawn until midmorning. After 10:00 A.M. most creatures seek cool forest hiding places to wait out the oppressive daytime heat. The helicopter goes to work then, since its snarling engine will no longer disturb the wildlife observations. Mounier and Frier film from the air during the day, and Jean-Michel sets out on occasional trips of aerial exploration.

In the late afternoon, when the forest and river grow active again, the helicopter is parked and the team floats off downriver again.

Two rules have been established at Tatunca's insistence. No one is to venture into the jungle alone, since it is easy to get lost, and no one is to leave the campsite without a gun or a machete. Venomous snakes are common here, Tatunca says, and so are large cats. A hundred yards from the tents, along a soft sandbank, he points out the tracks of an *onça*, a Brazilian name for the jaguar, the largest cat in South America. Tatunca says that *onças* come to the river's edge, dangle their tails in the water, then pounce on the curious fish that approach these unusual jigs.

The setting does not seem fraught with perils so much as ripe with tantalizing and benign discoveries. Macaws pass over in pairs, parrots in flocks. Yellow and black troupials, relatives of the Baltimore oriole, dart through the trees near camp. Tall and slender Mounier, sporting a Chinese "coolie" hat to shade his face and camera eyepiece, presents a whimsical appearance. Frier, capturing from the helicopter a rare shot of macaws in flight, rejoices loudly and turns lunch into a festive occasion.

And the work reinforces the mood of exuberance. Mounier films fish leaping from the river to snip leaves from an overhanging tree; they trim the drooping branches on a line above the water as clean and level as though a gardener had been at work with a hedge clipper. Underwater, Jean-Michel watches piranhas glide to and fro along a wall of shade. They hover yards away but never approach. He discovers a fish about fifteen inches long, as narrow as a dagger, with a snout curved like a scythe. It is translucent, with a

Opposite, above:
Along the banks of the Marupa River, a Tapajós tributary fifty miles above Itaituba, miners claim their sites simply by cutting forest trees. When cleared, the ground is excavated by water hoses until a layer of gold-bearing sand deposits is reached.

Opposite, middle:
Blasting out water pumped from the Marupa River, hoses eat away alluvial soil with such power that workers can support their entire bodies leaning against the roaring nozzles.

Opposite, below:
Paid by the mine owner in bags of gold-flecked soil, miners gain wealth but lead a lonely life in a site so remote it must be reached by bush plane.

157

ruffled dorsal fin. "Its clear body seemed to blush a hint of colors," Jean-Michel tells his comrades, "subtle colors, like autumn leaves." The curious fish approaches Jean-Michel and sticks its snout like a grappling hook over his raised camera to anchor itself in the current. "The fish probably used sunken logs usually, but I was available and motionless, so he hung on to me."

The night, too, is alive with enchanting oddities—with things that are not what one first assumes. Stepping into the river to wash dishes in front of the camp one night, Standard nearly strides onto a stone that turns out to be the back of a small *jacaré*. The *jacaré* makes a desperate exit downstream. Standard announces his find and the entire camp joins in a chase, plodding down the middle of the shallow Padauari until their flashlight beams illuminate a pair of dazzling ruby eyes along the bank. Mounier captures with high-speed film the plight of a confused crocodile surrounded by wobbly flashlights.

For soundman Zlotnicka, the night offers a bizarre library of polyphonous music. Lying in the darkened tent, he can list the solo performances, some of which are so exotic they command a listener to sit up in rapt silence, trying to imagine the form of the singer and the meaning of the message. There is a blipping occasionally, like the sound of a playing card in bicycle spokes. There is a donkeylike braying and a low, rumbling, hoglike honk. There are timid peeps and beckoning whistles that would turn heads on a New York City street. There is, as well, the brittle percussion of crickets and a constant chorus of rubbery oompahs from frogs.

Perhaps the most extraordinary sound is the melodic nighttime bark of the *jacaré*. It is like the sound of an excited guard dog, somehow modulated up the scale and softened, so that one has the impression that a horse-size bird is barking.

There is also a delicate high plinking, far in the distance, that sounds like tiny pebbles dropping rhythmically and ever so slowly into a crystal goblet. And there is an answer to the pebbles, perhaps a response to their crystal invitation, and it is different only as a whole note is to a sharp, sounding like a faraway piano tapped gently by the little finger of the right hand at the frail and tentative end of the keyboard.

On the ninth day of the Padauari mission, Tatunca leads Jean-Michel, Sumian, Mounier, and Zlotnicka into the jungle along an overgrown trail that passes only a hundred yards from the camp. The guide points out hack marks made by machetes along the way. Most of these tree scars are sealed by sap and time, and new buds have emerged. Where the scars look fairly fresh, Tatunca licks the cut and estimates its age—"a month" or "six weeks." It is his opinion that a hunting party from a distant Indian village has come through here in the past.

Tatunca spends the morning pointing out bits of jungle lore. He notices an inch-long ant. "Avoid him," he says, "because his sting hurts for twenty-four hours." He grabs a vine called *cipo de aqua*, which is as thick as a human arm. Cutting it open, the guide shows how fresh, cool water spouts from it. Interior channels in the vine draw water from the ground, purify it, and hold it like a giant drinking straw. "Inexperienced people have died of thirst in the jungle," Tatunca says, "while surrounded by *cipo de aqua* vines."

Opposite, above:
"Camp One" on the Padauari: *Papagallo* pilot Guy Gervais *(left)* delivers aviation fuel to Jim Standard, pilot of the helicopter *Felix* during the Padauari mission. Both men spent dozens of hours flying alone over trackless jungle.

Opposite, below:
"Camp Two" on the upper Padauari, where a Cousteau Flying Team led by Jean-Michel Cousteau experienced both raw beauty and surprises in one of the Amazon's most unpenetrated regions.

The men walk on, find and explore a long-abandoned Indian village, then halt when Tatunca bends to lick a machete mark and announces stolidly after a long pause, "This cut was yesterday." Suddenly time seems to stand still.

The guide is not certain of the tribe's identity, but he says they have never been contacted "by civilized people." They could be Yanomamö, the dominant tribe of the region. The Yanomamö have warned even missionaries to stay clear of their lands. Tatunca does not speak their dialect, but he knows enough of their ways to be certain the Indians have been watching everything the Cousteau team did during the entire stay at Camp Two, no doubt attracted by the helicopter.

"I don't think they will kill you," Tatunca says, "but they will eventually take you captive. Then I will have to go to my tribe and bring someone who speaks their language. We will try to negotiate." He crosses his arms before his chest, knuckles touching his shoulders, a sign that means "We want to talk." "It could take two weeks for your release, or two months."

The team is incredulous. Camp Two was supposed to be remote from any Indian presence.

"I think you should leave immediately," Tatunca says.

So the afternoon is spent breaking camp. Mounier is reluctant to leave before he is finished filming, so Jean-Michel sends him with Tatunca by helicopter to a spot far upriver, beyond easy reach of the Indians watching from the forest, a site they dub Camp Three. The two men will remain there for two days, then come out. The rest of the team will remain one more night at Camp Two, then return to Barcelos in several flights of *Felix* and *Papagallo*.

The night is an uneasy one, since the perceived reality of this lush setting has undergone a sullen transformation in the team's minds, reminding them of the axiom repeated frequently by jungle people, that nothing in the jungle is precisely what it appears to be. The bark is not a dog. The piranhas do not seem dangerous, but the ant does. The vine hanging in the air holds drinking water; the water of the river does not hold as much nourishment for the fish as the leaves of the trees. And the campsite thought to be isolated from Indians is not. Yet the night passes without incident, and the next morning the departures begin.

Sumian, the most experienced member of the team, is the last to leave. Waiting quietly to be picked up by the helicopter, he hears hacking sounds nearby in the forest. He rummages through the remaining supplies and equipment and makes a pile of food and other goods several yards away from the camp, in hopes these items will be understood as gifts to be left behind. Then, to indicate to his observers that he lacks both sinister intent and fear, he strips off all his clothes and goes for a leisurely swim in the middle of the Rio Padauari.

An hour later, the helicopter arrives and quickly departs with a much-relieved Dominique Sumian.

Jean-Michel is reminded again of the warning first given by Manoel, that the jungle is rife with deceptions. It is not really a matter of malevolence in the rain forest so much as ignorance among outsiders about the intricate details of jungle life. The face-to-face encounter of past and present intensifies in the Amazon these days, creating real and imagined conflicts.

Opposite, above left:
Looking like tiny chocolate chips, tree-frog eggs float in a flooded sand bowl scooped by adult frogs into a bank of the Padauari. The young remain in the bowls through tadpole stage and enter the main river as rising waters invade their unique nursery.

Opposite, above right:
Tatunca Nara—former *sertanista* (jungle Indian-contact man) and son of a chief of the Mongulala tribe—shows the team how to release fresh water stored in the hanging *cipo de agua* vine.

Opposite, below:
Considered a riverbank weed, this Papilionoid legume, *Centrosema*, is one of four hundred legume genera and ten thousand separate species in the Amazon.

From the upper Padauari, the team returns to Barcelos. Walking down the broken cement road from the airport to town at dusk one evening, three Cousteau team members pass within inches of a highly poisonous snake known locally as a *jararaca* and throughout the world as the deadly fer-de-lance. It causes more deaths than any other venomous snake in South America. But this creature appears perplexed by the cement road. It is about five feet long, olive brown with a creamy yellow underside. When the men notice the snake and return to study it from a safe distance, a young Barcelos man walks by with his wife and two toddling children. The snake is confused, having blundered onto a curiously hard clearing and into the midst of humanity. The young man breaks a limb from a tree and strikes the snake's head. The blow stuns the snake but does not kill it and it tries to slither quickly back into the sanctuary of the forest. Two more rapid blows, however, dispatch the frightened creature before it can escape.

The sight of the fleeing animal is pathetic, but no more so than a desperate, defensive strike by the snake at a curious child might have been. The young man tells of a woman in the village who has been paralyzed from the waist down for seven years from a *jararaca* bite.

In the Amazon at this time, beings from different realities seem to be penetrating one another's realms, each armed with formidable weaponry yet seeking only to survive and to prosper. The snake is probably just out looking for a meal, the young father moves merely to protect his children. The snake and the young father are both startled by the confrontation and neither comprehends that the other's ways and intentions are not really what they appear to be. Yet both are compelled to do what brains and nerves and genes dictate, to do what must be done to stay alive as their worlds collide...as the Indian must, and the settler, and the miner, and the *jacaré*, and the *onça*, and the piranha, and the yellow bird, and the ant.

162

Above:
Sumian and guide Tatunca Nara build a palm-thatched shelter at Camp Two.

Opposite:
Cousteau and Sumian explore virgin jungle near Camp Two.

SORROW IN A MAGIC LAND

Raymond Coll with an anaconda. The largest anacondas can swallow a 150-pound capybara whole, which explains their need to eat only once every two weeks. The giant snakes sometimes dangle from limbs overhanging water in order to drop on prey.

"CALYPSO" | RIO AMAZONAS | BRAZIL

On November 27, a weary *Calypso* crew steers the ship out of Manaus harbor and down the Rio Negro to the Amazon. It has been three months since the last break in expedition work, six months since the vessel sailed into the moist heat and persistent insects of Amazonia. It is time for a rest.

The plan is to stop in Belém for two days, where many crew members will board flights for France or the United States, then sail with a skeleton crew to Martinique. There *Calypso* will undergo two months of reconditioning before returning to Amazonia for the final phase of the expedition.

En route down the river, the scientific team carries out a series of sampling programs, anchoring at the mouths of the Madeira, Trombetas, Tapajós, Xingu, and Pará. These stations complete *Calypso*'s source-to-sea survey of the river's characteristics and water quality—an unprecedented investigation directed by Constans, Dustan, and Murphy.

J.-Y.C.—*Before our team is dispersed for Christmas at home, there is a final bittersweet duty to which we must attend. Our crowded vessel is an inadequate playground for a giant otter, and our future destinations will take us far from the world in which his species is comfortable. More important, Cacha is reaching sexual maturity. If he is to follow the dictates of his genes, he must find a mate.*

Unfortunately we cannot simply liberate our friend in a remote area where giant otter families still survive. Cacha's destiny was settled when he was first captured and confined in a zoo. He has been conditioned to expect friendship and food from human hands. In the jungle, trustfully loping up to the first human whose scent he perceived, Cacha would undoubtedly be shot. Though his species is protected in Brazil, this formality would mean little to a caboclo with the opportunity to sell a pelt worth three months' wages.

165

Fortunately, Robin Best and Silvio have succeeded in finding a young scientist who has adopted a male of the smaller river otter species. Roberto Huet Salva Souza has consented to add Cacha to his family and to seek a mate for him.

On December 5 Guy Gervais swoops low in Papagallo *and sets down near* Calypso *on the Rio Tapajós. He has brought Roberto with him to pick up Cacha. The plane glides to shore and anchors. Cacha's future awaits him on the riverbank.*

It is a sad leave-taking for all of us. Paul Martin and Bruno Vidal, who have been Cacha's constant playmates, spend an hour romping about the foredeck with him. Bebert, his personal fish delivery service, brings him a last meal, a small aruana *that Maurice Hervé had caught earlier in the morning for his own lunch.*

Jean-Michel and I wait in the water and take a final swim with Cacha, leading him toward shore. He whirls and darts with the abandonment of a dervish, but we know he won't take the opportunity to streak away and disappear into the wild. He has already proven his preference for Calypso. *When we were on the Rio Negro he managed to squeeze under the foredeck corral and dive from the ship's gunwale. While we rushed about the decks, Cacha took a pleasant swim, leisurely circling* Calypso *several times as if to flaunt his cleverness, barking to ensure that we were watching. When Bebert lowered a makeshift gangplank and dangled a fish, Cacha darted back onto the deck.*

On shore we watch Cacha's excitement as Roberto releases his own pet otter. The older and smaller creature is intimidated by Cacha and he races away as the exuberant youngster pounces gleefully toward him. When Cacha realizes this stranger is disappointingly reticent, he pauses along the water's edge, releasing a scent marker from his anal glands. He is undoubtedly leaving a message about his sex and receptivity in the sands, unaware that no potential mates are left in this part of Amazonia, and that soon he will be leaving, too.

Bebert, Martin, and Vidal set the plank from his pool against the doorway of Papagallo *and coax him into the plane. Moments later he is aloft, flying toward another new home, curious perhaps about this human species that first snatched him roughly from his jungle home, imprisoned him in squalor, then took him for a sail on wide rivers, and now lifts him into the air above the birds.*

We watch until Papagallo *has disappeared. The silence lasts for some moments, broken only by Bebert's gentle whisper as he turns away.*

"Bon courage, Cacha."

In mid-March the team begins to reassemble. *Calypso*, which returns to Belém on March 18, will spend three months in the lower Amazon, investigating large-scale Brazilian development projects and attempting to capture temporarily and to study both pink and gray dolphins. En route home, the ship will carry out scientific work in the Amazon "plume" that extends far into the Atlantic. Jean-Michel, meanwhile, will lead a team into Colombia and Peru, to investigate reports of a head-hunting Indian tribe and to assess the international drug trade that exploits the edges of the jungle.

Opposite, above:
Gervais arrives in *Papagallo* to carry the otter Cacha off to its new home.

Opposite, below:
The last swim: a gregarious, frolicsome creature, Cacha endeared itself to the entire *Calypso* crew.

On March 22, *Calypso* sails north from Belém, skirting the eastern shores of Marajó Island, and by March 27 she is anchored at the mouth of the Rio Araguari, just north of the Amazon delta. Along the South American coast the tides have reached their highest flows of the year, setting up a phenomenon known in Brazil as the *Pororoca* (the Big Roar). Eyewitness reports are enthralling. A wall of water as high as twenty-five feet rises from the sea during the spring tides, they say, and thunders up the Amazon, sweeping boats aside, chewing away the shorelines, dragging mammoth trees into the roiling water and sweeping them away. It is said this terrible wave races up the river for five hundred miles. In 1850 a *Pororoca* is reported to have cut through a 60-mile-wide island in the Amazon delta, leaving two islands in its wake.

Caboclos along the river tell Cousteau that it is a "beast," that its horrible roar can be heard twenty miles away. "Each year," one man says, "it takes away a little more of my land. Soon there will be nothing left."

Tidal bores like the *Pororoca* occur in many parts of the world. Victor Hugo's poem "A Villequier" mourns the death of his daughter, who reportedly drowned in the most famous tidal bore, the Mascaret, which travels up the lower Seine. But in the Amazon such a prodigious volume of water is involved in a bore that the event seems singularly dramatic. The tales of the *caboclos* invest this product of moon and sea with a mystical presence, yet the mechanics of the Amazon *Pororoca* are broadly understood, if little studied. When an abnormally high tide advances into a river mouth that is both shallow and funnel-shaped, the squeezing effect on the incoming water can cause it to pile up into a wave. Where these waves are greatest, they create the spellbinding illusion that the current of the river has magically reversed itself. Or, as *caboclos* perceive it, that a sinister water beast has risen from the sea and attacked the continent.

Ironically, the *Pororoca* was the first aspect of the Amazon ever discovered. When Vincente Yanez Pinzon, formerly a captain of Columbus's *Niña*, passed along the coast of South America in 1500, his sailors suddenly found themselves unable to control the ship. A brown wave of fresh water was carrying it toward shore. To their great relief, the strange wave diminished and the ship was saved, probably as the *Pororoca* subsided over a deep spot.

What the *Calypso* team witnesses on March 28, at sea beyond the river mouth, surprises them: a series of some thirty parallel water ridges forming nearly ten miles from shore and advancing toward land as a steady phalanx, ranks closed, with lines extending at least twenty miles from horizon to horizon. It is dawn, and Bob Braunbeck, on patrol in *Felix* to alert the team as the *Pororoca* appears, can barely contain his excitement as he radios back to *Calypso*. This is something new: the legion of rippling water ridges headed shoreward has never been documented before.

For the next hour, the team films the spectacle—Captain Cousteau, Mounier, and Frier shooting from the air; Prezelin, Amaddio, and Murphy filming, and Zlotnicka recording, from shore.

What they see does not reach the 15-to-25-foot heights attributed to giant *Pororoca* waves (though it does swell to more than 10 feet at times), but the might of the wall of water is nevertheless overwhelming. Maneuvering *Felix* only feet above the forward crest—looking to the photo team on the shore like a dancing dragonfly—Braunbeck clocks the average speed of the *Po-*

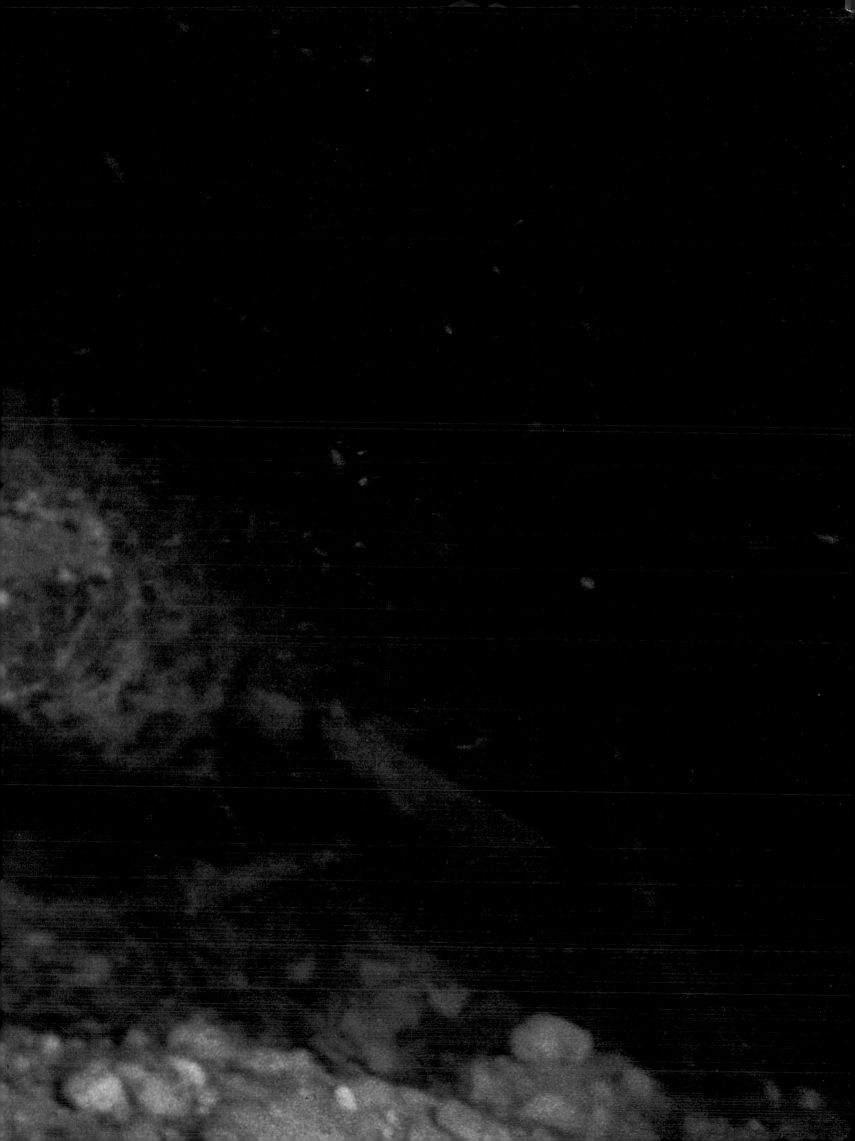

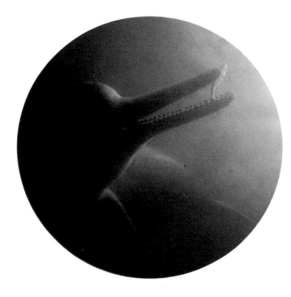

roroca at 25 knots, twice *Calypso*'s speed at full throttle. The velocity is a surprise to the men filming from the banks. Amaddio must make a last-second dash to avoid being swept away as the great wave suddenly swirls over his vantage point on shore. Murphy, running out of time to position himself for a photo, is forced to scramble up a spine-covered tree and snap his picture with bleeding hands. Filming from the helicopter, Cousteau is astonished as hardwood trees along the banks are ripped from the ground and tossed about like jackstraws.

During the night, Frier, Murphy, Amaddio, and Zlotnicka stay ashore to await the next advance of the *Pororoca*. They sleep on the floor of an empty *caboclo* hut. About 11:00 P.M., as they drift off, someone notices a peculiar sound—a loose piece of wood thumping against the hut. The significance of the sound eventually dawns on Murphy. The wood could only be floating. Leaping to the window, they find themselves only inches above rising water. Disaster seems imminent, but the water suddenly levels off. As they relax, Frier remembers seeing a farmhouse drifting down the Amazon when *Calypso* was sailing upriver nine months earlier.

"People, furniture, and animals," he says, "just floating." This night, the vivid memory flashed in his mind as the water rose about the hut. "Here we go, I thought, like those poor *caboclos*. We'll be carried into the Atlantic. We're going to be lost at sea in a farmhouse."

J.-Y.C.—*Despite the success we have enjoyed during these many months in Amazonia, we have failed in our attempts to approach the river's most inspiring creatures, the pink and gray dolphins, whose momentary appearances lend both lyrical grace and mystery to the great brown flood. INPA scientist Vera da Silva has agreed to join us if we can isolate dolphins in the wild; it could be an opportunity to gain vital information about the creatures' behavior. We are uncomfortable with the idea of capturing the intelligent animals, but in this case it seems unavoidable, since they cannot be approached in their own realm and therefore many scientific questions are left unanswered.*

At Bebert's suggestion, we sail Calypso *up the Rio Arapiuns, which empties into the Tapajós near its mouth, on the morning of April 15. With the help of the entire team, Bebert creates a temporary pool in a shallow inlet, closing it off with forty meters of wire fence. Our goal is to confine an individual or two as briefly as possible, then to release them.*

By mid-afternoon the pool is complete. Almost immediately a group of gray dolphins is sighted nearby. Surrounding the creatures in a shallow lagoon, using nets strung from our Zodiacs and the launch, the crew follows Bebert's shouted orders and quickly succeeds in capturing two individuals—a mother and her youngster. Bebert cradles the small dolphin while Xavier holds the mother, and they speed by Zodiac to the temporary pool. Ten minutes later, the creatures are gently carried into the corral. Xavier holds each animal in his arm for a few minutes, introducing them to the fence and calming them. Then the team leaves the water, staying away for the rest of the day so the creatures can become acclimated to their confines. After nightfall, the crew notices that the fence is shaking. Dolphins on the outside are attempting, unsuccessfully, to liberate their friends. "The underwater telephones are working well," says Bebert.

Above:
An *Inia* twists to catch a fish tossed by a Cousteau team member. Among the most unusual aspects of pink dolphin behavior is their ability to lie on the river bottom in a partial state of sleep.

Opposite, above left:
Silvio Barros approaches a bizarre *matamata* turtle, *Chelys fimbriata*. A leathery snorkel on its snout enables the turtle to float submerged among water plants just below the surface. When prey come near, the *matamata* opens its mouth quickly, creating a suction that pulls the victim into its throat. The knobby shell and flappy skin probably act as camouflage.

Opposite, above right:
In the Rio Arapiuns, near the dolphin pen, diver Sion tests the response of a freshwater crab. Like countless Amazon aquatic creatures, it closely resembles marine cousins. Fourteen families of marine fish are found in the Amazon, including sharks, sawfishes, anchovies, soles, and stingrays.

Opposite, below:
Barros strokes an iguana caught in a small Amazon stream. Like most of the jungle's larger animals, these giant lizards are hunted for food by some Amazon natives.

173

For two days we observe and film the dolphins, approaching them cautiously. As Xavier, Prezelin, and Frier gradually increase their time in the pool, the dolphins seem to relax. The youngster even appears to grow playful, turning somersaults and pirouettes in the water, dashing about in figure eights. Both remain distant from the divers, but on the second morning a curious thing happens. Prezelin is alone in the water and suddenly the mother rises from the river, standing on her tail in the maneuver common to dolphins trained to perform in captivity. Louis is astonished. He summons the rest of the team and for several hours the adult dolphin dances about as the men applaud.

When Vera da Silva arrives, accompanied by INPA assistant Miriam Marmontel Rosas, we ask about this surprising behavior. Vera is quick to point out that the dolphins of the Amazon remain a mystery for the most part. Very few field observations have been made of either of the two species. Most of the knowledge we have of their ways of life comes from the few animals maintained in captivity. To assign a motivation for the winsome display of dancing would be pure speculation.

Vera lists some of the sketchy facts that are known of the two species. Both have seasonal linkages with the rise and fall of the river, like nearly everything in Amazonia. Their young are born during times of low water, when feeding is easier because the available fish populations are limited to a more restricted space than during flood times. The gray dolphins, like the marine dolphins they so closely resemble, seem to appear in somewhat larger groups than the pink species, which is often seen making solitary forays into the flooded forest. The more social gray dolphins seem to prefer life in the main river and they hunt among the fish schools of the open water.

During the two days of contact with the gray dolphins, their shyness diminishes only slightly. Our underwater filming is successful, but because the creatures remain elusive and the water clarity is marginal, we elect to end the study and seek instead the more unusual pink dolphin species.

For several days the crew tries unsuccessfully to catch one of the pink dolphins, which cleverly evade the nets and escape under floating grass prairies. Finally, a large adult female is cornered and transferred to the pool. Two days later a second adult, a male, is caught.

From the beginning it is clear that the pink dolphins are stronger and more aggressive than the grays. Biologist Murphy assumes the job of befriending the creatures and monitoring their health and behavior, joined by Falco, Sion, and *Calypso*'s new medical officer, Dr. Jean-Louis Blanc.

Initially Murphy is taken aback by the pugnaciousness of the first captured animal. The creature promptly grabs fish offerings and appears perturbed when the fish are gone. She butts Murphy in seeming annoyance, occasionally surprising him from behind, even swatting him once with a flipper. The behavior is intimidating; the pink dolphin is nearly seven feet long and appears to weigh about two hundred pounds. Murphy realizes that he is dealing with a formidable animal, a master of its medium capable of inflicting harm should it choose to do so.

Opposite, above left:
Achuara chief Kukus walks along the oil pipeline that has bisected his tribe's hunting territory in northern Peru.

Opposite, above right:
An Achuara mother cleans lice and ticks from her children. Despite life amid insects and wild animals, it is the introduced diseases of civilization that most endanger the tribe. Smallpox, flu, and whooping cough are often fatal, especially to Achuara children.

Opposite, below:
Achuara women and girls carry the produce from their gardens and meat from a hunting expedition using a simple headband carrier. The pet monkey carried on the girl's head supplies company and a lice-removal service.

*J.-Y.C.—Hearing Dick's description of the pink dolphin, I am reminded of stories told me by a Brazilian fisherman at Praia Grande on the Rio Negro. It was his belief that the pink dolphins—*botos, *as he called them— were capable of monstrous behavior. Sometimes they steal a canoe paddle, he said, but sometimes they are more malicious. A pack of* botos *tried to sink the boat of a friend, he claimed. The fisherman repeated the legends of pink dolphins turning magically into men or women, then abducting humans. He himself had experienced a terrible thing, he said. A few years ago he had grown angry as a pink dolphin feasted on the fish catch in his net. He struck the animal repeatedly with a stick. The next day the* boto *floated to shore, dead. When the man returned home that evening, his pregnant wife had given birth prematurely and the baby resembled a dolphin. It lacked the rostrum, he said, but it was breathing through a blowhole. There was no doubt in the man's mind that the dolphin had evoked a dark magic in retribution. Neither he nor any of his fellow fisherman had ever harmed a* boto *since.*

Curiously, a caboclo *living alone on the outskirts of Iquitos had told me a similar story. His own mother had given birth to a dolphin baby, he said, a horribly deformed monstrosity. And he himself had been approached in his hut by a dolphin apparition that took the form of a comely bikini-clad temptress—a* chica preciosa, *he declared emphatically. She was trying to cast a spell over him, he said, to lead him to the river. He laughed as he explained how he had resisted the magic. "I told her I couldn't accompany her because I was cooking my lunch and it would burn."*

These stories, and others recounted by the two Amazon natives, were indisputable truth as far as they were concerned. Interestingly, the only discrepancy between the two accounts of dolphin; wizardry was in the species of the perpetrators. In Peru the sorcerors were gray dolphins; in Brazil they were pink.

On the second day of its captivity, Murphy and Falco notice a change in the behavior of the pink dolphin.

"Today the dolphin quickly realized when feeding time was over," Murphy writes in his journal. "She inspected me carefully in search of fish, but the aggressiveness was gone. She didn't nudge or hit me as before. Gradually, as the day passed, she became very docile and seemingly affectionate. At one point, she came to rest on my foot, leaning against my leg. I stroked her back, rostrum, and flippers. She rolled over and swam upside down in an arc around me as I scratched her belly. We both surfaced to breathe together, then as we descended in unison I took hold of her flipper and dorsal fin and she gave me a ride. She didn't seem to mind at all."

Over dinner in the *carré*, da Silva briefs the team on the facts that are known about the odd creatures. They are one of only four living species in the family Platanistidae (the others: a Ganges river dolphin, a Chinese river dolphin found in the Yangtze, and a La Plata river dolphin which ventures from the South American river into the sea and back). The Platanistidae were once a thriving marine family, but they appear to have declined as the more advanced delphinoid odontocetes evolved. Thus the Amazon's pink dolphins

are survivors of an ancient race, more primitive than common marine ceta-
ceans and separately evolved.

Captain Cousteau is intrigued by their unusually flexible bodies. Da Silva
explains that the creatures' vertebrae are more widely spaced than those of
other dolphins, allowing a greater degree of pliancy in their motions. When
the team reports that the creature occasionally stops along the bottom, da
Silva says this is thought to be common resting behavior.

When the second pink dolphin is captured and introduced to the pen, Murphy and Falco watch from a distance as the two creatures meet.

"It is impossible to know what the behavior of each dolphin meant," Murphy writes, "but the male dolphin seemed concerned only with escape while
the female dolphin seemed acclimated by now to confinement. She relentlessly pursued her new companion, repeatedly grasping his tail and flukes,
leaving traces of teeth marks. The contact wasn't harmful, but it was certainly
rough as the first creature badgered the second with nudges, pokes,
and rubbing.

"After a half-hour, the male calmed down and began to reciprocate in the
playful contact. He flinched only when he heard the click of my camera shut-
ter. Bebert and I watched in awe as the two dolphins continued to play. They
grew increasingly gentle, perhaps even sexual as they rubbed against one
another, twisting and rolling as if to caress. Occasionally one would open its
mouth wide and scrape its teeth over the other's head, flippers, tail, or
flukes."

While Falco, Murphy, and Mounier film the two dolphins, they notice a
third pink dolphin swimming back and forth beyond the fence. The three men
agree that they have accumulated enough film now to document the underwater behavior of the creatures, and they open the fence. The male departs
quickly, but curiously, the female dolphin lingers behind for several minutes
and does not swim away until the men encourage her with gentle pushes.

"It was a profoundly emotional experience for me," writes Murphy. "To
have spent so many hours with the pink dolphin, becoming used to one another, interacting almost as 'friends.' As we released them, the sun was just
setting. It was a magical moment—the white beach cast pink by the dusk light
and, in the river, all three dolphins swimming close together toward free-
dom—a moment to set aside science and photography and simply marvel at
the ability of dolphins to evoke in the human mind such profound and pleasurable emotions."

FLYING TEAM | RIO PASTAZA | PERU-ECUADOR BORDER

While the crew of *Calypso* investigates the mystique of river
dolphins, a Flying Team organized by Jean-Michel makes
contact with an Indian tribe whose reputation for extraordinary fierceness has made them a living Amazon legend. The Jívaro people
of northern Peru and Ecuador seem to fit the image of primitive forest tribes
sensationalized in jungle fiction. Over the centuries, accounts by outsiders

Opposite, above:
Taught as a boy to shrink the
heads of enemy warriors, Kukus
today grapples with modern
threats from encroaching oil
drillers and loggers.

Opposite, below:
Itinerant merchants range far
up Amazon tributaries in boats
that represent floating variety
stores. On this day the Achuara
sold peccary skins, living
turtles, and chickens. With the
garnered cash they bought
blankets, clothing, ammunition,
cookies, and salt.

have claimed that they specialize in poison-dart attacks, that they glory in revenge killings, that they practice the eerie necromantic tradition of head-shrinking.

The Jívaro have been exalted in folklore since a Spanish expedition first penetrated their isolated forest haunts in 1549. Boiling with indignation, the leader of the first expedition, Captain Hernando de Benavente, dispatched a letter to the monarchy in Spain: "I say truly to Your Highnesses," Benavente wrote, "that these people are the most insolent that I have seen in all the time that I have traveled the Indies and engaged in their conquest." Arriving with the idea of establishing a settlement, Benavente was instead forced by the hostile Jívaro to beat a retreat out of their territory.

In his 1972 book *The Jívaro*, anthropologist Michael J. Harner fixed the place of the tribe in history:

> Only one tribe of American Indians is known ever to have successfully revolted against the empire of Spain and to have thwarted all subsequent attempts by the Spaniards to reconquer them: The Jívaro."

Though Spanish armies dominated the tribe for half a century, the Jívaro arose in 1599, attacking two gold-mining settlements and pouring molten gold down the throat of the Spanish governor. A contemporary account estimated the loss of Spanish lives at about thirty thousand, with only the "serviceable women" spared death. It was nearly three centuries before outsiders—Jesuit missionaries—succeeded in establishing a new permanent white settlement in Jívaro country.

The question on the minds of Cousteau team members is how such a resolute people are faring today. To set up a possible visit, Jean-Michel meets with anthropologist Luis Uriarte of the University of Chicago. Uriarte has studied the tribe over several years, lived among them, and learned their language. He explains that there are actually five separate tribes comprising the Jívaro people, with distinct languages, practices, and territories. Uriarte contacts the village where he is known—a group called the Jívaro Achuara—and after several weeks of communications, the tribe grants permission for a small Cousteau team to visit them.

In early May the crew assembles in Iquitos. Sumian acts as expedition leader, Cornu as cinematographer. Recently arrived from France, Jean Hamon serves as radio and sound engineer. Anne-Marie Cousteau joins the team as still photographer. Uriarte agrees to accompany them as a guide and translator. When commitments in the United States permit, Jean-Michael will join the others.

The team boards a Wings of Hope amphibious bush plane in Iquitos and flies to the foot of the Andes near the Ecuadorian border, alighting on the Rio Pastaza near the Achuara village of Rubina.

Standing on the bank to greet them is a powerfully built, handsome man with black hair cascading down his back. Two tightly wrapped cords of hair hang to his chest in front. Uriarte introduces the chief of the Achuara, Kukus. Polite greetings are exchanged. To break the ice, Sumian asks about the size of the tribe. There are only about forty people here in the village, Kukus says, but his extended family, upon whom he can call for help in times of conflict,

numbers between three hundred and five hundred. He is not certain of the exact number. He has seven wives, and in-laws represent a kinship tribe scattered in several villages. A good hunter, Uriarte says, can support several wives.

Kukus leads the team into his village of chonta palm huts. When they are seated on the dirt floor of his house, bowls of *masato* are offered around. Sumian and Cornu notice that the fermented saliva-and-manioc brew resembles the beverage they have tasted in other Indian villages. Uriarte says that each wife produces her own supply for her husband. Kukus has seven bowls of *masato* at his side. He says he can tell who made each one.

Eventually someone diplomatically asks the inevitable question: Do the Jívaro Achuara shrink heads? "When I was a boy," Kukus answers, "my father taught me to prepare *tsantsas* [shrunken heads], using monkeys and sloths. The true *tsantsa* imprisons the spirit of a dead enemy warrior, so that it cannot avenge the death. The Achuara have not made human *tsantsas* for forty years."

"Gradually," Cornu remembers later, "Kukus allayed our fears about the ferocity of the Achuara. We were prepared to encounter dangerous warriors. We found instead a group of nice people facing grave problems."

Nearly every night in Rubina, the team is kept awake by sporadic fits of coughing in village huts. For all their defiance of white invaders, the Achuara, like all Amazon tribes, are helpless to repulse infectious white diseases, which race through villages as deadly epidemics of whooping cough, measles, smallpox, even the common cold. Children are especially vulnerable. Kukus has fathered forty-two children. Only eight are still alive. The relentless siege of misery and childhood deaths casts a painful cloud over Achuara existence. To combat the diseases, they turn to the age-old sources of rehabilitation—the village shamans. Some shamans are truly knowledgeable about the herbal pharmacopoeia of the jungle. Some are charlatans.

The Jívaro people believe that events are controlled by a supernatural world. Daily life is an illusion. The passports to the supernatural world are hallucinogenic drugs of the forest. Shamans are intermediaries who enter the other world in drugged states and influence events. There is a general acceptance that white people's diseases are not caused by witchcraft, but tradition and mistrust of white medicine compel the tribes to rely on shamans to cure even these maladies.

Late one afternoon, Kukus invites Jean-Michel (who has joined the team during its third week in Rubina), Anne-Marie, and Cornu to accompany him by canoe to the house of a shaman. Kukus is suffering from arthritis, and one of his young sons has an unknown illness.

Jean-Michel later records in his cassette-tape journal: "In the dim glow of a fire, the shaman—Nyashu—took a hallucinogenic drink brewed from what is called in Peru *ayahuasca*, a vine that is boiled to create a tea. Kukus lay on a mat on the floor, the boy on an adjacent mat. As the shaman entered a trance, he began to suck on Kukus's afflicted joints, ritually drawing poisons from them, then loudly and eerily spitting out the sources of the pain. Alternately he would take up branches from a tree considered bewitching and shake them like castanets above Kukus's body. The treatment went on for hours, late into the evening; then the witch doctor turned to the boy and repeated the performance far into the night."

Opposite, above:
An Achuara hunter guts one of several peccaries killed during the visit of the Cousteau team.

Opposite, below:
Two Achuaras fell a buttressed tree that will be used in the construction of a new village hut. To fashion a dugout canoe the trees must be even larger.

Like other Jívaro tribes, the Achuara can be moved to take revenge if a shaman assigns the responsibility for a death to an enemy or to outsiders. During the second week of the Cousteau team's presence in Rubina, when all signs point to their acceptance by the tribe, an incident takes place that nearly results in tragedy. Innocently, Sumian and Cornu accept a gift of deer meat from a villager who has killed the animal as it grazed in his garden. Two days later, the villager's son dies of whooping cough. Suddenly word is passed to the Cousteau team that the village shaman has blamed the death of the child on them. He is calling for vengeance. Stunned by the turn of events, the team goes to Kukus. Deer are sacred animals, they learn. The Jívaro believe that their ancestors are reincarnated in the bodies of deer. The shaman is demanding death for the outsiders.

Sumian and Cornu decide to confront the problem directly, to explain their innocence to the shaman. When they arrive at his hut, they find him in the midst of curing a baby. Dressed in the Western garb of a *mestizo*, the man is puffing on a common cigarette and blowing the tobacco smoke in the face of the coughing infant. They are convinced that their accuser is a charlatan taking advantage of the power wielded by witch doctors.

Three tense days pass. To avoid exacerbating the situation, the team remains quiet, restricting filming activities and remaining alert to any signs of hostile activity. Finally Kukus arrives, smiling. He has convinced his people to ignore the exhortations of the shaman. When, a week later, the shaman again castigates the team for photographing the felling of a tree, the entire village ignores his accusations.

The Flying Team spends six weeks living with the people of Rubina. During that time four Achuara children die, evoking mass ceremonies of sorrow with each tragedy. Anne-Marie writes later of the experience:

"About 8:30 one night we were sitting quietly in our hut when suddenly we began to hear some wild, wailing sounds—the voices of women keening. These were lamentations, there is no other word for it. They started down the hill toward us, and Luis was able to make out what was going on: a baby had died, and the women were going in a procession down to the river to meet the canoe bringing the body back from the shaman. In the pitch dark we followed, and soon we could hear answering lamentations from the canoe. It was almost like a song, but from the stomach and throat—instinctive, visceral cries of pain, whimpers like those of a dying animal. It was a little frightening.

"All night the women went through stages of crying and wailing, and then quiet—from fatigue, I imagine. Then after each period of silence, one voice would begin, joined by another, then another, increasing in pitch and tempo until the sounds would slowly die out again. Their suffering was so heartfelt it brought tears to our eyes.

"The following morning they buried the child. They let us come but not film. It turned out that no one really knew why the baby had died, just that it was a white man's disease, so the shaman couldn't cure it.

"The grave was dug by men who were not part of the immediate family, and the mother never came near while it was being dug, or went near the body. Older women painted the face of the baby, then wrapped the body in a hammock and placed it in a tiny canoe. It was buried in the hut, under the mother's bed, and every villager brought a gift.

Above:
The traditional woven-palm roofs of Achuara houses provide shelter from rain while allowing cool breezes to circulate during the hottest of days.

Opposite, above:
Achuara tradition, unlike that of many tribes, demands that baskets be woven only by men.

Opposite, below:
A hut to be occupied by Kukus's son goes up near the center of Rubina.

"The mourning continued for three days, with sad songs punctuating the work routine of the village. Then Kukus led everyone down to the river for a bath of purification and it was over. Time to forget. For three nights a bowl of masato was put in the garden to feed the baby's spirit; the baby was female, and the garden is the province of the women."

Slowly the Cousteau team wins the trust of the Achuara. Learning that Sumian is knowledgeable about machinery and medicine, Kukus asks him to look at the infected finger of a village woman and at a broken outboard motor. The team leader finds the finger gangrenous and urges that the woman be taken to Iquitos immediately for medical treatment. Then he disassembles and repairs the motor in an hour. That evening, women from the village bring the team firewood, fish, manioc, and two chickens.

Jean-Michel and Kukus spend hours discussing the tribe's plight. The problem of diseases is a continuing sadness, but the long-term threat in Kukus's opinion is the matter of land ownership. Peru acknowledges the rights of its natives to own land, but in order to qualify, Indians must obtain an identity card. To do so, males must serve in the national armed forces. To enroll in the army, they must cut their hair. Yet to the Achuara, Kukus says, long hair is the badge of masculinity, of strength. Cutting the hair of an Achuara man is the same as emasculation.

Without ownership, the Achuara have little control over *mestizos* from outside, who invade their territory to cut valuable trees or encroach around the edges with cattle ranches. Hunting grounds diminish and the large trees, sacred to the Achuara and used for dugout canoes, disappear with the arrival of chain saws. "During the past year," Kukus says, "*mestizos* cut twelve hundred big trees along the river." Kukus had a sign made in Spanish and posted it: OUR PROPERTY! NO ONE ALLOWED TO TAKE TREES! The cutting continued. "A friend of mine," Kukus says, "had to walk five miles to find a canoe tree, so many were gone." Unable to halt the poaching, Kukus personally planted eight hundred trees on Achuara territory. "Not for me or my children," he says. "The trees will not be large for many years. They are for the grandchildren."

In the world where Kukus has grown up, the loss of trees is a serious resource depletion. It is from forests that the Achuara obtain poles and thatching for their houses, wood for their canoes, vines that serve as ropes, herbs and roots for medicinal purposes and hallucinogenic ceremonies. Shelter, travel, construction, health, ritual.

Without knowing the precepts of Western ecology, Kukus has also initiated an Achuara project to preserve *paiche (pirarucu)*. The giant fish are declining as settlers arrive at the edge of Jívaro territory. The Achuara have set aside one lake as a *paiche* reserve. Kukus wants the fish population to increase and to provide a continuing food reserve for future generations.

Fish protein becomes all the more important to the Achuara as their hunting successes diminish. Traditionally, Jívaro hunters seldom range more than ten miles from their villages in search of monkeys (howler, squirrel, capuchin, and black), birds (parrots, toucans, doves, and curassows), armadillos, peccaries, and agoutis (rabbit-size rodents). Though they use rifles to kill ground-dwelling animals, the blowgun is employed most commonly to procure monkeys and birds. The Achuara are, in fact, the acknowledged masters among the Jívaro tribes in the making of blowguns, and their territory supplies the strongest curare poison in the region. Other tribes have long traded with the Achuara for these necessities.

Game has been culled from the surrounding jungle over many centuries, however, and the encroachment of *mestizo* hunters further limits the hunting prospects. While the Flying Team is living in Rubina, a small herd of peccaries happens to pass nearby. "The entire village emptied in a matter of minutes to join in the hunt," recalls Anne-Marie. "They killed several, and the women staggered back to the village carrying the carcasses on their backs in baskets supported by headbands around their foreheads. It was a time of plenty."

The feathers and skins derived from hunting, as well as blowguns, baskets, and pottery, are bartered for Western products from *mestizo* traders who periodically travel up the Pastaza in motorboats. The Cousteau team films the negotiations one day, as a crowd of Achuara offer up their peccary skins along the bank. The trader begins by purchasing these pelts at low prices, then recaptures all of his investment by selling his goods at high prices. Aware of this profiteering, Kukus has recently begun to send one of his elder sons directly to Iquitos with a boatload of Achuara products. The practice has brought the tribe better prices, but new complications have arisen. The son is stopped by soldiers patrolling the river, who demand that he display his identity card. The young man has taken the sacrificial step of cutting his hair short in order to pass unnoticed and has adopted the white name Walter. One day, as Cornu is filming Kukus along the river, Walter returns deeply upset. Soldiers have prevented him from passing and threatened his life. They have also warned him that they might follow him to the village and cut off the long hair of Kukus. The old man is enraged. He grabs a rifle from another villager and plants himself in a firm stance on the bank. "Let them come!" he shouts. "I will kill them!" At that moment, a military patrol boat appears around a bend in the river. There are five uniformed soldiers in the boat and one is holding an automatic rifle. As Cornu watches in amazement, the boat heads towards Kukus, then veers away and speeds on.

Shortly before the Cousteau team leaves Rubina, Kukus takes his new friends to see something that provokes his outrage. In 1971 a petroleum company began to scout Jívaro territory by helicopter. The search was successful and now there are PetroPeru/Occidental Petroleum drilling rigs pumping oil near Rubina, on territory claimed by the Achuara. Kukus leads the team through the woods to a cleared corridor bisected by a pipeline that disappears over a nearby ridge. "Wildlife has fled from our hunting grounds since the pipe was laid and the helicopters began patrolling it," Kukus says.

The oil field, at a site called Andoas, produces a hundred thousand barrels a day. PetroPeru takes half of the production, Occidental keeps half.

"The oil is coming out of our land," Kukus says. "We cannot stop this. But we went to the white engineers. We asked for two barrels of oil a day for our motorboats. Only two barrels from their thousands and thousands." He shrugs. "They refused."

"There is a scene I will remember always," Jean-Michel records on the day the team leaves Rubina. "It was early morning in the Achuara village. Hunters would leave soon to seek birds or monkeys or an agouti. The women were

Opposite, above:
Occasionally kept as pets, agoutis (*Dasyprocta aguti*) are nocturnal rodents that live in burrows.

Opposite, below:
While this Achuara girl was chewing manioc for the tribal beer supply, her pet parrot arrived to eat the mash from her lips.

finished sweeping their houses with branch brooms and would soon begin to make *masato* or to weave cloth. The children began to assemble in the village center and the adults stood around patiently. I had no idea what was about to happen. Then an elder walked into their midst and stood at the base of a wooden pole. In his hands was a Peruvian flag. The children fell into ranks, and as the old man raised the flag, they put their hands on their hearts and began to repeat the national pledge of allegiance. The Jívaro, I learned, are compelled to carry out this ceremony every day. It struck me as a pathetic irony. The bureaucratic forces of the government do not extend civilian rights to these people, yet they force them to affirm an oath of fidelity. The children before me probably did not comprehend the act. It would be years before they discovered that in the eyes of the white government that is gradually enveloping them they have no more rights than the termites and peccaries of the forest. I searched the crowd for Kukus. He was standing in the rear, watching silently. Other adults were joining in the pledge, but not Kukus. He would not obstruct the ceremony, but he personally would not tarnish the memory of his ancestors by participating. It was a matter of principle. It was a matter of dignity."

Left:
Young Achuara boys become serious hunters by the age of twelve, wielding blowguns with great skill to pick off monkeys and birds.

Opposite, above:
As the *Pororoca* smashes into the Amazon's banks it rips away huge trees as if they were children's toys. Settlers fear the great wave and call it a beast that rises from the sea to eat their land.

Opposite, below:
Occurring during the highest spring tides, the *Pororoca* rushes over Amazon banks as it swells in from the sea, leaving a flooded brown world behind.

Overleaf:
An awesome phenomenon begins: waves of the giant tidal bore known as *Pororoca* (Big Roar) begin to rise from the sea off the Brazilian coast. Stories are told of waves cresting in a wall of water sometimes twenty-five feet high and racing up the Amazon as far as five hundred miles. The Cousteau team observed waves no more than ten feet high, but was the first to document the formation of these preliminary waves as far as ten miles at sea.

186

THE RIVER OF THE FUTURE

FLYING TEAM | RIO CAQUETÁ | COLOMBIA

In the quiet isolation of Amazonia's least-penetrated regions, local human sociey often appears enigmatic to outsiders. Cousteau team members notice that a separate reality sometimes lurks behind the perceived nature of many villages, tribes, boats, passing faces. There are shades of color to these ambiguities: the obstinate solitude of the Quechua in their high Andean sanctuarics, the casual revenge killings of the trc ctor-driving Txukahamëi on the Xingu, the undivulged presence of Indians keeping watch from the shadows of the Padauari forest, the hidden cargoes of illicit skins and captive animals in the holds of river craft, the ghostly medicine of Achuara witch doctors. To visitors at the far edges of Amazon civilization, it feels as if a sinister resonance hangs in the air, invisible, indefinable, but as heavy on the skin as humidity.

Along the western fringes of the jungle, this secretive attitude cloaks two spreading underground activities. In Peru, Jean-Michel's Flying Teams have skirted the edges of the Andean guerrilla movement called *Sendero Luminoso* (Shinging Path) as well as a hidden but vast Amazon illicit drug industry. Since the expedition is ecological, not political, the decision has been made to avoid contact with the leftist guerrillas, but the workings of the vast drug business appear to have an impact upon the focal point of the mission—the future of the river, forest, and local human environments.

Although scores of mind-altering chemicals are produced by jungle plants, in Amazonia today the world "drug" is synonomous with cocaine. Most of the cocaine arriving in the United States and Europe comes from coca plants grown along the eastern flanks of the Andes in Bolivia, Peru, and Colombia. As a rule, the leaves are turned into a paste locally. The process of refining the paste into cocaine and the dispersal to other nations takes place, for the most part, in Colombia. Increasingly, the tremendous income potential leads local Amazon farmers and even some Indian tribes to uproot food crops and

For two days the Yakuna maintain a mildly euphoric state by chewing powdered coca leaves. Some celebrants blow the powder directly into each other's noses through hollow bamboo shafts.

replace them with fields of coca plants, and to clear new areas of forest for coca farming.

The plant itself, for all the international glamor and intrigue attached to its euphoriant properties, is a drab-looking shrub. The conquistadors found it in use by the Inca nobles, and there are tales (still debated by historians) that the Spanish conquerors dispersed it among the peasants as a means of controlling them. Herndon reported the Quechua use of coca leaves in his 1849 book *Exploration of the Valley of the Amazon.* Among the Americans who read his account was a young man in Missouri named Samuel Clemens. When he set out down the Mississippi for New Orleans—in the voyage that led to his job as a steamboat captain and was later celebrated under the pseudonym Mark Twain—Clemens was actually bound for the Amazon. His plan was to create a business importing these magical coca leaves to America. In New Orleans he discovered that no ships sailed from that port to the Amazon. When his $50 in savings was gone, he took a steamboat job, sailed back upriver, and forgot his money-making scheme. It is a little-known irony: America's most famous writer nearly became its first coca dealer.

Coca refined into cocaine first appeared in Western society in 1885, when it was used as an eye anesthetic. A year later, an American pharmacist mixed cocaine into a beverage that soon gained a vast popularity: Coca-Cola. The drink was only one of many cocaine-enriched tonics available, but by 1914 cocaine's dangers were widely recognized and it was prohibited in the United States for all but medical purposes. Chemists working for Coca-Cola developed a process to extract the flavoring of the leaf without the alkaloids, which produce the drug, and the company remains the largest legal importer of coca. They sell the residual base to pharmaceutical companies, which continue to use it to produce an anesthetic for the nose and throat.

Nearly a year before, the Land Team that climbed to the Amazon's source witnessed the centuries-old and legal tradition among Andean Indians of chewing coca leaves to quell hunger and to experience a minor stimulation. Among Quechua Indians, chewing coca leaves is the equivalent of smoking cigarettes or drinking beer in the Western world.

When the visit to the Jívaro Achuara is complete, Jean-Michel asks his Flying Team to join him investigating and filming within the clandestine Amazon world of coca growers and traffickers. He makes the mission voluntary. Murderous violence goes hand in hand with massive profit in the cocaine underworld. Cornu, Zlotnicka, and Sumian volunteer. Anne-Marie Cousteau and Scott Frier will join portions of the mission as still photographers. Karen Brazeau will fly to Lima to carry out the difficult work of obtaining official permissions for filming and to coordinate the team's logistics. Dr. Gabriel G. Nahas, a pharmacologist at the Columbia University Medical Center and a Cousteau Society Advisor, will accompany the team as a consultant during parts of the mission. Dr. Nahas also puts the team in contact with Dr. F. R. Jerí, a leading Peruvian clinical neurologist, who is instrumental in paving the way for the filming work.

The Cousteau team learns that the coca leaf takes on a near-mystical role among a tribe living, not in the Andes, but in the jungles of Colombia. In seasonal fetes, they are said to consume copious amounts of coca leaves. To witness this ritual, Sumian, Cornu, Zlotnicka, Calvo, and Anne-Marie join an-

Opposite, above:
The coca plant, *Erythroxylon coca:* leaves of this shrub, picked at the western edges of Amazonia and processed into cocaine, bring a higher price, ounce for ounce, than gold.

Opposite, middle:
During a thanksgiving festival among the Yakuna Indians of southern Colombia, masked dancers imitate creatures of the forest. The fete celebrates jungle resources, especially coca. Though the masks are similar, the dancers portray different animals with movement.

Opposite, below:
A Yakuna dries coca leaves, which will be pounded into powder and mixed with the ashes of cecropia leaves. The limey ashes release the narcotic alkaloids in the coca.

thropologist Martin von Hildebrandt on a journey up the Japura River from Brazil into Colombia aboard *Anaconda*, then transfer to canoes in order to reach Puerto Rastrojo, a remote village of the Yakuna tribe on a tributary of the Rio Caquetá.

Four times each year the Yakunas descend upon one of their villages and hold a festival that celebrates the gifts of the rain forest: fruits, vegetables, medicines, game... and coca. Yakuna guests arrive by canoe for the two-day revel, then don masks and become elements of the forest for a series of ritual dances that lasts through the night and the following day. As the marathon winds on, through endless meals and dances symbolizing aspects of Yakuna life (hunting, fishing, sexual potency, jungle fertility), a canister appears in the center of the *malloca* (meeting house). It is filled with coca leaves ground into a green powder and mixed with the ashes of cecropia leaves. The village chief and shaman ceremonially dispense the coca throughout the crowd. With their cheeks packed full of coca and catalyzing lime ashes, the elders sing for hours about God's benevolent award of coca to those who will use it properly. Already exhilarated by the merriment, the dancers seem to gain from the coca an emotional amplification that fuels their tiring bodies and sensitizes them to the cacophony of drum music.

After nearly forty-eight hours of continuous revelry in a mild coca stupor, the Yakuna festival ends. With Hildebrandt interpreting, Cornu asks an old Yakuna man about the modern practice of intensifying the coca experience by processing the leaves into cocaine. "White people contaminate coca," he says. "They mix it with kerosene [one of the processing agents] and it harms their brains. It is crazy, crazy." The old man adds sadly, "Unfortunately, some young Yakunas are now doing this, too."

The rising "contamination" of traditional coca use parallels other intrusions of the outside world into Yakuna life—Western clothing, tools, weapons, and Christianity, which radiates into the forest from scattered missions. Hildebrandt tells the team of an Indian he visited downstream from the Yakuna village. The man had been converted to Christianity, but he was reluctant to abandon the beliefs of his tribe. His life has become an amalgam of two faiths. In his jungle hut there was a small altar with a plastic statue of Christ. Each day he knelt reverently before the shrine and blew coca powder onto it.

FLYING TEAM | TINGO MARIA | PERU

The acknowledged capital of the illicit cocaine trade in Peru is a village named Tingo Maria on the eastern slopes of the Andes, about a day's drive westward up a winding road from Pucallpa. It is estimated that some 95 percent of Tingo Maria's 35,000 people are directly or indirectly involved in the growing or selling of coca. Some of the coca action is legal: Peru permits registered landowners to grow coca for pharmaceutical purposes, and the government purchases the crop. However, some 90 percent of Tingo Maria's coca acreage is thought to be unregistered and its production sold to the illicit industry. Once an agricultural center, the valley around Tingo Maria has turned into a checkerboard of coca patches. The crops breed prosperity—taxi drivers retire to beautiful homes, the poorest shacks are surrounded with new cars—and the prosperity breeds violence. A prefect who sought to clean up the city was badly wounded in a church shooting. An investigative journalist was dead four hours after arriving in Tingo Maria. The age-old suspiciousness of Andean highlanders is here escalated into a brutal underworld where trespassers are dealt with savagely.

Curious about this lawless drug center, Jean-Michel and Cornu first enter Tingo Maria in September, staying with Franciscan monks. When they express an interest in filming, they are quickly warned to be careful. Now, some nine months later, when they make inquiries in Lima about a trip to Tingo Maria, they receive a frantic message from the monastery. Word of their interest has spread. There are rumors of death threats to the team if they arrive with cameras. The Flying Team assesses the danger for three weeks, contacting authorities in Lima for assistance. They learn that two separate police agencies are operating in Tingo Maria: the national investigative police agency known as PIP (Policia de Investigaciones de Peru) and a special drug force called UMOPAR (Unidad Movil de Patrullaje Rural). UMOPAR is financed in large part by the U.S. Drug Enforcement Agency (DEA) as part of a drive to stop the flow of cocaine at its source.

During the next few weeks, the team makes two trips to Tingo Maria. On the first trip, led by Jean-Michel, the men are accompanied by a PIP patrol. They witness the destruction of a coca field by chemical spraying north of Tingo Maria, and then in the city they watch as the patrol confronts two pretty teenage girls at a bus stop, each holding a baby. Something looks odd to the police. They discover a pound bag of coca paste strapped around each girl's waist. They have been paid a total of $75 to carry the material, worth about $100,000 after processing and retail sale. At police headquarters, the two girls learn that their act could cost them a minimum of ten years in prison.

Because the danger appears to be escalating, the team is escorted to Tingo Maria on the second trip by a special UMOPAR protective unit of two officers and seven armed guards as well as DEA agent Federico Villareal as interpreter. During the ensuing mission, the nine guards never leave the team's side. They reconnoiter the commercial plane before allowing the Cousteau team to board, sleep at their sides in Tingo Maria, and escort them into every restaurant booth and bathroom.

For three harrowing days Cornu, Sumian, Zlotnicka, and their bodyguards explore the tense world of the drug capital. They are allowed to accompany a UMOPAR squadron on daily rounds, patrolling the nearby Huallaga River in search of coca-laden boats, driving the streets of Tingo Maria in efforts to ferret out pedestrians and vehicles carrying the drug, roving about mountain roads on the lookout for unregistered coca fields.

Following a tip, the UMOPAR patrol halts along a mountain road and follows a steep trail into the forest. After an hour's walk, they come across a recently abandoned processing plant, where coca paste is extracted from dried leaves. Coca leaves, kerosene, and sulfuric acid are macerated in a pit lined with sheets of black plastic. A pale yellowish white residue with the consistency of moist plaster is skimmed from the mash and formed into balls—the coca paste—called *pasta basica de la coca* (PBC). In this form, the drug is shipped by traffickers to refining plants in Colombia, where a second treat-

Opposite, above:
Wearing dust masks, Jean-Michel Cousteau and Silvio Barros tour the extraordinary gold mine at Serra Pelada, where as many as 45,000 men dig for one of history's largest bonanzas.

Opposite, below:
Cousteau finds an unusual angle from which to photograph the human drama of the world's most spectacular present-day gold rush.

Overleaf:
Looking like soiled sugar cubes, the land claims of Serra Pelada are only six by nine feet each. The varying speed of the gold diggers accounts for the mismatched levels.

ment produces the common cocaine sulphate (cocaine "base") and a third treatment produces the common cocaine powder, cocaine hydrochloride. It takes about two hundred kilos of leaves to make one kilo of commercial cocaine. Two hundred kilos of leaves would bring a Peruvian farmer the equivalent of about $500 for a legal sale to the government, perhaps $2,000 for a black-market sale, about three times the annual per capita income. Processed and sold on a U.S. street corner, the derivative cocaine from this transaction could bring between $100,000 and $150,000. In Peru, as the saying goes, cocaine is worth more than gold.

While the Cousteau team is filming the clandestine processing plant, Cornu nearly trips over a ground wire. A UMOPAR agent quickly pulls him away, averting tragedy. The trip wire is attached to a jerry-rigged shotgun hidden in the brush—a defensive trick of the processor. To illustrate the danger, the agent clears the team away and pulls on the wire. The homemade gun, made of pipe, fells a small tree nearby. Cornu realizes the weapon was pointed directly at his legs.

One afternoon, on a side street of Tingo Maria, the UMOPAR patrol suddenly leaps from their jeeps and confronts a passerby. The man dashes away but is soon caught and handcuffed. In his haste, he has dropped behind him a bag containing more than seven pounds (3.5 kilos) of coca paste. Dominique Sumian asks how they could detect the coca paste from the jeeps. An officer explains that the man looked uncomfortable, so they decided to experiment, pretending to arrest him. His attempted escape confirmed the suspicion.

Cornu, Sumian, and Zlotnicka ask to visit the Tingo Maria prison, and after some bureaucratic debate, the request is granted. The team enters an old stone building with dark medieval corridors. They are led into a cramped open courtyard partially covered by corrugated tin awnings. Within the bleak barracks live some two hundred inmates. About 90 percent are coca smugglers. Female prisoners are segregated into an unlit chamber about the size of a school classroom. There are twenty-eight women crowded into the cell, most of them young, many with babies, the majority facing long sentences within this same dank space. Among the faces around them, Cornu recognizes one of the teenage girls arrested at a bus stop during the team's first trip to Tingo Maria. Her sentence, they learn, was ten years here. She says she will keep the baby until he is finished nursing, then send him to relatives outside. He will be nearly eleven years old when she is released. The three Cousteau team members find themselves deeply moved by this fresh-faced girl suddenly trapped like a frightened animal in a squalid pen. "She and her friend probably acted on a whim, to earn food money," Cornu says, "never suspecting they would lose their youth and their babies in the process."

As Tingo Maria has risen from a modest village of farmers and shop owners to become an epicenter of the lucrative coca trade, say the UMOPAR officers accompanying the team, a kind of cultural malignancy has spread. Though it brings prosperity to many, it devastates the innocent poor, like the girls at the bus stop, and it ignites a wicked callousness among the greedy. Among the many stories heard by the Cousteau team in Tingo Maria, one is especially chilling. A bus driver on the Tingo Maria to Pucallpa run—a highway used by smugglers to transport drugs to the Amazon River—noticed one day that a baby carried by a young woman sitting in the rear looked seriously ill. At a stopover point, he asked the woman if he could get some water for the infant, who appeared pale and feverish. The mother seemed unconcerned, so much so that the driver grew suspicious. At the next stop, he called the police. They discovered that the baby was dead, and the corpse was stuffed with bags of coca paste. The infant had been kidnapped a week earlier. The same thing has happened three times, says a UMOPAR agent.

The extraordinary profits of the coca trade engender not only virulent crime but the wherewithall to outmaneuver enforcement agencies and to bribe corrupt officials. During their work in Tingo Maria, the Cousteau team rents a taxi plane to film the coca fields around the city. They take with them an officer of UMOPAR. It is the first time he has seen the region from the air. Despite funding from the U.S. DEA, UMOPAR cannot afford to equip its agents in Tingo Maria with a plane. During the hour-long flight, the officer is astonished to discover two new airstrips cleared in the jungle by drug runners at sites never suspected by his enforcement agents. One, a long cement runway designed for private jets, has been built in less than a month.

When the Flying Team finishes its work in Tingo Maria, they return to Lima. Their worried bodyguards accompany them to the boarding ramp of the plane, clear other passengers from the seats before allowing the team to enter, and carefully check the passengers as they file in.

FLYING TEAM | LIMA | PERU

For years, the flourishing cocaine trade in Peru and other South American nations was sidestepped by government enforcement agencies because the hard currency it generated was a major component of their economies. But a crackdown has begun, in part because of pressure from the United States, where the DEA estimates as much as sixty-two tons of cocaine arrive each year, representing an illicit industry worth about $25 billion annually. A more compelling reason for the efforts to curb the cocaine industry may be its boomeranging effects on South American society. Like designer jeans and rock music, coca paste has become stylish among the young elite in cities like Lima, where North American fads are emulated. Some estimates place the number of coca paste "addicts" in Lima at about 150,000, most of them middle- and upper-class youths. This represents a significant portion of the next generation of governing elite, causing authorities to call the problem a threat to national security.

Nevertheless, progress in eradication of cocaine is painfully slow. At the headquarters of PIP in Lima, the Cousteau team witnesses a major event in the government program. Under the watchful eyes of the Minister of the Interior, agency personnel display a mass of plastic bags packed with some three tons of confiscated coca paste. Chemists test each bag to confirm its illicit contents. When the tests are complete, the bags of coca paste are carried to an open truck and driven to a building-size incinerator twelve miles out of Lima, where the Interior Minister ceremoniously tosses the first bag into the flames. An hour later, some $25 million worth of coca paste has turned to smoke drifting eastward toward the mountains where it originated.

As Peru's young people have rushed to experience the euphoria of coca

Opposite, above:
A constant storm of dust in the pit leads bag carriers to use whatever is available to fashion masks.

Opposite, middle:
Bag carriers and shovelers at Serra Pelada endure conditions and toil reminiscent of ancient slave gangs. The difference is: an exhausted and dirt-caked worker may find the world's largest gold nugget at any moment, as two men have recently done.

Opposite, below:
Miners at Serra Pelada cross every social strata but that of the already rich: among them are doctors, schoolteachers, rubber gatherers, accountants, and the unemployed.

paste, which is packed into an emptied filter cigarette and smoked (the cigarettes are called "Exocets" after the French rockets used by Argentina against the British during the Falklands/Malvinas war), their parents wring their hands in frustration. Some now turn for help to doctors and clinics in Lima, where experimental cures are being developed to halt coca addiction. (Though cocaine is not commonly associated with the drugs producing classic dependence syndromes, such as heroin, researchers use the term "addiction" because of the profound craving it creates in the brain of the user. Experiments have shown that cocaine is the only known food or drug that research monkeys will self-administer to the point of death, from the drug's effects, or starvation, from the loss of interest in food.)

The most extreme of these procedures, one that has caused heated debate throughout the international medical establishment, was developed by a psychiatrist, Dr. Teobaldo Llosa, and a brain surgeon, Dr. Humberto Hinojosa. The two men have pioneered an operation in which a tiny part of the limbic system of the brain is removed. The technique is based on a popular theory that the forebrain contains specialized circuits that motivate necessary human behavior by rewarding the body with pleasurable sensations (such as the tastes of food, the quenching sensations of water, the stimulations of sex). Some researchers associate our most profound drives and emotions with neurochemical regulatory mechanisms commonly called "pleasure centers." Drug researchers have found evidence that cocaine and other drugs affect these pleasure centers, altering normal behavior and creating a craving for continued consumption of the drug. Llosa and Hinojosa theorized that the surgical removal of a part of the cingulum—an area in which these neurochemical motivating mechanisms are concentrated—would remove the craving, the addiction. They call the procedure a "cingulotomy." Unfortunately, it is not known for certain what other effects may result. It is possible the patient could be deprived for life of other pleasurable sensations.

Dr. Llosa tells Jean-Michel that the idea for the operation came from his experiences with young people who were desperately dependent upon PBC. He began to consider a radical cure three years ago when he confronted the case of a twenty-eight-year-old father who had sold nearly everything his family possessed in order to purchase coca paste. Conventional psychiatric therapy had failed. When the young man attacked his mother in a frantic attempt to steal money, tearing off her earrings and leaving her near death after beating her, Llosa decided he was "hopeless." The idea of the cingulotomy came to him and he found Dr. Hinojosa, who was willing to perform the surgery. A total of twenty-eight young patients have now undergone cingulotomies. Jean-Michel asks about the success rate of the operation. Llosa says about two thirds of the patients have abandoned coca use; the other third has reverted.

In Llosa's private clinic, Jean-Michel meets a boy of sixteen who is scheduled to undergo the operation in forty-eight hours. To protect his anonymity, the youth is referred to as Patient 29. He tells Jean-Michel that he has smoked coca paste for more than two years and has consented to the cingulotomy out of fear he is headed in the same direction as an older brother, a coca-paste addict who committed suicide.

The next day, the Cousteau team is permitted to make the first film record

Opposite, above:
Traffic moves up and down the walls of the Serra Pelada pit from dawn to dusk, as bag carriers remove worthless dirt. A misstep can mean tragedy as a ladder-full of workers plummets to the pit bottom. Appropriately, the ladders are called *"adios mamas."*

Opposite, below:
A young Serra Pelada miner reflects the exuberance and optimism of the men in the "hole," some of whom celebrate the mineral they seek, and reveal their obsession, by implanting grains of gold in their teeth.

Overleaf:
To the Cousteau team, the engulfing sound of this sea of humanity was like the inside of a beehive amplified.

of the operation. In surgical gowns and masks, Jean-Michel, Cornu, and Zlotnicka watch in a Lima operating room as the skull of Patient 29 is opened by a hand drill and saw, an incision is made, and what appears to be a gelatinous bud is suctioned out of the brain. A month later, the team returns to film an interview with the youngster. Superficially at least, the boy's behavior and intelligence seem unimpaired. Llosa emphasizes strongly that the operation does not change mental abilities.

However, for the team as for countless others familiar with this irreversible alteration of the brain, the process evokes haunting worries. Llosa maintains that none of the acceptable techniques has proven effective with the most compulsive cases of coca-paste addiction—neither psychotropic drugs nor psychotherapy. He explains that he screens potential candidates rigidly before coming to the conclusion that all other treatments have failed and that the patient cannot avoid "destroying himself socially, academically, occupationally, and as a family member"—leading ultimately to insanity, suicide, or a life of crime. In Llosa's word, the candidate is "irrecoverable."

The vehemence of Llosa's critics is an indication of the profound ethical arguments the cingulotomy procedure has created. Some charge that the two doctors are experimenting with living human beings, others that the expensive operation, even if 100 percent successful, is hardly a cure for the majority of coca addicts (a conclusion Llosa readily acknowledges). The most volatile question involves the naked issues of psychosurgery itself: Is it ethical to directly alter the behavioral mechanisms of a human being? Is it appropriate to create humans potentially devoid throughout their lifetimes of the pleasures that make life worth living? Could the process lead to tyrannical abuses, such as the medical subjugation of political enemies?

Jean-Michel concludes in his taped diary: "As I watched the operation today my mind kept returning to the same thought: whatever the ethics of this violent intrusion into the brain, the fact it is even considered is a sign of the virulence of the cocaine menace. So radically is it contorting the lives of countless people that responsible professionals with the best of intentions are ready to consider, and now even to carry out, such an unthinkable procedure, believing it is the last possible remedy.

"The contagion in Peru ends here, in young brains exposed on operating tables, but along the way it inflicts many kinds of violence—on peasant farmers, parents, policemen, reformers, and young girls giggling with their babies at bus stops.

"Moreover, the poisonous effects of cocaine appear to be employed as a weapon in international warfare. In the Colombian jungle, Jean-Paul and Arturo met a coca trafficker who agreed to be interviewed on film. He was about thirty years of age, college-educated, and highly articulate. He said that his business, purchasing coca and transporting it, earned him about $250,000 each year. This in a country where the average annual income is just over $1,000.

" 'But I have never used the drug and don't do it for the money,' he said earnestly. 'I do it to destroy the United States. This is a war.' His profits, it seems, are used to buy weapons for guerrilla groups, and his mind-altering products are sent into the U.S., insidious chemical bombs made of white powder, designed to weaken the populace and wear down the machinery of

Opposite, above left:
Jean-Michel watches as a gold bar is formed from Serra Pelada nuggets at a government-run gold-purchasing center near the mine.

Opposite, above right:
A seventeen-year-old bag carrier.

Opposite, below:
Cousteau (*in hat, left center*) and Barros (*to his left*) watch as profits are distributed among a partnership exploiting a single claim. During the year in which the Cousteau team visited, the partnership made nearly $9.5 million.

government. Hearing of his claims, I was reminded of similar tactics used by the Chinese during the Opium Wars. He was an educated young man merely seeking ways to combat what he perceived as a colonial power whose economic dominance enslaved his Third World nation. From what we have seen, the chemical weapon he wields is a frightening one, inflicting widespread casualties among his faraway adversaries and devastating as well the lives of the people he is trying to champion.

"As our teams try to understand the future of Amazonia, we wonder if the dark brutality of the drug underworld will continue to spread like a cancer, or will fade into history as only a brief nightmare of agony."

TRUCK TEAM | TRANSAMAZON HIGHWAY | BRAZIL

The illicit fortunes derived from a stimulating shrub leaf in western Amazonia are matched in the east by a burgeoning harvest of mineral treasures. In mid-April, on the last leg of their highway odyssey, the Cousteau Truck Team reaches an area south of Belém, between the Rio Xingu and Rio Tocantins, that today is swirling with activity at three sites envisioned by the planners of Brazil's future as "El Dorados."

Following a new tar-covered spur road west from Marabá, the team enters a series of rounded mountains called the Serra dos Carajás. As night falls they arrive atop a flat summit strewn with earth-moving machines, building materials, and temporary housing. To Brazilians, this mountain is the site of "the project of the century," the centerpiece of a $60 billion expenditure to make this region an economic mecca.

The red dirt the team steps onto as they leave the trucks is the magic ingredient in the Carajás story. The entire mountain beneath them and several mountains in each direction are immense mounds of iron ore. Discovered accidentally in 1967 by a Brazilian geologist whose helicopter was forced down, the Carajás lode is now estimated to contain the purest, and one of the two or three largest, deposits of iron in the world—18 billion tons. As geologists surveyed the bonanza, they discovered a series of mind-boggling surprises. The mountains were also laden with an estimated 1 billion tons of copper, 60 million tons of manganese, 40 million tons of bauxite, 47 million tons of nickel, 100,000 tons of tin, 100 tons of gold, and commercial deposits of six other minerals as well.

The next morning, Carajás engineers guide the team around snaking dirt roads to witness rail lines under construction and scrubby forests being cleared. Though still meager, production has begun. Immense shovel-trucks, each able to carry 120 tons of ore at a speed of 30 miles per hour, bounce past on 9-foot-high tires. Dynamite explosions rumble in the distance and walls of red earth cascade in dusty avalanches. Eventually, say the directors of the project, Carajás will produce 50 million tons of ore a year, making Brazil the world's largest exporter of iron ore and enabling the country to cut back its huge foreign exchange losses by $15 billion a year and to employ one million out-of-work citizens in the process.

It will take two more years of preparation, the team is told, before production is significant. A 550-mile railroad must be laid eastward through the jun-

Bathed in mud all day, Serra Pelada miners have only trickling brooks in which to clean up each evening.

gle to the Atlantic port of São Luís, where the ore will be shipped worldwide. But then—then!—they say, Carajás will fuel a burst of economic progress in Brazil, possibly supporting grandiose development projects elsewhere in Amazonia. The developers of Carajás plan to do their share. The Companhia Vale do Rio Doce, a corporation owned on a two-to-one basis by the Brazilian government and private shareholders, intends to open huge farms, cattle ranches, and forestry projects along their railroad to the sea.

The depth of Brazil's commitment to Carajás is starkly illustrated by its creation of a $3-billion hydroelectric project designed principally to run the mining and refining operation. A hundred miles north of Carajás, en route to the nearly completed Tucuruí dam, the Truck Team passes more construction gangs and rising villages along more new highways. Scheduled to start working within a year, the project will eventually produce nearly 8 million kilowatts of electricity—more than all but the Itaipu (southern Brazil), Grand Coulee (U.S.), and Guri (Venezuela) dams. Tucuruí will back the Tocantins into a lake covering 850 square miles of jungle. It is a measure of Brazil's optimism that the lake has appeared on national maps since the mid-seventies, nearly a decade before it was due to be formed. The energy capacity of Tucuruí could run a city of 4 million people, and its electrical transmission lines will run to Marabá, Tucuruí, and Belém; yet its principal purpose is to keep the mines and smelters and electric trains of Carajás roaring.

Through the regional division of its national electrical utility, Eletronorte, Brazil has spared little to ensure Tucuruí's success. A labor force of 25,000 men pour 13,000 cubic yards of concrete a day to erect a 200-foot-high, 7.5-mile-long barrier across the Tocantins.

The imminent success of Tucuruí is encouraging planners to replicate it throughout Amazonia. A brochure handed to Raymond Coll by Eletronorte officials identifies nine other Amazon dam projects either planned or under construction. Eletronorte executives list more than twenty other sites they are considering, and say the potential projects far in the future could be three times that number.

An executive of Eletronorte captured the prevailing spirit when he told two visiting American journalists, "We could be the Saudi Arabia of hydropower." With its overabundance of flowing water, Brazil could create enough energy to process its ample bauxite riches into exportable aluminum and become a major supplier of this increasingly valuable metal. It is this litany of monumental possibilities that intoxicates the international banking community and keeps the loans coming to Brazil despite its current economic turbulence. While the country's economists dream of prosperity, its ecologists wring their hands over the potential forest devastation that would accompany the construction of dams and cities and highways and jungle-engulfing lakes.

For sheer human drama, however, nothing in the Amazon surpasses the mud-caked spectacle underway south of Tucuruí and Carajás on the top of a small knoll rising from the jungle like a brown swelling. Its name in Portuguese means Naked Mountain, an apt description. Yet to the masses of poor in Brazil, nothing about Serra Pelada is barren. The words quake with excitement when they echo through the hovels of the south. Serra Pelada is a chaotic, magnetic gold rush contained in a single hole in the ground. In and out of the hole swarm as many as 45,000 men on a given day, their bodies coated in dust and mud, their minds riveted on the stories of phenomenal discoveries that float about the camp: the man who found $6 million worth of gold rocks in a single day, the man who found a single nugget weighing sixty-six pounds, exceeded shortly afterward by another *garimpeiro* whose nugget weighed eighty pounds. There is no gold mine in the entire world like Serra Pelada, and its epic brown pageant of moving bodies looks, through the powdery air, like the largest crowd of extras ever assembled in history's most expensive cinema fantasy. One thing it does not look like is reality.

Even the tale of how gold was discovered at Serra Pelada has appropriately mythical elements. In 1980 an immense tree was blown over during a violent storm on the hill, the story goes, and *caboclos* passing the site noticed that the soil in the gaping hole beneath the tangled roots was studded with gold rocks. A month later there were twenty thousand people maniacally shoveling into the top of the mountain. Ten months later they had already extracted more gold than had ever been mined in a year's time in the whole of Brazil. Three years later the value of the gold already carried out of the mountaintop pit was nearly $800 million, and no one could see an end in sight.

When the Cousteau Truck Team first arrives in Serra Pelada on April 20, the 200-foot-deep open pit has been half flooded by the rainy season, halting most of the work. Raymond Coll is told that the water will be gone in another month and the *garimpeiro* population will return to dig feverishly, since the government has threatened to end public access to Serra Pelada within six months, turning it over to a state-run mechanized mining company.

On June 21 Jean-Michel flies to the mine in *Papagallo* with a team composed of Prezelin, sound engineer Francis Bonfanti, Camargo, and Barros. Ten days later, in a tiny motel near the open pit, Jean-Michel describes on cassette the team's experiences:

"We had been flying for an hour or so over the forest when Guy Gervais pointed to a freakish cloud sitting on the treetops in the distance. As *Papagallo* droned toward it, the cloud took on the appearance of a smoky glow rising from the middle of the jungle, as if something was erupting from the bowels of the earth. It was ethereal, but it was nothing compared to our first glimpse as Guy descended into the miasma of dust and banked so that we could look down upon the 'great hole,' as it is called. The scene below us staggered our imaginations. It was epic, a vision from the age of the Pharaohs, from Babylon. Or from the insect world. Streaming to and fro were thousands and thousands of organisms the color of the soil, marching in endless files that brushed against one another as they poured in and out of the hole, going and coming, disappearing into the dust and emerging from it, swarming in an orderly way like ants excavating an underground nest. Even the hole itself was an arresting sight, an inverted pyramid pointing toward the center of the earth, its walls honeycombed with notches and scaled by countless ladders.

"It was dusk when we landed, so we waited until the next morning to take a close look from the ground level. I was awakened at 5:30 A.M. by a low hum. From the door we could see long trails of people coming from the left and

A pure gold bar in a Rio de Janeiro processing plant—the object of passions that have swept dreamers across continents to California, the Yukon, and the Amazon.

right, heading toward the hole, meeting in a human river that disappeared into the ground. The sound rumbling in our ears was produced by thousands of feet stomping the ground.

"We followed. At the edge of the pit the sound escalated, as if we were listening to a microphone thrust into a beehive. There were shouts when a large stone would tumble toward people below, but seldom did one voice rise above the humming melee. The constant motion was hypnotic—men carrying, climbing, shoveling, scurrying, building canals to divert the springs coming out of cliff walls, passing us with bags of soil. We could hear stones grinding against one another in the bags, but they weren't gold. These were worthless bags of earth being carried out of the way. In essence, the entire mountain was being moved upon human backs.

"During these ten days we met winners and losers. We talked with a man named 'Kinko,' Joaquim Bezerra Bomfim Sobrinho, who is a partner in one of the plots in the hole. He and his friends found 128 kilograms of gold last year, worth nearly $2 million. This year they expect to double that. He explained that the government sent militia to establish order and safety here four months after the gold rush began. Women are not allowed at Serra Pelada, neither are alcohol or firearms. A miner can claim a plot called a *barranco*, which is only six feet by nine feet. He keeps 75 percent of the gold he finds; the government keeps the rest. If a plot is abandoned for seventy-two hours, it is redistributed. There are prospectors who own several plots and employ diggers; there are partnerships exploiting a single plot. Men without claims come to work as bag carriers and shovelers. Some carriers are paid by the bag (40¢), making about sixty trips per day. Shovelers make a daily fee of about $15. Workers sometimes labor for free, under an arrangement giving them about 5 percent of the take if gold is discovered. It is a serious gamble. They leave Serra Pelada either wealthy or penniless.

"Some never leave. Two men died and a third lost his leg during our first day here. The miners tell us about thirty people have died in the hole. The problem is that the plots are dug at different speeds, and none are at the same level. The surface of one plot may be five or six 'stories' above the adjacent one. Men slip and fall to their deaths off high places, and rock avalanches occasionally crash down on men in deep plots. As the pace increases to beat the approaching closing of the mine, accidents multiply.

"Other men lose everything *but* their lives. I spoke with a miner who has been here three years. In the beginning he made good money, but recently his claim has yielded nothing. To pay his workers, he sold his house and all of his belongings. Still nothing. Now the end is approaching. Once a 60 percent shareholder in his claim, he has been forced to sell all but 10 percent. When his story ended, he looked me in the eye and said philosophically, 'Win with class. Lose with class.'

"In the fantasy land of Serra Pelada, resilient spirits mix with mysticism. We talked with Advernon Vincente Lopes, the *garimpeiro* who uncovered the eighty-pound nugget, the world's largest. He told me that one night he had a dream that his daughter was covered with excrement. When he began to clean her, the filth turned to gold. When he awoke, he knew it meant that this was the day he would find gold. He dressed in his Sunday suit and walked to the hole. Miners laughed as he stalked to his claim through the red mud. At

Calypso docks at Jari, a paper pulp plantation the size of the state of Connecticut developed by American billionaire Daniel K. Ludwig. The plant in the center of the photo was barged to the Amazon from Japan. Before being sold to a Brazilian consortium, the Jari plot was the largest tract of land on earth owned by an individual.

the plot, with thousands watching, he told his partners to step aside. He knelt down and plunged his arms to the elbows in the wet soil. A minute later, after churning about in the mud, his hands hit a rock. It was the size of half a watermelon. As he drew it out, cheers erupted. The stone was 92 percent gold.

"There are as many stories here as *garimpeiros*, and the militia officers who oversee the project are quick to warn visitors that imaginations in Serra Pelada are as rich as the ground. The main gathering place here is called The Plaza of Lies. There is the story, for example, of the miner who cashed in a fortune and tied the money in bundles hanging from his backside. 'All my life I have been running after money,' he said, 'now the money will be after me.' Yet our favorite story has been verified by a witness. It vividly illustrates the ultimate dream of the men who flock here—Brazil-nut pickers, fishermen, rice farmers, urban unemployed, foundry workers, rubber gatherers—the dream of near-supernatural transformation that accompanies the discovery of gold...the dream of instant respect...the dream of winning with 'class.'

"An impoverished *garimpeiro* who had shoveled on his own plot for two years suddenly struck it rich. He had never had more than a few *cruzeiros* in his pocket all his life. He exchanged his gold, filled several suitcases with cash, and left Serra Pelada behind him, flying back to his family in the south. When he reached the São Paulo airport, he ordered two taxicabs to take him home. When his suitcases and belongings were easily loaded into the first taxi, the driver of the second car asked why two taxis were necessary. The miner briefly opened a rear door of the empty taxi, then returned to the loaded car and signaled both drivers to proceed. He was going home as a winner with 'class.' The second taxi was carrying his hat."

"CALYPSO" | RIO JARI | BRAZIL

W hile headlines tout the mineral treasures to be plucked from Amazon lands, a less-publicized search continues for the secrets to cultivating botanical riches in the ground that sustains the largest vegetation formation on earth. Understandably, investors look at Amazonia's prodigious forest and, while admitting its fragility, refuse to believe a scheme cannot be devised to exploit its productivity in a commercial way. Many scientists in Peru, Colombia, and Brazil are taking a pragmatic approach. They tend to eschew immense land-clearing agricultural projects in favor of small-scale husbandry, pointing out that the only continually successful harvesters of the jungle to date are the region's Indian tribes. The goal is to develop a sustainable agriculture for local people, one that does not require cutting away great tracts of the rain forest. Cousteau teams have visited experimental farms in all three nations and noted the optimism of agronomists. Near Iquitos, at an experiment called a "Sun Station," Coll spoke with Peruvian scientists who are planting crops in the standing forest and raising peccaries and turtles in uncleared jungle corrals. Cornu and Sumian have seen a similar experiment in southern Colombia, at Araracuara, where cacao trees are planted amid rain-forest species, and the raising of capybaras and agoutis as meat-producing livestock has begun. At

other sites, scientists test cash crops such as cacao, peach palms, Brazil nuts, coffee, and cassava, all of which thrive in the jungle, seeking to create local prosperity while discouraging tree removal and soil destruction.

The immensity of Amazonia's wilderness, however, continues to create immense dreams, and governments hungry for revenues prefer to nourish ideas that could lead to copious profits. The most famous agricultural enterprise in the Amazon today, known simply as "Jari," was begun in 1967 by the American shipping magnate Daniel K. Ludwig, who purchased the world's largest plot of land owned by an individual—a tract larger than Connecticut—and set about creating a colossal wood-pulp and agriculture empire. Ludwig's plantation straddles the Jari River, which descends from the north to empty into the Amazon near the delta.

Jari is not the first herculean farm operation attempted in Amazonia by a captain of American industry. In 1927 Henry Ford bought 2.5 million acres of jungle on the Tapajós—an area almost twice the size of Delaware—and proceeded to install a giant rubber-tree plantation. Ford was angry at British and Dutch suppliers of Far Eastern rubber, who raised prices and restricted output to maximize profits. He decided to create his own source, buying a fleet of 199 ships to carry supplies and construction materials into the Amazon—and rubber out. For his five thousand workers he built homes, two hospitals, roads, water and sewage systems, schools, nurseries, and churches. The instant community was called Fordlandia. Eighteen years later, the dream was dead. Ford, the essence of stubborn and visionary capitalism, was defeated. He sold the land for a loss estimated at nearly $8 million and withdrew from Amazonia like a humbled Goliath.

Captain Cousteau and Jean-Michel visited Fordlandia during *Calypso's* voyage downriver in early December, speaking with a plantation foreman who told them the trees Ford planted are still tapped for rubber, though the production is small and the government-owned operation languishes.

The Cousteaus asked what caused the failure of Fordlandia. A series of errors and bad luck, they were told. The project manager, a sea captain, discovered that his loaded ships could navigate the Tabajós only during the high-water season. Diseases plagued the workers. Because the closely planted monoculture was vulnerable to epidemics, it was devastated when South American Leaf Blight struck in 1935. To improve the situation, a second planting area was opened downriver at Belterra. But in 1942 the trees were nearly destroyed by swarms of caterpillars. After World War II, Far Eastern rubber prices declined, making Amazon rubber less attractive. Then the final blow: the flooding of the market with synthetic rubber.

Ford's sudden departure left behind a calamity for the workers dependent upon the operation, and it discouraged other companies from investing in Amazonia. Nothing important was begun for years, the foreman said, not until Daniel Ludwig came to Jari.

Jari. From the beginning, the press reveled in the dramatic engagement: one of the world's most daring entrepreneurs pitted against the world's most forbidding jungle. Ludwig was celebrated, like Ford, as an indomitable billionaire with imagination. It was generally assumed he would succeed. For more than fifteen years, Ludwig tinkered in colossal fashion with his piece of

Amazonia, creating the largest tropical forestry company anywhere. He was convinced of an impending international fiber shortage, and Jari would help him corner the market. Typically, Ludwig had innovative ideas. One was a species of tree called gmelina, which his researchers found in Nigeria. Under ideal conditions, gmelina can grow a foot a month. Ludwig would clear native forest and replace it with his "miracle" tree. The second innovation was a highly mechanized operation for stripping away and hauling the trees.

Like Ford, Ludwig erected a solid infrastructure costing more than $1 billion. He built a $269 million, seventeen-story-high pulp mill in Japan and floated it all the way to Jari on a barge. He cut 2,600 miles of roads and a 45-mile railway through his land, built workers' houses and an airstrip, and planted rice fields to diversify his production.

Almost immediately, the jungle retaliated. The two stratagems on which his profit projections rested began to fail. Despite all his planning, Ludwig had made the classic Amazon mistake: he overestimated the potential of the soil. The gmelina never approached growth rates common in its native environment, and the heavy machines badly compacted the delicate soil. Jari was forced to switch to hand clearing, which had a ballooning effect on Ludwig's overhead, requiring not only the payment of wages for some 30,000 workers and executives, but the construction of a complete city in the jungle to house them.

Ludwig persevered, experimenting with other tree species. Gmelina plantations were eventually supplemented with eucalyptus and Caribbean pine. Gradually Jari began to show an annual profit, though hardly enough to justify or recapture the enormous investment. When Ludwig sought financial aid from the govenment of Brazil, he was turned down. When he asked that his legal title to the land be verified, the bureaucracy refused—or was incapable of defining ownership in a land where title is often vague. In 1982 Ludwig's patience ran out. He sold controlling interest in Jari to a consortium of twenty-seven Brazilian firms. The estimates are that he recouped less than one third of his billion-dollar investment.

To comprehend the situation, Cousteau assembles his own tiny coterie of specialists for a visit to Jari: Howard T. Odum, the pioneering American ecologist who has developed quantitative methods of evaluating human and natural systems and the effects of each on the other (by using energy as a common denominator); Mark T. Brown, the director of Odum's Center for Wetlands at the University of Florida; and Cousteau Society biologist/ecologist Dick Murphy and engineer Jacques Constans. The group tours the plantation on the ground and from the air and engages in rigorous discussions with the directors and scientists running Jari today.

Several things become clear in the conversations, which at times shift into amiable debates. The management team that has inherited Jari from Ludwig believes the giant experiment can still prosper. In fact, in their eyes it is a success now. So far the soil is supporting growth; fertilizer is used only minimally; pulp is being produced and sold to foreign markets. About 50 percent of the plantings are gmelina, 35 percent Carribean pine, 15 percent eucalyptus. The Jari pulp is of a high quality, used for such paper products as disposable diapers and tampons. "It's working," they say.

Professors Odum and Brown have reservations. The net profit is still insuffi-

cient to pay off the initial investment, making it a questionable idea for others to follow. Also, the pulp plant is presently fueled by the trees cleared for plantations. When clearing stops, Jari will need 40 percent of its developed acreage just to grow fuel wood. The question of soil potential persists as well. Eventually costly fertilizer may have to be added to the overhead. (The Cousteau team recommends using the phosphorus-rich ashes from the power plant as a fertilizer.)

In the final analysis, both sides agree, the world market for pulp and the price of petroleum will largely determine Jari's success or failure. Declining pulp prices and a rise in the cost of petroleum—which fuels the mechanized systems—could signal the end of Jari. The management of Jari, however, maintains that no such major changes will occur.

As a final suggestion, Professors Odum and Brown recommend that the layout of the plantation be altered to leave wide corridors of natural forest throughout the areas to be cleared. This way, they explain, should the worst happen, should Jari fail, the rain forest could re-cover the exposed areas. If huge clearings were left behind, the seeds of the largest native trees could not disperse across them. The open areas would require centuries to recolonize and to become mature forests.

When the visit is complete, Odum and Brown leave with data they will add to a major study of Amazon management strategies, funded by The Cousteau Society. Both men are skeptical, believing the world energy future could doom Jari as it is presently set up.

Planners in Brasília tend to think otherwise. The interministerial council drawing up the agricultural programs associated with the Carajás mining complex has announced plans to create plantations there twenty-four times the size of Jari.

"CALYPSO" | MARAJÓ ISLAND | BRAZIL

As befits a still-virgin frontier so often compared to the American West of the nineteenth century, the most widespread invasion of the jungle comes not from miners or farmers but from cattle ranchers. Nearly 70 million acres of Amazonia today are devoted to pasture for beef cattle—an area as large as the state of Washington. Although most of the land is composed of natural grassland, government incentive programs in recent years have encouraged the replacement of nearly 5 million acres of forest with cleared pasture land, the largest chunk of the total Amazon area developed. It is big business conducted by big corporations. Volkswagen owns 343,000 acres of pasture; a consortium of Armour-Swift/Brascan/King Ranch owns 177,000 acres. Liquigas, an Italian multinational, owns 1.6 million acres.

The motivation behind cattle ranches is not always the production of beef. Like most agricultural activities, grazing operations quickly exhaust the treeless soils. Most Amazon ranches produce a meager supply of beef per acre. Yet the fact that development has taken place causes pasture lands to skyrocket in value. As a result, speculators buy forest tracts and clear them for pasture merely to reap profits from the appreciation. Herds of cattle are almost incidental.

219

Among the first regions of the Amazon devoted to heavy ranching was the Switzerland-sized island built up by sediment deposits in the delta, Marajó. The world's largest fluvial island, Marajó is a patchwork of swamps and jungle. Cattle and water buffalos have long grazed its eastern savanna. The location is ideal, because the nearby port of Belém is five shipping days closer to U.S. and European beef markets than are major Brazilian competitors, such as Argentina and Australia.

Captain Cousteau visits Marajó during the final phase of the expedition, dispatching the helicopter and hovercraft from *Calypso* and sending *Anaconda* up a shallow river that winds through a forested tract of the huge island.

J.-Y.C.—*As we prepare to leave the Amazon, Marajó treats us to a last feast of spellbinding sights. Aboard* Anaconda, *Prezelin, Desmier, and Murphy are once again tourists with cameras in a biological antiquity. A tarantula passes them, swimming on the surface of the river. Garlands of orchids, among the most complex of earth's plants, dangle like ornate earrings amid strands of liana vines. Turtles watch from sandbars, praying mantises from camouflaging foliage, monkeys from shadowy upper limbs. The men recall the words of a Peruvian zoologist: "The jungle has more eyes than leaves."*

In Felix, *Braunbeck and I skim the treetops and come upon something extraordinary—red roses scattered along the upper canopy. Suddenly the flowers leap into the air and converge in a brilliant cloud that whirls and turns above the jungle. Bob banks in pursuit and for ten minutes we chase like elated children. The streaks of red below us are scores of scarlet ibises, fluttering en masse through the green crevices of the forest ceiling. My mind stores away still another unforgettable image.*

Felix lands in a marsh and we rendezvous with a team led by Falco in the hovercraft. For hours we glide across the wet lowlands of Marajó, passing cattle herds and vaqueiros. *The swamps inundated by the surging Amazon remind us that Amazonia is a waterlogged world. The cattle remind us of its future.*

The unfolding confrontation between primal jungle and humanity will not be settled within my lifetime. But change is inevitable because the primary agents of great territorial change are streaming into Amazonia— the dispossessed but growing young families and the resource miners, independent and multinational, who are running out of mineral-rich, timber-rich, opportunity-rich regions of the planet. It is urgent that far-sighted planners devise limited-development programs that will not endanger the Amazon's colossal but fragile fecundity. If the seeds of wise management can be sown at this moment in history, perhaps Amazonia can be saved from despoliation, as a legacy and as a model for future generations.

Meanwhile, we leave with some concerns. What will happen to the stability of the ancient forest regime if it is viewed only as an obstacle to be cleared away and the land beneath it only as a commodity? The fallacy of the jungle's omnipotence has been exposed. The pattern is this: if the rain forest is attacked from deep within, its vast breadth and exuberance

The Yanomamö engage in frequent warfare, village against village, along a prescribed system of escalating violence, from ritual chest-beating to club fighting to massacre. The Yanomamö also are chronic users of hallucinogenic plants, which they gather in the forest.

tend to prevail over human enterprise. But if it is attacked from its periphery, beaten back from riverbanks and highways, cropped inward from its edges, the jungle succumbs.

What will happen as new kinds of development ideas take root? The governments of the Amazon are flirting with the idea of creating an interior waterway between the continent's north and south. The connecting link would be the Casiquiare Canal, a natural channel—the only one of its kind known in the world—that leads from the north-flowing upper Orinoco River of Venezuela into the south-flowing Rio Negro. A team led by Raymond Coll explored the Casiquiare for us in a huge Zodiac. It is a quiet sanctuary now, flowing through the homeland of the Yanomamö Indians. But if it is dredged and filled with heavy shipping, the virgin country of northern Amazonia will be immeasurably altered.

What prospects lie ahead for the embattled Amazon Indians, whose forest mythology is powerless to make bulldozers disappear? As native cultures are incorporated into the modern world, their encyclopedia of forest knowledge—about medicines, useful and harmful plants, hunting and agricultural strategies—passed orally from generation to generation over millennia will disappear. It will be as if an ancient library has burned down, and the books must be researched and written again from scratch.

And as the legends of this enchanted land dissolve, what will happen to creatures like the dolphins, which have been protected from harm by generations of forest dwellers fearing their mystical powers? Fisherman of the prosaic future might not tremble at the thought of killing dolphins that snatch fish from their nets, or of overfishing waters now revered as sacred.

What will befall the life of the river if the floodplain trees that feed it are cut for timber or to create seasonal pasturage or rice fields? The river would continue to feed the varzea *with its rich sediments, but there would be fewer cascading feasts of fruit and seeds for the fish, fewer fish for the fishermen and the dolphins, ultimately fewer fishers.*

Our overriding worry involves the very element of Amazonia that is its allure, its vitality, its irreplaceable gift to the planet. The Amazon is trillions of discrete living organisms, each solving the riddles of survival in a dissimilar way, each providing goods and services for other organisms and in turn dependent upon its neighbors in the soil or river or foliage or air. The prodigal mass of living pieces has been sewn together by evolution into a homeostatic, continent-spanning system that acts very much like a stupendous single organism. Amazonia brings to mind the writings of Teilhard de Chardin, who described three infinities: the infinitely big, the infinitely small, and the infinitely complex. This almost inconceivable diversity of Amazonia must be guarded valiantly as a precious treasure.

Why? Because it is the greatest scientific laboratory on earth, conducting genetic experiments that began millions of years ago. From it have come bizarre beauty and mesmerizing invention: the strange, torpid sloth; the knobby, flap-skinned mata mata turtle; the beak-dwarfed, rainbow-hued toucan; the fungus-farming leaf-cutter ant; and the water-spouting cipo de água *vine.*

The awesome alchemy of the jungle, however, produces more than peculiar life forms. New medicines and new raw materials and new foods lie

Cousteau: "The awesome alchemy of the jungle produces more than peculiar life forms. New medicines and new raw materials and new foods lie hidden in Amazonia's unstudied sea of diversity.... How tragically shortsighted it would be to eradicate these wonders before they are even discovered."

hidden in Amazonia's unstudied sea of diversity. Nicole Maxwell, who has collected knowledge of the native pharmacopoeia over several decades, took me for a walk in the jungle near Iquitos. Pointing to a leaf here, a bark or herb or root there, she identified sources of medicines used by Indians for everything from arthritis to contraception. In Colombia, Cornu watched a shaman search the forest for a particular species of black ant, then set the creatures on the wound of a man suffering from a venomous snake bite. The next day he was robust and healthy. A medical researcher in Bogotá told Cornu that he had tested one hundred plants used medicinally by Indians and had found sixty of them effective. The other forty may have been tested improperly, he admitted. Through the ages, a cornucopia of products has been discovered here, from rubber to quinine to chocolate. What discoveries still lie sealed in the countless species undiscovered, unnamed, unstudied? The biological diversity of Amazonia's forest is as valuable a future resource as the minerals under the forest floor. To diminish diversity of species here is to lose that enormous opportunity forever. There may be at this moment Amazon plants that Western eyes have never seen, dull and nameless vines or roots, churning out the base chemistry that could lead to miracle cures we have long awaited. How tragically shortsighted it would be to eradicate these wonders before they are even discovered.

Almost a year to the day since we first saw the meeting point of the Atlantic and the Amazon, Calypso crosses northward again from the plume of brown fresh water into blue-green salt water. As I write, our last scientific program is underway, an atmospheric study being conducted aboard Calypso by a research team from Harvard University. They are hoping to learn more about Amazonia's storage and transfer of vital gases to the atmosphere that sustains every living thing on the planet. It is a final reminder of the global significance of this rain forest and river, and it leads me to remember not only the worries we take away as mementos but the signs of hope as well.

For one thing, we are now convinced that it is not too late to save Amazonia. Though inexorable forces are at work to alter it, huge areas remain vibrant and little changed. We have flown for hours over vast unbroken sheets of tree cover still beyond the heavy machinery of human trespassers, and our samplings of the river have revealed only scattered signs of pollution.

If Amazonia is to retain its exuberance, development planners must set aside immense islands of rain forest and rivers as effective wilderness preserves. Some researchers today are trying to identify the critical regions and the necessary size of such protected sanctuaries. It is clear that the only way for this scheme to be effective is for the preserves to be large enough, to be characteristic of each ecological province, and to be actually off limits to human exploitation. That the idea is prevalent in many offices of government is at least reassuring.

Most important, however, we leave encouraged by the dedication and reverence toward Amazonia we have witnessed among so many who dwell within it—the scientists laboring to understand and to protect it and the hardy people of the river, for whom the waterways are main streets and *back alleys and the forests are shopping centers. Their mighty green bene-factor provides them with staples for the body and gods for the spirit. They fear it, but they do not want it demolished.*

The last thought to record comes from an ironic source. "Amazonia is the last place in the world where man hasn't taken over yet," says Breno Dos Santos, the geologist from Belém whose forced landing on a jungle mountain led to the discovery of the vast Carajás iron deposit, the treasure Brazilians celebrate today as their portal to the future. "And in world history," says Dos Santos, "when man goes into a region like this, he always goes in destroying the land and killing other men. He's never gone in using his head. This is the last chance for man—he gets a chance here to show either that he's no longer a child, or that there's no more chance for man."

Mounier and Braunbeck are aloft again, filming for the last time the point where a thousand journeys by a thousand Amazon rivers come to an end in the sea. Beyond in the open ocean, vapors are rising into the winds to fly as mist across the jungle, to collide with the Andes and slide back across the land, irrigating in the process the trillions of shiny pieces of life in Amazonia. Below us in the ocher liquid are the specks of detritus shaken from this infinity into the rolling river—the empty husks of insects, bits of pulverized Andes rocks, the molecular residue of leaf flesh and bird bones and fish scales and human hair—all ready-mixed to fertilize new life, all streaming into the sea, the world's blood system. How will this prodigious outflow change as the decades and centuries pass? I recall other crossings of Calypso *and the comparisons reverberate in my mind: the Nile, a rav-aged river of antiquity, the Danube and St. Lawrence and Mississippi, profoundly damaged rivers of the modern industrial areas. The Amazon, still practically untouched, is the river of the future. And its future is at our mercy.*

FLYING TEAM | LIMA | PERU

For Jean-Michel Cousteau, there remains a final mission. The six-week-long visit of a Flying Team to the Jívaro Achuara Indians in Northern Peru has been among the richest experiences of the expedition. A friendship has grown between the Achuara chief, Kukus, and the younger Cousteau, a camaraderie strengthened in mid-July when Jean-Michel takes time off from filming the cocaine story to fly Kukus and Walter from Iquitos southwest to Yurimaguas, where there is a district land office. Accompanying the two men into the busy bureaucratic center, Jean-Michel and Luis Uriarte attempt to translate and to clarify the Indians' requests. They want to file papers to establish their title to Achuara lands. It is their second trip to Yurima-guas. The result of their long canoe trip here months before is that "the previous application has been lost," explains a clerk across the counter. With the help of Uriarte and Jean-Michel a second application is tendered. There is little optimism that it will be fruitful.

The experience sparks an idea in Jean-Michel's mind. He decides to at-tempt to arrange the impossible, a direct meeting between the chief of the

jungle tribe and the President of Peru. Perhaps the exchange would lead nowhere. Perhaps it would initiate some small step toward understanding. Jean-Michel asks Karen Brazeau to make overtures to the President's office in Lima and he returns to join Cornu, Sumian, and the rest of the Flying Team.

A month later, late in the evening on August 12, Jean-Michel sits in his room at the Gran Hotel Bolivar in Lima and tape-records the events of the day, which marks the end of the essential work of the expedition.

"This morning as we sat at the Lima airport awaiting the arrival of the commercial flight carrying Kukus from Iquitos, I wondered what might be going through his mind. He was at the moment flying over the Andes, which he had never heard of, on his way to an audience with the leader of Peru, who has never seen his village of Rubina. I recalled the time I met him at the Iquitos airport in July at the end of his first airplane flight. He had never seen so many people in one place. He stood transfixed in the terminal building gazing at what seemed to be nothing. Then I realized that he had never seen stairs before, never seen a second floor. When his plane arrived in Lima today, we embraced him at the base of the passenger ramp. He was barefoot, dressed in his finest feather headdress, a new T-shirt, and a new sarong woven for the occasion by one of his wives. Luis Uriarte, who had accompanied him in the DC-8, said he was invited by the crew to look down upon the Andes from the cockpit. He stared silently for several minutes and then turned to Luis. 'Where are the trees?' he said.

"We left the airport in an old Cadillac limousine and drove into Lima. The sky was leaden, loaded as usual with dust and industrial smog. I think this was one of his first shocks, but there must have been countless others. Every sound was new—horns honking, tires squealing. Every sight caught his eye—armed militia trucks parked in the Plaza San Martin, traffic lights, the vaulting architecture of the presidential palace and the iron gates guarding it, through which he would venture in the afternoon. He asked Luis how so many people could live so closely and how they could all find enough food. His eyes searched relentlessly. 'His radar is on,' Jean-Paul said.

"We checked into the Bolivar, passing through its ornate domed lobby, then we allowed Kukus to rest before joining us at a long table for lunch. He ate sparsely, tasting each dish but finding nothing very palatable. At the end of the meal, the restaurant presented us with a bottle of champagne. It was the second bottle Kukus had seen; a restaurant in Iquitos had also offered us champagne. He was not interested in tasting it, but he was fascinated by the large cork that somehow fit into the tiny mouth of the bottle. At Iquitos I had told him of the old French custom: the cork is a bird and the wire muzzle is a cage. When two friends share a bottle, one keeps the bird, the other the cage. When they meet again, the friend who fails to produce the bird or cage must buy the next bottle. At Iquitos, Kukus took the bird. Now, in Lima months later, I jokingly produced my cage and asked, 'Where is the bird for my cage?' To my amazement, Kukus plunged his hand into his shoulder bag and withdrew the dried cork, raising it in the air with childlike pride. His stoic countenance broke into a broad smile. I realized that he had cherished this foreign compact of friendship and had kept his little bird in the bag at his side since my departure.

"The meeting with the President was held at 4:00 P.M. President Belaunde was gracious, genuinely interested, but noncommittal. He affirmed his support of Indian rights and told of visiting many parts of the jungle. He emphasized the benefits to Indians of the changes taking place, such as the dispersal of modern medicine into the rain forest. He declared it important that all of the cultures that comprise modern Peru be carefully preserved.

"Kukus looked idly about the elegant office as the President spoke. When the remarks were over, the old Indian made an eloquent statement through Luis about the untenable situation of his people, about the oil drilling and the military harassment. They were two men of about the same age, each representing a people, neither fully aware of the complex forces compelling the other man. Luis made a strenuous representation of the Indian's despair, and I prodded diplomatically. Perhaps we will never know if these thirty minutes had an impact, if the President was listening, if the President has the power to control the advance of his populace into Achuara country. Regardless, the meeting was a step in the right direction.

"This evening we drove out of Lima and down to the coast. Kukus had shared his world with me; I wanted to show him for the first time my world, the sea. As we drove, I remembered riding with him in a canoe to visit Nyashu, the shaman. The scene had struck me as a childhood fantasy come to life—the dream of being an explorer in the time-honored sense, witnessing an exotic, hidden world. I was in a dugout with an Indian chief who had learned to shrink heads, paddling to the jungle hut of a witch doctor who wore feathers and face paint and cured with invocations of a dark magic. I was sitting on bark bags containing the meat of a wild boar and as I watched the glassy water around the canoe I saw a green snake slither silently across the surface and disappear. Halfway to the shaman's house, Kukus began to feel some pain from his arthritic joints and he leaned forward as he stood in the canoe, using my shoulder as a support. It was a small gesture, an older man seeking some strength from a younger man, but it was a barrier crossed. I felt an obligation to honor this trust, and to deepen our friendship. Tonight I would extend to him the largest gift I could give—the sea.

"We came to a long beach, parked the car, and climbed down boulders to the sand. I guided him to the surf as night fell quickly about us. He tasted the salt water and laughed in puzzlement. He made a face that I took as a comment about the coldness of the water. He looked as far out to sea as he could for a few moments and then he said, 'Where is the other bank?'

"Luis translated my answer: 'It is not a river. The other bank is beyond the reach of your canoe. It is called the sea.'

" 'Where does this water go?' he asked.

" 'It goes everywhere,' I said.

"He bent forward to touch the strange white foam again, then looked far out to sea—Kukus, chief of the legendary Jívaro Achuara, his head wreathed in macaw feathers, his face painted with *achiote* grease, his back bolt upright as if it were a shrine to the memory of his illustrious ancestors. He was a single being in whom all of the rich and mysterious jungle past confronted all the tumultuous change of the future, like the Amazon itself an extraordinary ancient presence at the curious edge of the rest of the world. It was one of those rare, quiet moments when the distinction between endings and beginnings seems blurred."

A rainbow as gaudy as the plumage of Amazon macaws tinges the sky near Santarém, Brazil.

EPILOGUE

C hanges large and small continue to pulse through the extraordinary world of Amazonia, revealing in glimpses the array of interior and exterior forces converging there, heightening curiosity about the shape of its future.

Here are some of the developments added to the Cousteau Society's Amazon File since the last team member left the area:

• In the aftermath of eighteen months of research and exploration in Amazonia by Cousteau personnel, eight team members have been treated for malaria contracted in the jungle: Jean-Michel Cousteau, Anne-Marie Cousteau, Jean-Paul Cornu, Guy Jouas, Dominique Sumian, Arturo Calvo, Francis Bonfanti, and Ayrton Camargo. Paula DiPerna has been tested for an intestinal disorder that doctors so far have been unable to identify. Dick Murphy has been treated for hookworms. Murphy also sports a permanent skin discoloration on his neck resulting from exposure during the climb of Mt. Mismi.

• The plantation owned by Pepe Parodi on the Rio Apurímac in Peru (see page 87) has been seized by armed leftist guerrillas, reportedly members of Sendero Luminoso. Parodi, who had farmed the land for thirty years, was in Lima at the time. His wife managed to escape during the attack, aided by the Indian guide Policarpo, who carried her across the Apurímac to safety.

• Father Mariano Gagnon, the Franciscan priest who founded a mission and hospital along the Apurímac at Misión (see page 88), has received a series of threats from the guerrillas because of his associations with humanitarian and religious organizations based in Canada and the United States.

Entering the world's largest river, *Calypso* heads up one of the many arms of the Amazon near its delta. The colossal volume of water flowing in the Amazon system nearly equals all the water carried in the next six largest rivers on earth.

• A band of fifty Piramasco Indians shooting poisoned arrows attacked a road-building crew working for a Shell Oil subsidiary in the eastern Peruvian jungle. One worker was wounded. The tribe was trying to protect its hunting grounds, which the oil firm is opening up for petroleum exploration.

• Three months after the Cousteau team's visit to the Serra Pelada gold bonanza (see page 209), a *garimpeiro* named Julio de Deus pulled from a plot in the hole a gold nugget that broke the previous world record. The nearly pure rock weighed more than 140 pounds. Shortly afterward another prospector, Marlon Lopes Bidde, found a gold boulder on his plot weighing 2,954 pounds and worth about $20 million.

There was other news. The threat of mass evictions as a state-owned company took over the mine has dissolved. The miners formed an association and purchased the concession rights to Serra Pelada. Though the government will continue to inspect the site, the miners will now be responsible for the entire operation.

• At the site of another gold boom, however, the news was calamitous. The village of Jirau on the Madeira River (see page 135), where diving miners scoured the river for gold flakes, was struck by a malaria epidemic that resulted in five hundred deaths. Most of the miners have moved their barges and the settlement has disappeared.

• A preliminary report from scientist Dennis Powers, who is analyzing fish caught near the Madeira River gold site (see page 137), showed that mercury concentrations in the fish were two times higher than in fish from other areas, and the concentration of mercury in people who eat the fish is two to five times higher than in people not eating fish from the region. The conclusion is that, at present, the levels are "subtoxic." There is reason for concern (about thirty tons of mercury have entered the river) but not yet alarm. However, continued dumping could create a potentially grave situation, and The Cousteau Society is recommending to the government of Brazil that the mercury be completely contained or its use discontinued.

• The governor of the Brazilian state of Amazonas has declared his intention to change the laws and permit hunting of endangered species in his state, the largest single territorial division of Amazonia. Governor Gilberto Mestrinho said that by legalizing the unpreventable harvest the government can substantially increase its tax revenues.

• The Harvard University research team that worked aboard *Calypso* collecting atmospheric samples has communicated some preliminary findings to Jacques Constans. The goal was to evaluate the production of gases by the Amazon rain forest. The scientists have found that Amazonian terrestrial ecosystems "play a significant role in the budget of atmospheric nitrous oxide," and that, overall, the moist tropical forest systems of Brazil "play a central role in regulating the chemistry of the atmosphere." They note that the rapid expansion of timber harvesting and agricultural clearing is "likely to lead to significant future change in the source of nitrous oxide."

- Brazil's economic picture has continued to darken, with inflation rates hitting 200 percent. A commercial bank loan involving 250 banks and totaling $6.5 billion, the largest in the history of international finance, has been added to a long list of loans extended to the government. With more than 800 bank creditors around the world, Brazil is buoyed up by bankers because the alternative, failure to meet its loan payments, could initiate a major worldwide economic collapse, according to some economists. The situation adds to the ambiguities about Amazonia's future. The pressures to rapidly bring Carajás and other development sites into production are intensified. But ironically, the tightening budget also means that less money is available for the large-scale development projects that most threaten Amazon ecology.

- Meanwhile, eight more manatees are headed for Curua-Una Lake (see page 112). That will bring the size of the herd to fifty and ensure successful interbreeding. And, in a development with significant implications for the future of Amazonia's beleaguered manatees, Eletronorte, the national utility building the mammoth Tucuruí dam on the Tocantins (see page 208), has decided to employ manatees to help keep the immense lake behind the dam free of vegetation.

- Cacha, the giant otter, has grown acclimated to his new home and new companion, Roberto Souza. The young scientist has incorporated the frisky mammal into his research program. At this writing, Souza is searching for a mate for Cacha.

BIBLIOGRAPHY

For those interested in additional reading about some of the topics in this book, here is a list of texts and articles available at most libraries.

Amazonia. Washington, D.C.: Brazilian Embassy, 1976.

Ayensu, Edward S. *Jungles*. New York: Crown Publishers, 1980.

Collier, Richard. *The River that God Forgot*. New York: E. P. Dutton Co., 1968.

Cousteau Almanac. Garden City, N.Y.: Doubleday and Co., 1981.

Dolinger, J. *Inca Gold*. Chicago: Henry Regnery Co., 1968.

Drozdiak, W.; Mehta, N. S.; and Scott, G. "Tackling the Last Frontier." *Time*, 18 October 1982, p. 48.

Encyclopedia Brittanica, 30 vols. Ed. by Warren E. Preece.

Fittkau, E. J. *Biogeography and Ecology in South America*, vol. I. The Hague: Junk N.V., Publishers, 1968.

Foreign Area Studies. *Area Handbook for Brazil*. Washington, D.C.: American Univ., 1975.

————. *Area Handbook for Peru*. Washington, D.C.: American Univ., 1972.

Furneaux, Robin. *The Amazon*. New York: G. P. Putnam's Sons, 1969.

Goodman, E. J. *The Explorers of South America*. New York: Macmillan Co., 1972.

Goulding, Michael. *The Fishes and the Forest*. Berkeley: Univ. of California Press, 1980.

Herndon, William L. *Exploration of the Valley of the Amazon*. New York: Grosset and Dunlap, 1952.

Kelly, Brian, and London, Mark. *Amazon*. New York: Harcourt Brace Jovanovich, 1983.

Lathrap, Donald. *The Upper Amazon*. New York: Praeger Publishers, 1970.

Lost Empires, Living Tribes. Washington, D.C.: National Geographic Society, 1982.

Machado, B. R. "Farquar and Ford in Brazil." Ph.D. dissertation, Ann Arbor: Univ. of Michigan, 1975.

Majcherczyk; Pietowski; and Chmielinski. *In Kayak Through Peru*. Polish Expeditions Cunoandes, 1981.

Maxwell, Nicole. *Witch Doctor's Apprentice*. New York: Collier Books, 1961.

McIntyre, Loren. *The Incredible Incas*. Washington, D.C.: National Geographic Society, 1978.

————. "The Lost Empire of the Incas." *National Geographic* 144(6), 1973, p. 729.

Meggers, Betty. *Amazonia: Man & Culture*. Arlington Heights, Ill.: AMH Publishing Corp., 1971.

Moran, F. Emilio. *Developing the Amazon*. Bloomington: Indiana Univ. Press, 1981.

Randall, R. "Peru's Pilgrimage to the Sky." *National Geographic*, June 1982, p. 60.

Sabbag, R. *Snowblind*. Indianapolis: Bobbs-Merrill Co., 1976.

Shoumatoff, Alex. *The Rivers Amazon*. San Francisco: Sierra Club Books, 1978.

Smith, H.H. *Brazil—The Amazons and the Coast*. New York: Charles Scribners' Sons, 1879.

Smith, Nigel J. H. *Man, Fishes, and the Amazon*. New York: Columbia Univ. Press, 1981.

————. *Rainforest Corridors: The Transamazon Colonization Scheme*. Berkeley: Univ. of California Press, 1982.

Sternberg, Hilgard O'Reilly. *The Amazon River of Brazil*. Wiesbaden, West Germany: Franz Steiner Verlag.

————. "Man and Environmental Change in South America," *Biogeography*. Edited by Dr. W. Junk. The Hague: Monographie Biologicae Series, 1968.

Wallace, Alfred R. *Narrative of Travels on the Amazon and Rio Negro*. London: Reeve and Co., 1853.

PHOTOGRAPH CREDITS

All photographs courtesy The Cousteau Society, Inc.

Key to the placement of pictures on the page: t. = top, m. = middle, b. = bottom, r. = right, l. = left

Raymond Amaddio: 226

Ayrton Camargo: 17 m., 23, 29 b., 74 b., 94 m. and b., 104 b., 115, 116 b.r., 127, 128, 130 m., 135, 136, 139, 140, 141, 142, 144, 146, 149, 150, 152–53, 154, 156, 159 t., 195, 196–97, 198, 200, 202–3, 204, 206, 216, 218, 221, 229

Raymond Coll: 26–27, 130 b.

Anne-Marie Cousteau: 24 t., 35, 38–39, 47, 82, 86 b., 174, 177, 179, 180, 182, 183, 184, 186, 190, 193, 224

Jean-Michel Cousteau: 10 t., 72 t., 94 t., 104 t., 160 t.

Xavier Desmier: 22 t.

Scott Frier: 1, 2–3, 4–5, 6, 10 b., 12 t., 17 b., 24 b., 29 t., 45 t. and m., 49, 50 t., 53, 54, 56, 57, 58, 61, 63, 64 b., 67, 69, 70, 72 m. and b., 74 t., 76, 78–79, 80 t.r. and b., 86 t r., 88 b., 91, 110 b., 113, 114, 116 t.l., t.r., b.r., 118, 121 b., 122 t. and b., 124, 143, 159 b., 160 t.r., 162, 163, 167, 168 b., 187, 188–89, 210, 212 t., 214–15, 223

Claus C. Meyer: 208

Richard C. Murphy: 12 b., 15, 19, 20, 30, 33, 37, 40, 41, 45 b., 71, 77, 80 t., 85 b., 86 t.l., 88 t. and m., 97, 98, 100, 103, 168 t., 170–71, 172 t.r., 173, 212 b., 230

Haroldo Palo: 106, 108, 109, 110 t.l. and t.r., 112, 121 t., 122 m.

Louis Prezelin: 42, 50 b., 64 t. 92–93, 164, 172 t.l. and b.

Mose Richards: 130 t.

P. V. Rose: 48

Dominique Sumian: 105

Yves Zlotnicka: 17 t., 132

Project Director: Robert Morton
Designer: Judith Michael

LIBRARY OF CONGRESS CATALOGING IN PUBLICATION DATA

Cousteau, Jacques-Yves.
  Jacques Cousteau's Amazon journey.

  1. Natural history—Amazon River. 2. Amazon River.
I. Richards, Mose. II. Title. III. Title: Amazon
journey.
QH112.C68 1984   508.81'1   83-15374
ISBN 0-8109-1813-7

© 1984 The Cousteau Society, Inc., Paris

Endpapers:
Many of the Amazon's 1,100
tributaries, such as this river in
Peru's Manú Park, cut endlessly
meandering courses as they
cross the vast flat floor of the
Amazon basin, an expanse so
large it represents one twentieth
of all the land surface on
earth—2.7 million square miles.

Page 1:
A *Heliconia*, related to banana
plants.

Pages 2–3:
A Cousteau diving team
prepares to explore the
red-brown waters of the
Rio Negro.

Pages 4–5:
Thunderstorms forty times more
powerful than those of
temperate zones irrigate
Amazonia's lush vegetation,
sometimes passing overhead in
only a few minutes.